THE MAKERS OF
ENGLISH FICTION

THE MAKERS OF ENGLISH FICTION

BY

W. J. DAWSON

NEW YORK   CHICAGO   TORONTO

FLEMING H. REVELL COMPANY

LONDON AND EDINBURGH

THIRD EDITION

New York: 158 Fifth Avenue
Chicago: 80 Wabash Avenue
Toronto: 27 Richmond Street, W.
London: 21 Paternoster Square
Edinburgh: 100 Princes Street

CONTENTS

THE FATHER OF ENGLISH FICTION

*Daniel Defoe, born 1661, in the parish of St. Giles, Cripple-
gate, London. Served in King William's army, 1688. Published a satirical poem, "The True-born Englishman," 1701;
"The Shortest Way with Dissenters," 1703. Imprisoned in
same year; released in August, 1704. Published "Robinson
Crusoe," 1719; "Memoirs of a Cavalier," 1720; "Moll Flanders," "The Journal of the Plague Year," "The History of
Colonel Jacob," 1722; "Roxana," 1724. Died in Ropemakers'
Alley, Moorfields, April 26th, 1731, and was buried in Bun-
hill Fields.*

PROSE fiction, which has come to occupy so large
a part in English literature, was relatively a late
growth. It first takes definite form in Lyly's
"Euphues, the Anatomy of Wit," published in 1579.
This book had an extraordinary success, due less to
the story it unfolds, which is slight enough, than to the
novelty of its style. Shakespeare was well acquainted with Lyly's masterpiece, for it is tolerably
clear that he occasionally parodied, or perhaps imitated, its trick of antithesis, and its passion for ornament; but Shakespeare did not perceive that it marked
the genesis of a new kind of imaginative literature
which was destined to usurp the place of the acted
drama. Perhaps it appeared to him, as to all his contemporaries, an illegitimate form of art. The drama

held the field. To find plots for his dramas Shakespeare ransacked the Italian novelists, without perceiving that Boccaccio and Bandello had invented a form of art capable of expressing all the passions of human nature not less successfully than the drama itself. Nearly two hundred years later we find that the plays of the older dramatists were widely read. " I know, my dear, that you love to read plays," writes Miss Byron to Miss Selby, in " Sir Charles Grandison." Very slowly it came to be realised that the real drama, whether designed for the closet or the stage, was a cumbrous form of fiction.

What was it that the dramatist set himself to do? He endeavoured to present his public with a transcript of human life, but under certain inexorable and highly artificial conditions. All that he had to say must be packed within the narrowest space. The subtilties of character and of thought must be indicated rather than expounded. He must trust to single phrases for the illumination of the greatest intricacies of motive. He must crowd a lifetime of vicissitude and experience into a few moments by the aid of histrionic art. It needed the actor to complete the indication of the dramatist; it needed his voice, his emphasis, his gesture, his personality; it needed in a less degree the painted scene. Take away from the drama these elements which are constituent to it, and three-fourths of its power is sacrificed. Very few dramas can be read as literature. Even Shakespeare himself gains so much at the hands of a Kean or an Irving, that not to have seen their interpretation of his genius is to form a totally inadequate estimate of it. Moreover, to read drama imposes a severe tax upon the attention. That which moves rapidly and with ease before the visual eye moves cumbrously before the mind's eye. The sketch, the hint, the mere indication of character, to which the actor gives vital form, is apt to appear empty and crude to the reader, and irritatingly inadequate. The question, therefore, was certain to arise whether there was no better way of presenting a transcript of life to the reader than by the art of the dramatist. What was wanted was a method more leisurely, an art more deliberate, a broader canvas and more room. The novel came as answer to this demand.

Daniel Defoe was the first English writer to perceive the uses of the new method of imaginative expression. He stumbled upon the truth rather than discovered it. In 1702 he published his famous pamphlet called " The Shortest Way with Dissenters," in which he advocates, with the greatest sobriety of reasoning, that all Dissenting ministers should be hanged and their congregations broken up and outlawed. It is a sardonic masterpiece. Its supreme merit lies in the perfect fidelity with which Defoe acts the part he has set himself to play. Not by the merest hint does he allow his real opinions to escape him. What he desired to do was to state the logical issue of the High Church argument against Dissent, and this he does with an art so perfect that no one perceives that his argument is meant to be absurd. He had unconsciously hit upon the primary principle of fiction, that fiction is a kind of lie, and that it is useless to lie unless you can lie so like the truth that you are believed. In this case, however, Defoe lied too well for his own profit. The pamphlet was accepted as genuine. He had duped and fooled both parties. When the fraud was discovered, both parties turned upon him. He was pilloried, fined, and imprisoned; and when he came out of prison at the end of a year, he found his family starving and his prospects ruined. Under such disastrous auspices did modern fiction begin.

Defoe had, however, discovered the real bent of his own genius. He could lie like the truth. He could make a tissue of invention, a fabulous story, a pretended argument, appear absolutely real and sincere. He was not slow to take advantage of his discovery. In 1705 he published his " True Relation of the Apparition of One Mrs. Veal." It is said that this brochure was written at the instigation of a publisher who could not sell one of the dullest books ever published, " Drelincourt's Book of Consolations against the Fear of Death." If this be so, the publisher of Drelincourt deserves immortality as the most sagacious of all publishers. Defoe, to whom no sort of hack-work came amiss, did as he was bade, and the result was a ghost story told with such inimitable gravity, with such attention to detail, with such apparent sincerity, that it completely deceived every one. He himself acts the part of the impartial witness. He weighs the circumstantial evidence for the the case with the scrupulous care of an agnostic lawyer. He makes the apparition talk of trivial things, such as a scoured gown which no one but a certain Mrs. Watson knew to be scoured— an excellent touch of art, for the very triviality of the subjects discussed gives the conversation an engaging air of credibility. He writes in a blunt, commonplace, homely fashion, admirably suited to his theme; for he was shrewd enough to perceive that any attempt to decorate such a story with fanciful effects would at once arouse suspicion. The entire method of Defoe's art is illustrated in this brief theme. He is a convinced Realist. He is consistently faithful to his own principle, that "lies are not worth a farthing if they are not calculated for the effectual deceiving of the people they are designed to deceive." It is part of his method to affect a gravity which, to the ordinary mind, must appear inseparable from truth. It is equally part of his method to accumulate details after the most approved fashion of modern realistic fiction. He had deceived the whole town, and both political parties, with his sober argument for the hanging of all Dissenting ministers; he again deceives his readers with this invented ghost tale, but with more happy results for himself. Henceforth Defoe knew that the proper expression of his genius must be found in realistic fiction, so plausibly presented that it should appear as truth.

All Defoe's subsequent fictions are built upon the same method. In 1719 he produced "Robinson Crusoe," one of the few immortal books in English literature. He was now fifty-eight, a broken, battered politician—a striking instance of how long a man may wait before he discovers the nature of his own powers. So like the truth is "Robinson Crusoe" that it was accepted on its publication as a real narrative, and to this day multitudes of the uninstructed probably regard it in the same light. It bears some resemblance to the authentic story of Alexander Selkirk, but it is in theme rather than in incident. What finer justification of Defoe's method can be found than that the invented story of Crusoe appears quite as probable as the real story of Selkirk? Charles Lamb found the story altogether too homely, and said that it was better fitted for the kitchen than the drawing-room.   Dickens complained of " an utter want of tenderness and sentiment" in the account of Friday's death, and said that it was the only great novel which excited neither tears nor laughter.   Later critics have lamented its lack of psychological interest.   But these criticisms, after all, amount to nothing more than this, that Defoe chose to tell his story in his own way.   He does not pretend to describe emotions; he is content to relate facts.   The state of Crusoe's mind is of less importance than his expedients to get the means of life.

Opportunities of brilliant description such as Stevenson would have seized with eagerness, opportunities such as Tennyson has used to the utmost in his " Enoch Arden," Defoe ignores, as incompatible with his method.   Perhaps it would be juster to say that he does not so much as perceive them.   He was essentially a bluff, masculine, matter-of-fact man, and he tells his story in a matter-of-fact way.   Prosaic accuracy of detail serves him perhaps better than heroics. The man he paints is a sturdy, plain-minded seaman, who sets himself to solve the problem of how to live under conditions which would have overwhelmed a more sensitive mind.   It is the indomitable courage of Crusoe which charms us.   He is typically Anglo-Saxon in his stolid endurance of fate, his practical grasp of circumstances, his ingenuity, his fertility of resource, his determination to make the best of his unfortunate situation.   He behaves after the manner of his race.   Having by chance become the monarch of a desert island, he sets himself to govern it to the best of his ability, and to arrange his life with decent orderliness.   There is something much more affecting in the indomitable courage of Crusoe than there would be in any amount of sentiment. One supreme imaginative incident illumines the book—the finding of the foot-step on the sand; but, apart from this, Defoe is content to kindle the imagination by mere truthfulness of detail in common things. And he does this so successfully that we are affected quite as deeply by Crusoe's pain-ful attempts to keep house and record the passage of time as we are by what may be regarded as the su-preme imaginative incident of the book.

None of Defoe's later fictions have obtained the popularity of "Robinson Crusoe," yet they are all memorable productions. It has been the custom of critics to rate them much lower than "Crusoe," but this is a verdict which may be justly disputed. "Moll Flanders" and "Roxana" are much greater works than "Crusoe." They have a unique value as human documents and records of contemporary life. It is true that they are often unsavoury in detail, but so is "Oliver Twist." The man who sets himself to write about criminals can scarcely avoid the unsavoury. Vice, folly, and crime; Newgate, the hulks, and the plantations of Virginia; the exploits of highwaymen, and the duplicities of courtesans; wickedness unde-tected, prosperous, and triumphant, and wickedness scourged to the bone by the undelaying fates,—these are the themes of Defoe's later fictions. How far he wrote them with a moral purpose it is difficult to deter-mine. Probably he persuaded himself that his main purpose was good. There is no reason to doubt the sincerity of the frequent homilies on the rewards of folly with which he interlards the progress of his nar-rative. If he wrote coarsely, it was because the age was coarse. Shakespeare, too, can be coarse, for his age permitted it. The question of coarseness must not be confounded with the question of immorality. It is quite possible for a book which possesses the utmost refinement of language to be much more perilous to innocence than a straightforward narrative of a vicious career, which is expressed in blunt and homely language. Defoe's chief fault is lack of discrimination in incident. He writes his account of vicious people in the spirit of a police-court journalist. He must needs tell everything, and he proceeds to do so with meticulous honesty. He does not perceive that the half may be more than the whole. He will leave nothing to the imagination. His passion for detail is so excessive that he does not omit things which might very well have been omitted without disadvantage to his narrative. But when we say these things, we must recollect that Defoe was the pioneer of an art entirely new in English literature. He had grasped only its primary principle, which was to produce the illusion of reality in a fictitious narrative. If, in working out this principle, he does not discriminate very subtly on the use of his material—arguing, as many a later novelist has argued, that because a thing is true in life therefore it is true in art—he should be readily forgiven an error which it has taken a century and a half to unlearn.

Apart from this fault, inherent in the man and the age, the later fictions of Defoe are very wonderful productions. With what extreme vividness does he make us see his creatures and the scenes through which they move! We know all about what they eat, drink, and wear; their houses, and the way in which they are furnished; the expenses of their tables and of their

journeyings; the interest they obtain on their invest-
ments; the methods of the trades in which they are
engaged; and so on, through a mass of detail, by which
we derive a truer picture of life two hundred years
ago than any history has given us. Defoe is almost
humorously exact in all that relates to money. One
has often occasion to wish that modern novelists would
tell us how their heroes and heroines contrive to live.
The housekeeping bills of the splendid adventurer of
modern fiction would interest us quite as keenly as his
exploits. Defoe leaves nothing to seek in this respect.
He audits the accounts of his sorry heroines with the
exactness of an actuary.

He has also an admirable, though unconscious, eye
for scenery. We get to know the road from Harwich
to London as if we had travelled it, and few pieces of
descriptive writing are more impressive than his account of the storm at sea between Holland and Harwich. His sea-captains, merchants, and highwaymen
are genuinely alive. His very absence of sentiment
makes for lucidity of vision. He knows very well
that the need of money is the mainspring of social
life, and he is at no pains to disguise the truth. His
women are frankly mercenary; they are coolly count-
ing their profits when they seem to be most the slaves
of passion; they know nothing of love that scorns
banking accounts. Defoe never parades his power of
analysis, but it exists; and in his portraiture of women
it is frequently subtle and acute. The successful attempt of Moll Flanders to pass as a woman of fortune
on £500 makes very diverting reading. Defoe may or
may not have known women of a different order, but
it is certain that the women he has chosen to depict he

knew to the bone. In his frank, daring, and almost brutal display of motive he often reminds us of Kipling, as he does also in his insistence on trivial detail. Crude as his stories are, considered merely as stories, yet they move and live. There are no dull moments, except when he preaches. His work may not be art of the first order; it may be but a sort of superb journalism, as many critics have declared; but it is vital work. The same thing has been said of Kipling. Probably it will continue to be said of men whose power of vision exceeds their power of artistic combination. Yet the power of vision, the all-observant eye, is after all the great thing, and the most marked feature of genius; and this power Defoe had in a very high degree.

One other observation may be made on the material of Defoe's fictions. It is commonplace, coarse, and often squalid, and no doubt the modern reader will wish that so great a genius had been devoted to themes more worthy. But it is a thing apparently inevitable in the beginnings of any new form of literary art that it should find its material in the grosser emotions of humanity. The tales of Boccaccio and Bandello are cases in point. So also are the plays of the Elizabethan dramatists. Just as the child loves crude, strong, primary colours, so the early novelists and dramatists used primary passions for their art. Their pictures are masses of light and gross shadow. The plain elemental emotions attract them, and they deal with them fearlessly. It needs the culture of many generations to educate the eye to softer gradations of colour, to produce the delicacy of touch which can coax the subtler workings of the soul to light, which can so refine both taste and art that the thoughts of a simple girl like Maggie Tulliver shall become as dramatically absorbing as the shudderings of a Moll Flanders under the shadow of the gallows. Defoe is scarcely to be blamed for using his new-found art upon gross themes; it was a necessity of the art itself. He laid his hand upon the most dramatic material he could find, which was the "Newgate Calendar," just as the Elizabethan dramatists seized upon the violent and criminal episodes of Italian history, constructing from them dramas of tremendous force, which took small account of taste. The only moral question involved is whether work of this kind is done in a masculine, healthy, robust fashion. As far as Defoe is concerned, the question is easily answered. He is always masculine, and his very coarseness is a sign of health. He is a big, rough-fibred Englishman, who has no idea that any one can be offended in him because he tells the blunt truth, and his art is so full of wholesome vigour that it partly redeems its material.

Of the later works of Defoe, the "Journal of the Plague" is the most memorable. His art of obtaining verisimilitude by the accumulation of detail never reached so high a point. The complete triumph of his method is proved, as in the case of "Crusoe," by the fact that this imaginary fiction has been constantly accepted as authentic history. Defoe, as we have seen, did not attempt fiction till he was virtually an old man. He probably had no idea of the value of the art which he had discovered. He was not the sort of man to give himself airs upon the invention of a new literary vehicle of expression. He wrote for bread, wrote carelessly and hastily, and cared very little for anything beyond the immediate reward of his exertions. Nevertheless, he was a great man; of limited but intense imagination, of infinite invention, of immense force; who built better than he knew, for much that he has written is immortal, and no defects in his writings can be weighed for a moment against the claim that he must justly be regarded as the Father of English Fiction.

II

RICHARDSON, AND THE NOVEL OF SENTIMENT

Samuel Richardson, born 1689 in Derbyshire. Published "Pamela" in 1740; "Clarissa Harlowe," 1748; "Sir Charles Grandison," 1753. Died 1761.

DEFOE'S method found its greatest imitator in Swift. " Gulliver's Travels," published in 1726, is a book which perhaps would never have been written but for the success of " Robinson Crusoe." Swift was quick to realise the potencies of the new literary vehicle which Defoe had invented. But he brought to the practice of the new art a mind of incomparably greater range. Defoe was capable of describing ordinary human actions with admirable and vivid realism; Swift created an absolutely unreal world, yet with such perfect accuracy of detail that it appears real. Robinson Crusoe is an ordinary human creature; Gulliver is a human creature too, but he is made to move in a totally imaginary world. The voyages to Lilliput and Brobdingnag are, humanly speaking, impossible. The imaginations of a child may accept pygmies, dwarfs, and giants as credible, but the more sophisticated imagination of the man rejects them. Defoe makes the ghost of Mrs. Veal credible, but he was incapable of inventing Lilliput and Brobdingnag. To do this required a prodigious and sustained power of invention. Each part of the narrative must be fitted and proportioned with an infinite nicety. The least fault in invention destroys the entire structure. The story is inherently absurd; it is only by the most delicate proportion of its parts that it can impose its illusion upon the mind. Swift is the only writer who has perfectly succeeded in this most difficult of arts.

In saying this we should not forget Bunyan, or so modern a writer as Mr. Lewis Carroll. Each creates an impossible world, sustaining his illusion by constant ingenuity of invention. But even Bunyan is not uniformly successful. The picture Bunyan draws of the Slough of Despond is a case in point. Morally considered it is intelligible enough, and Bunyan was right in reckoning on the moral intuitions of his readers for its interpretation. But considered as a piece of fiction it does not for a moment impose upon the imagination. The Slough is said to be in a field, quite visible, and therefore easily avoided; yet Christian falls into it. Christian does not appear to be aware of its existence until he begins running; and yet it was close to his own home, and he must have seen it every day. Swift never makes such errors as these. His imagination is constantly controlled by the strongest logical faculty. Having once granted his premise, that a Lilliput or a Brobdingnag may exist, his logic moves without a flaw. Gulliver behaves exactly as a human creature would behave under the conditions depicted, and the pygmies and giants among whom he moves behave exactly as such creatures would behave if they were equipped with human reason. There is a sort of mathematical accuracy in Swift's method. Every part of his picture is consistent, harmonious, proportionate, and the most impossible incidents are narrated with such perfect gravity that the reason and imagination are equally satisfied and delighted. Defoe's principle of lying so like the truth as to be believed is here carried to its ultimate expression; for in " Gulliver's Travels " we have a record which we know to be false, and never for a moment imagine to be true, yet we find nothing absurd in it, nothing that is not logically convincing.

In the proper sense, or at least in the accepted sense of the term, it is doubtful, however, if Swift should be ranked among the writers of fiction. He is rather an instance of a man of supreme genius who took up a literary medium which happened to suit him, and bent it to his own ends, without the least regard for its true uses. He wanted an effect; he cared as little how he got it as Turner did when he stuck a red wafer on his picture to represent the setting sun. He did nothing to advance the art of fiction; he only showed us what could be made of it by a man who strangely combined pitiless logic and intense imaginative power with an embittered mind and a foul heart. One cannot acquit Swift of an indecency which goes deeper than the use of coarse material; it is an indecency of the heart. He loathed the human race so thoroughly that he took a rancorous pleasure in its degradation. Mankind was to him a race of Yahoos, foul, unclean, brutal, and incapable of redemption. " A Republic of the Beasts " displays far higher virtues, a nobler temperance, a finer magnanimity, a loftier intelligence. In the tenth chapter of his " Voyage to the Houyhnhnms " Gulliver breaks out into passionate vituperation against mankind and all its ways, thanking heaven that at last he has found among the beasts what human society could not give him—a world where there was "neither physician to destroy my body, nor lawyer to ruin my fortune; no informer to watch my words and actions, or forge accusations against me for hire; no gibers, censurers, backbiters—no encouragers of vice by seducement or examples; no dungeons, axes, gibbets, whipping-posts, or pillories—no scoundrels raised from the dust for the sake of their vices; or nobility thrown into it on account of their virtues," and so on, through an interminable catalogue of all the basest things in human nature.   What filled the heart of Swift with this ferocious rage against his kind is an unanswered question.   There is something too awful in it for either blame or pity—something that goes beyond reason and the rebuke of reason; it excites only the kind of terror which we experience when we listen to the ravings of the mad.   Yet through it all the genius of the man shines so resplendent that we cannot refuse a sort of resentful admiration.   Such vast powers of mind scarcely any other English writer has possessed; and never was power so abused.

The work of Swift was rather an aberration than a development in the art of fiction.   The seed sown by Defoe had fallen into a strange soil, and had sprung up in a monstrous flower, but it was clear that the line of right development must lie in other directions.   The new development was to come from Samuel Richardson, who published his "Pamela" in 1740.

Nothing could have seemed more unlikely than that such a man as Richardson should give new impulse and direction to English fiction.   He was intellectually and morally a small man, with very strict and narrow

views of life. He was in spirit a sort of eighteenth-
century Martin Tupper, precise, commonplace, full of
little moral maxims, devoted to the proprieties, fond of
adulation, the idol of female coteries, knowing nothing
of life in its larger aspects, sedulous in skirting the
edge of its most virile realities, and perfectly convinced that his quiet corner of the world stood for the
entire universe. Richardson reminds us of a comfortable cat who purrs on ladies' laps, treads delicately,
and makes no more adventurous pilgrimage than to the
kitchen area. Defoe and Swift at least have masculine
and massive good sense; Richardson is an old maid.
He has all the tedious garrulity of an old maid who
finds the interest of life in trifles. He is prolix beyond
all example. His books are to be measured, not by
pages, but by volumes. " Pamela " or " Sir Charles
Grandison " would be excellent books to take with one
to a desert island; there we might find time to read
them ; and it is certain they would last a long time, for
even a marooned bishop could not read much of them
at once. The modern reader simply despairs over
them. He sees no reason why they should ever have
been begun, and none whatever why they should end.
A stupefying atmosphere of dulness seems to emanate
from them. There is something soporific in the very
aspect of the close-packed page. Nevertheless, few
books have exercised so wide an influence, and have
more completely won the praise of those whose praise
is best worth having. Macaulay has told us in a well-
remembered passage, how entirely he succumbed to the
charms of " Clarissa Harlowe," and how the residents
of an Indian station were so infected with the same
enthusiasm that they fought for the book and read

it with tears. It is still more astonishing to find French critics and novelists equally enthusiastic over Richardson. Balzac and George Sand give him hearty admiration; Diderot ranks him with the great Greek classics; and—strangest thing of all—so thoroughly modern a writer as Alfred de Musset speaks of " Clarissa Harlowe " as the first romance in the world.

By what strange power or virtue did a man so essentially homely achieve this prodigious fame? The secret is, after all, quite simple: he was the originator of the Novel of Sentiment. The charge which Dickens brings against Defoe of an entire lack of tenderness and sentiment in his death of Friday is a charge which lies against all Defoe's work. Defoe never thinks of touching the fountain of tears, and probably could not have done so had he wished. The lack of sentiment is even more marked in Swift, for he takes a cruel pleasure in exposing human frailty, and has no tears even for the most pitiable of human miseries. Richardson strikes a new note. He introduces sympathy and pathos into English fiction. He investigates the human heart, not to sneer at its emotions, but to dignify them. His sympathy with women is remarkable. He understands them perfectly, he reverences them, and he applies to them an analysis which is as delicate as it is acute. No wonder he found himself the idol of female coteries: he was the anointed Prophet of the Feminine. Women read his books with a kind of breathless interest which the sentimental tales of Dickens excited in our own day, and wrote him passionate letters, imploring him not to kill his heroine, or to save the soul of his hero, much as the early readers of Dickens implored him not to kill Little Nell. One of his favourite correspondents, Lady Bradshaigh, has vividly described her emotions over "Clarissa Harlowe." She wept copiously over the book, laid it down unable to command her feelings, could not sleep at night for thinking of it, and needed all her fortitude and the active sympathy of her husband to enable her to persist in her agonising task.

There is no reason to doubt the sincerity of this confession. We have become inured to the sentimental novelist, and are on our guard against him. Our feelings have been outraged so often, that if we yield ourselves to his spell it is with deliberation, and with a due regard to the consequences of our weakness. But Richardson dealt with unsophisticated readers, rich in virgin emotions. He produced a kind of writing which had not been seen before, and it surprised the world by its novelty, as well as charmed it by its sympathy. Richardson thus began a movement whose effect was to be lasting. Henceforth fiction was to engage itself mainly with the interpretation of sentiment, and the influence of Richardson is as obvious in Goethe and Rousseau as it is on our own long array of sentimental novelists. If any man has the time and patience to explore Richardson, he will not go unrewarded. In spite of all his prolix moralisms and wearisome preachings he was an artist. The method of novel-writing he adopted was detestable: it was that most unsatisfactory of all methods, a story told in letters. Yet it must be confessed that, when the initial irritation of the method is surmounted, one is surprised to find how real is the grip which the story takes upon the imagination. The very repetition which the method involves gives a wonderful definiteness to the characterisation. The actors in the drama appear again and again: not in a single part, but in a variety of parts; so that in the end we know them, not by a solitary phase of emotion, but through and through.

Sir Charles Grandison himself is an earlier edition of the " Egoist." He is made to reveal himself from every point of view, until his superb priggishness in all affects us with something like a sense of humour. Not that Richardson is ever guilty of deliberate humour: he takes himself much too seriously. He is a good, solemn, homely man, whose main object is to write a useful tract on the wisdom of being good and the extreme folly of all kinds of ill behaviour. It is this moral quality in Richardson which Dr. Johnson praised when he said that Richardson made the emotions move at the command of virtue. He does so far too much at times, for never was virtue more tiresome than in Sir Charles Grandison. Yet in spite of all—in spite of a cumbrous method, of a mind overwhelmed with copy-book maxims, of an acquaintance with life that never went beyond a narrow range of society—this respectable homely bookseller was an artist, as any one of discrimination will readily discover by a careful study of the latter half of " Clarissa Harlowe."

In the development of English fiction Richardson is the greatest name, because he settled the trend of the novel for many generations. Among those who were the first to imitate him were Sterne and Goldsmith, but each in his own way. Sterne had an undoubted power of sentiment, unfortunately mixed with a fatal pruriency of taste. His humour and his pathos are equally remarkable and vital, yet both seem artificial, owing to his lack of any real depth of feeling. Goldsmith, on the contrary, is exquisitely sincere, and his one novel, " The Vicar of Wakefield " (1766), is the finest example of the sentimental novel in English literature. One rarely weeps with Sterne, because there is ground for legitimate suspicion that Sterne waits for our tears only to laugh at us ; and he plays pranks with our emotions rather than purifies them. Goldsmith succeeds by his sincerity and his simplicity, for in him sentiment is genuine. Sterne will always be read by the student of literature with mixed feelings of admiration for his wit and dexterity and contempt for the man ; Goldsmith will be read by the humble and the wise, the cultured and the illiterate alike, with a genuine delight, and with a growing sense of personal affection for the writer.

The novel of sentiment did not take possession of the public mind without opposition. The eighteenth century was a particularly masculine age, and Richardson was a feminine writer. There will always be a large class of readers whose taste resents the sickly sweetness of the sentimental novel ; and such readers will demand a more robust treatment of life. Just as in our own day we find that after a long debauch of sentiment the public demand a rougher and plainer meal, the novel of adventure ousting for a time the novel of emotional analysis, so, even while Richardson's sway was unquestioned, a counter-movement had begun. The revolt was led by Henry Fielding, whose story of " Joseph Andrews " (1742) was meant to be a burlesque on Richardson's " Pamela." Richardson felt the insult keenly, and described Fielding's book as " a lewd and ungenerous engraftment " on his own story. Nevertheless, it marked the rise of a new school of fiction. Fielding was a man wholly different from Richardson at every point. He had moved in a large world; he knew life at first-hand; he knew how rough and bitter a thing life could be, and he boldly used in fiction the material he had won in many hard experiences. He was, in the full sense of the term, a great artist. He told his stories directly, not through a cumbrous mass of letters, and he took pains to perfect his plots. He was also a master of style. No better model of pure, strong, nervous English can be found than in Fielding's pages. Nor is he destitute of sentiment; there are pages in " Amelia " which affect us much more deeply than anything in Richardson, simply because the sentiment is masculine and restrained.

With Fielding must be ranked Smollett; but it is method which unites them, not equality of genius. Smollett is more of the humourist, but only in the sense that his humour is broader, more farcical, and therefore more easily apprehended. Fielding's humour is subtle, and always has behind it the energy of a powerful thinker, who has a real philosophy of life to unfold. The old comparison which ranks Fielding with Thackeray, and Smollett with Dickens, is not altogether wrong. It is significant that Dickens himself preferred Smollett's " Roderick Random " (1748) to any work of Fielding; no doubt its spirit of caricature was more agreeable to his own genius than the more reticent art of Fielding. But, after all, such comparisons are misleading, because the true student of any art must be prepared to admit that the spirit of art may manifest itself through widely divergent forms, and until he does this he contracts prejudices rather than acquires culture. Both Fielding and Smollett speak in a language not suited to the present day. "Tom Jones" has again and again incurred the condemnation of the fastidious. Yet we may remember that our forefathers, and the best-bred women of an earlier time, read "Tom Jones" without the least sense of impropriety. Clearly Fielding is not refined— he paints human nature in its less pleasing aspects; but neither was his age refined, and art follows rather than sets the standard of manners. In any case an age which permits Tolstoi and goes mad over Gorky can have little to say against Fielding and Smollett. They, at least, mark a great advance upon Defoe and Swift, and it is still a matter of question whether Coleridge was not right when he held Fielding to be a sound moralist.

For the man who really desires to learn something of the origin of English fiction, it will be enough to know that Smollett and Fielding are first-rate forces in the history of its development. With them the first period of English fiction closes. The pioneer work was now done; the foundations were well and truly laid. The pleasanter task now remains of seeing how upon these foundations there rose stage by stage the splendid edifice—how this new land of art was gradually civilised, developed, and fashioned into a stable kingdom, becoming at last a glorious heritage, of which any nation and any literature might be proud.

III

FROM FIELDING TO JANE AUSTEN

Henry Fielding, born 1707, died 1754. Tobias George Smollett, born 1721, died 1771. Laurence Sterne, born 1713, died 1768. Oliver Goldsmith, born 1728, died 1774. Jane Austen, born 1775, died 1817.

A GREAT period in the history of English fiction closes with Fielding and Smollett. They had created the novel of masculine realism, as Richardson had created the novel of sentiment, and each of these forms of fiction was to prove enduring. The latter half of the eighteenth century produced no novelist who could contest their primacy. It did, however, produce an immense crop of fiction, much of it wholly feeble; some of it execrable, both in style and matter; and a part of it really noteworthy because it marked the birth of the romantic spirit.

The new tendency towards romance began with four books which appeared between the years 1761 and 1770, viz., Macpherson's "Ossian" (1761-63), Horace Walpole's "Castle of Otranto" (1764), Bishop Percy's "Reliques of Ancient English Poetry" (1765) and Chatterton's "Poems" (1770). The influence of Macpherson, Percy, and Chatterton upon English poetry was decisive and far-reaching. The influence of Walpole upon the development of fiction was scarcely less remarkable.

Walpole, cynic, coxcomb, and dilettante as he was, nevertheless had a real literary gift, in spite of the fact that he avoided literary men, and thought that poets were like birds, who sang best when they were half starved. His conduct to Chatterton is well known, and admits of no excuse. Instead of recognising "The Marvellous Boy" as a fellow-craftsman, working toward the same end, he denounced him as a forger, telling him that "all the house of forgery are relations," and that he who forges poems is in danger of forging promissory notes. It is eminently characteristic of Walpole that he detests men of letters because "they are always in earnest, and think their profession serious, and reverence learning." Throughout his long life, spent in comfort secured by a State pension of £2,000 per annum, which he had done nothing whatever to merit, it is not known that he stretched out a kindly hand to any one of the great writers who were making the century famous. Dr. Johnson, working at literature at fifteen pence a day, and writing his fine fiction "Rasselas" in order to pay for the funeral of his mother; Goldsmith, producing his immortal "Vicar of Wakefield" under cruel conditions of precarious fortune; Chatterton, writing a poem of several hundred lines for ten and sixpence, and receiving the same remuneration for sixteen songs, had nothing to expect from Walpole, who owned no kinship with them, and in his heart despised them. Yet Walpole, under all the cold polish of the cynic and the affectations of the fop, had a genuine sense of literature, and may claim to have invented the romantic novel.

Curiously enough, he who rebuked Chatterton for representing that his poems were the work of the monk

Rowley, recovered from the muniment chest of St. Mary's, Redcliff, Bristol, adopted the same method in publishing his fiction, and gave ground for the bitter imprecation of the disappointed boy:

> Walpole, I thought not I should ever see
> So mean a heart as thine hath proved to be;
> Thou, who in luxury nurst, beholdst with scorn
> The boy, who friendless, fatherless, forlorn
> Asks thy high favour. Thou mayst call me cheat.
> Say, didst thou never practise such deceit
> Who wrote " Otranto "?

The full title of Walpole's book is " The Castle of Otranto, a Gothic Story; translated by William Marshall, Gent., from the original Italian of Onuphrio, Muralto, Canon of the Church of St. Nicholas, Otranto." It abounds in absurdities, such as helmets that fall without visible agency, portraits which emit sighs, and blood that falls from the nose of a statue; yet it is remarkable for a powerful, if crude, imagination. The element of the supernatural is never managed with the plausibility of Defoe; Walpole's object is merely to create terror by devices which may be called mechanical. Yet there can be no doubt that terror is created, and beneath all the absurdities of the book there is a genuine spirit of mediæval romance which was to find many imitators and interpreters.

For the remarkable thing about Walpole's story is not in the attempt he makes to represent the supernatural, but in his effort to reproduce the spirit of mediævalism. If there was one thing about which Walpole was in earnest, it was his genuine admiration for mediævalism. His villa at Strawberry Hill was a pasteboard imitation of a Gothic castle, which he himself described as a bauble " set in enamelled meadows in filigree hedges." He was an eager collector of armour, china, old pictures, carvings, and so forth, in a day when the taste for connoisseurship was scarcely born. His book is a reflection of these tastes, which excited only contempt among his contemporaries. To them he appeared a trifler; yet he was not trivial. It was his singular destiny to create a new taste in the public corresponding to his own, to turn the attention of men of letters from the commonplace life of the eighteenth century to the varied and wonderful life of the fifteenth century, and the romances of Scott, the poetry of Coleridge, and the Oxford Movement of Newman may all be traced to the influence of Walpole.

The greatest of Walpole's imitators were Mrs. Radcliffe, Maturin, and Beckford. Mrs. Radcliffe, in her famous " Mysteries of Udolpho " (1794), has carried the art of creating terror to a point never reached by Walpole. There is the same kind of mechanism, mysterious vaults, pictures, panels, and trapdoors; but there is a new element—the creation of mysterious persons, stained with unknown crimes and vices, who inspire fear by something supernatural or profoundly melancholy in their aspect. " There was something in his physiognomy extremely singular, and that cannot easily be defined. It bore the traces of many passions, which seemed to have fixed the features they no longer animated." We can readily discern the genesis of Byron's " Lara " in such a description, and of many another mysterious personage in melodramatic fiction. There is also in all Mrs. Radcliffe's romances a singular sensitiveness to the larger aspects of nature, which, perhaps, was due to the reading of " Ossian." Few writers have utilised the gloom of impenetrable forests, the suggestions of wild sunsets or melancholy dawns, the terror or magnificence of tempests, with more effect.

Maturin pursues the same method, but he relies less on violent mechanism to produce the sense of terror; he suggests terror rather than describes it. It is he who has created the truly great figure of Melmoth, which fascinated the imagination of so great a writer as Balzac—Melmoth, the man who has purchased immortality at a price so terrible that its secret is incommunicable.

Beckford's name lives in fiction by his one romance of " Vathek " (1786). It opens with a passage which will strike the modern reader as absurd: Vathek's

figure was pleasing and majestic; but when he was angry *one of his eyes* became so terrible that no person could bear to behold it, and the wretch upon whom it was fixed instantly fell backward, and sometimes expired. For fear, however, of depopulating his dominions, and making his palace desolate, he but rarely gave way to his anger.

Nevertheless, the book rises at times to grandeur, though it scarcely deserves the praise that has been awarded it, as " the finest Oriental tale written by an Englishman." Some of its descriptions are intrinsically impressive—as, for instance, the description of Vathek's tower (Beckford's own passion for building towers amounted to a mania):

His pride arrived at its height when, having ascended for the first time the eleven thousand stairs of his tower, he cast his eyes below and beheld men not larger than pismires, mountains than shells, and cities than beehives. The idea which such an elevation inspired of his own grandeur completely bewildered him; he was almost ready to adore himself, till, lifting his eyes upward, he saw the stars as high above him as they appeared when he stood on the surface of the earth.

The close of the book, with its famous description of the Hall of Eblis, reaches something nearly akin to sublimity:

They reached, at length, a hall of great extent, and covered with a lofty dome, around which appeared fifty portals of bronze, secured with as many fastenings of iron; a funereal gloom prevailed over the whole scene; here, upon two beds of incorruptible cedar, lay recumbent the fleshless forms of the pre-Adamite kings, who had been monarchs of the whole earth . . . each holding his right hand motionless on his heart; at their feet were inscribed the events of their several reigns, their power, their pride, and their crimes.

The sense of terror inspired by such a scene as this is very different from that inspired by the gross machinery of Walpole's " Castle of Otranto "; it is legitimate, as his was illegitimate; it is intellectually impressive, as his was intellectually absurd.

The success of this new form of fiction was immense. It seemed as though the vital and strenuous work of the earlier novelists was entirely forgotten. The public taste grew by what it fed on, and numberless romances appeared, in which no attempt was made to paint any single aspect of human life with fidelity or truth. The more horrible and blood-curdling the tale, and the more abnormal and monstrous the actors in it, the more certain was the author of success. Yet it must be remembered that, however crudely and coarsely this new romantic spirit expressed itself, it possessed the secret of a genuine literary impulse. "Monk" Lewis—so called from the immense success of his story "The Monk" (1795)—deals in crude horror with a hand much less scrupulous than Mrs. Radcliffe's; but he also contrives to resuscitate the spirit of feudalism, and it was this element in his work which arrested the attention of Scott. In later literature Hawthorne, Poe, and Stevenson have been practitioners in the same school as Maturin. Mrs. Shelley's "Frankenstein" and Shelley's own boyish romance of "Zastrozzi" belong to the same movement. Yet upon the whole it must be said that the novel of terror has enjoyed but a precarious success in English literature. Now and then a writer of great genius has been able to handle his theme with supreme art, as in the "Dr. Jeykll and Mr. Hyde" and the "Thrawn Janet" of Stevenson; but as a rule the writer of the novel of terror fails through extravagance of conception or puerility of invention. The best fruit of the movement is not found in prose literature at all, but in poetry, and particularly in "Christabel" and "The Ancient Mariner" of Coleridge.

In the meantime other influences were at work on the development of the English novel. While Fielding painted life with uncompromising realism, and Mrs. Radcliffe created romances which had no relation to life, there were others who had begun to see that fiction afforded an excellent vehicle for the expression of theories and ideas. The nascent influence of the French Revolution began to be felt. Rousseau had sown the mind of Europe with the seed of new truth and untruth; he had accused the whole social order; he had counselled a return to nature, by which he meant that man in his natural condition was a much worthier creature than he appeared under the artificial conditions of an elaborate social system. Rousseau had also utilised prose fiction for the expression of his doubtful gospel, and his example was contagious. A considerable list might be prepared of late eighteenth-century novels in which some portion of the revolutionary teaching of Rousseau is expressed but the greatest exponent of these ideas is unquestionably William Godwin (1756—1836). Just as some of our most popular modern writers have achieved fame by the interpretation of the religious doubts or social theories which were in the air, so Godwin deliberately used fiction for the interpretation of what was essentially a new political gospel. Godwin's creed was that the extension of liberty meant the decay of vice; that the vices of men were not inherent, but were the result of bad institutions; that among the bad institutions which produced human misery, and prevented human perfectibility, were the throne, the church, the army, and the law; and that therefore these institutions should be abolished. With these theories we are not concerned, but the remarkable thing is that Godwin should have sought to express them in fiction. His " Adventures of Caleb Williams " is a fine novel, which has escaped oblivion by its real art; and if it still merits attention, it is not because of its philosophy, but because of its art. Novelists who write with a purpose may still consult Godwin with advantage, for no writer of fiction affords a better example of how to combine a serious aim with that genuine power of characterisation without which the novel with a purpose is nothing better than a ponderous tract.

But, after all, the real aim of the novel should be the interpretation of life ; and to this plain work of interpreting life, without bias of creed, whether religious or political, the novel was bound to return. Miss Burney's famous novel " Evelina " (1778) marks this return. She brought to her task a mind of singular vivacity, an eye characterised by a power of acutest observation, and a heart capable of the intensest feeling. The claim has been made for her that she invented the novel of domestic satire, and it is a just claim. Yet it is rather as a forerunner of a yet greater woman of genius, whose supreme power lay in domestic satire, that Miss Burney is remembered. Jane Austen, born in 1775, at Steventon, is one of the true immortals of English literature, yet she found no easy road to fame. Few novelists have written three great novels without the prospect of publishing one of them, yet this was Jane Austen's fate. And when we remember that all the great names we have already mentioned are the names of persons moving more or less in a large world, cheered by the praise or stimulated by the opposition of their contemporaries, and drawing their knowledge of life from ample sources, perhaps the most extraordinary characteristic of Jane Austen's life is its singular isolation.

Jane Austen had no literary adviser, and indeed knew no one even remotely connected with the world of letters. She read " The Spectator," but did not like it, and thought it coarse. For Cowper and Crabbe she had an abiding love, and this is not surprising, since we find so much in her own nature akin to theirs.

Not that she had any of Cowper's melancholy—a person of more cheerful vivacity never breathed. But she had Cowper's happy faculty of discovering delight in simple and common things, and she gathered with unfailing diligence " the harvest of a quiet eye." She had a touch also of Crabbe's unflinching realism, but without his pathos and compassion. She strikes no deep chords, moves us with no deep passion, thrills us with no great thoughts or poignant emotions. But neither Crabbe nor Cowper, nor any one else, we might almost add, could paint still life with a precision and charm such as hers. Her highest claim as an artist is that she inaugurated the novel of still life.

In a day when people wept over the mock pathos of Sterne, and were thrilled with the sensationalism of Mrs. Radcliffe, it needed an unusual degree of courage, of resolute self-poise, and of detachment of mind to accomplish this task, and for the development of these qualities solitude was necessary. And, to the discerning, there is genuine dignity and pathos in the picture of this quiet, cheerful, clear-eyed woman, far away from the great interests of life, sitting down to write books which no publisher was to venture on for years, and yet so absolutely assured of the rightness of her method, and so full of the quiet enjoyment of her own work, that her patience is never wearied, her temper never soured, her brightness never dulled. She wrought for pure love of her work, and without thinking much about it. She wrote at her little desk by the sunny window, carefully covering up her papers when a stranger entered, and breathing no word to any one outside the family circle of the nature of her pursuits. Sometimes she wrote amid the chatter of conversation, and found it no detriment. She wrote on, unconscious of her own genius, and content that no one should recognise her as an unusual person. Before her, as she sat at her desk, all the little world she knew lived and moved, and it was all the world she wanted. She was content to love and be loved, and did not ask for praise. Perhaps public praise would have spoiled her; it was best that so delicate a gift as hers should mature itself in silence and seclusion. Literature was not her life, but her pastime; had the making of books been the real bread-winning purpose of her life we should still have had a great writer, but not the Jane Austen we know. One can fancy that such books as hers could only grow by slow processes of crystallisation, in the stillest of atmospheres, and that any enlargement of life which might have come from contact with a tumultuous world would also have meant the arrest of her genius and the deterioration of her style. But, however this may be, there can be no doubt of the greatness of her work, though it is a kind of work too true and delicate ever to be appreciated at its real worth by minds destitute of critical discrimination.

IV

JANE AUSTEN, AND THE NOVEL OF SOCIAL COMEDY

Jane Austen, born at the Rectory, Steventon, Hampshire, December 16th, 1775. Published four stories anonymously during her lifetime, viz., "Sense and Sensibility," 1811; "Pride and Prejudice," 1813; "Mansfield Park," 1814; "Emma," 1816. Died July 18th, 1817, at Winchester. "Northanger Abbey" and "Persuasion" were published in 1818, when her authorship of the whole six novels was first acknowledged.

JANE AUSTEN stands for so much in the development of English fiction that the nature of her genius and influence demands careful consideration. "Pride and Prejudice" was written when she was only one-and-twenty; her last book, "Sense and Sensibility," in 1797-8. Two of her best-known novels, "Northanger Abbey" and "Persuasion," were published after her death. Her entire literary life was comprised in the twenty-one years between 1786 and 1817.

It has often been said that an original writer has to create the taste by which he is appreciated; it may be remembered also that the original writer often unconsciously discerns an altered or a new taste in the public before the public itself is quite aware of the change. One of the most remarkable characteristics of the closing decades of the eighteenth century was the rapid change of literary taste. The tone of society had altered. Morals were perhaps not less corrupt than in the days of Defoe, but sentiment had become more refined. The common life of the time was still coarse, and abounded in the abominations which Hogarth has exposed with a truth and realism unrivalled in art; but there was also a genuine movement towards a more delicate apprehension of life. The brutality of Swift had become disgusting to the new generation; the frank realism of Defoe and even the masculine satire of Fielding were scarcely less palatable. There was room therefore for a new kind of fiction, which should be a comedy of life and manners.

Among novelists Jane Austen ranks as a supreme mistress of comedy. Macaulay has boldly compared her with Shakespeare, and Mr. Goldwin Smith has said that " the hand which drew Miss Bates, though it could not have drawn Lady Macbeth, could have drawn Dame Quickly, or the nurse in ' Romeo and Juliet.' " She brought to her task of social comedy a singular combination of rare gifts—a wit and satire of wonderful delicacy, a mind of great penetration, a style absolutely pellucid and effortless. No novelist has ever been more thoroughly an artist both in her attitude towards her own work and in her respect for her own limitations. She is so impersonal in her attitude that one may seek in vain for any trace of her own opinions or thoughts in her writings. Her respect for her own limitations is equally remarkable. " I must keep to my own style," she says, " and go on in my own way; and though I may never succeed again in that, I am convinced that I should totally fail in any other." Within her own limits she comes as near perfection as any human genius can, and those who object to the material and scale of her art should recollect that a dewdrop may be as perfect a creation as a star, a grass-blade may be fashioned with as high a skill as the most wonderful of tropic flowers.

In order justly to appreciate Jane Austen, the first duty of the reader is, then, quite obvious; it is to respect the limitations of her art, as she herself did. It is foolish to expect from her what she does not profess to give, such as romance, or high-flown sentiment, or the tragedy of great passions. She painted the world she knew; her claim is that she not only painted it with fidelity, but with sympathy; with a lively sense of its blemishes, and with an ever-present satire, no doubt; but also with a true insight into its redeeming pieties and virtues. It is not her fault that romance and sentiment and large passions are not found in her pages; they were not found in the world she knew.

Like the Brontës, Jane Austen was born and bred in an English parsonage, and lived in a by-road far from the main roads of life. But the Brontës had a far better opportunity than Jane Austen. They at least lived among a people in whom the primitive passions were strong and very imperfectly suppressed. The country which lay at the back of Haworth was as wild as the people, and had a primeval beauty and savageness of its own. One could conceive of great dramas, full of intense love and passion and revenge, being enacted on such a stage; there is a suggestion of the Titanic in the very scenery. But Jane Austen was born into a world of unredeemed dulness. Everything around her was prim and trim and proper. Instead of thunder-scarred hills there are leafy parks and smooth lawns.

The people who move across these strictly regulated Edens have the unconscious self-poise of very proper persons; they love with discretion and sobriety; they are disappointed in love, but take it calmly; and even in the very height of a successful passion are quite capable of discussing, with a suitable attention to elegance of phrase and the four per cents. (they were four in those days), their marriage settlements. What material could be less likely to provide a great novelist with the plot and movement necessary to a great novel than this tiresome mediocrity of eighteenth-century village life?

Yet it was from this material that Jane Austen has contrived to extract stories which have survived for a century, and seem likely to endure to quite unprophesied generations. The means by which this success has been achieved are quite clear to any one who will study her works with even casual attention. She had the clearest eyes that ever detected the foibles of human character. The very limitation of her range of vision explains its intensity. She accurately described her method when she spoke of herself as a miniature painter. Broad and tumultuous effects she not merely cannot achieve—she dislikes them. But she can lay touch upon touch with an infinite patience and fineness, until the finished picture is as near perfection as one can well conceive. It may perhaps be but miniature-painting—a work of art wrought upon three inches of ivory; nevertheless, to write " Pride and Prejudice " demands as fine a genius as the production of " Ivanhoe " or " Kenilworth." This no one knew better than Sir Walter Scott, who, after reading " Pride and Prejudice " for the third time, says: " The big bow-wow strain I can do myself, like any now going; but the exquisite touch which renders ordinary commonplace things and characters interesting from the truth of the description and the sentiment is denied me." It is this exquisite touch which Jane Austen possesses, and in a degree that is unrivalled. She has successfully contrived the apotheosis of the commonplace, and clothed dulness with distinction.

In Jane Austen it is the very naturalness of the picture which makes it seem uninteresting. Without perhaps saying it, or even analysing our thoughts so far as to express it, we all of us favour a little exaggeration in art. We do not object to emphasis; on the contrary, it attracts us. A bit of clear blue sky and greyish-blue down is not enough for us; its simplicity seems to us commonplace, and its truth foolish. And in the same way a book that is no more nor less than an exact reflection of life, which does not attempt to group people with an eye to stage-effect, or to put speeches into their mouths which invite applause, repels us by its very fidelity. Beyond doubt many readers will be similarly affected by Jane Austen. But upon reflection they will begin to discover how wonderful a gift this is, which can gaze on life with so unembarrassed an eye and report its vision with so perfect an exactitude. After a while the bit of blue sky and grey down charm us. The quiet and simple tones of colour soothe and delight us.

The genius of Jane Austen lies in this perfect and even severe simplicity. Her characters evolve themselves without any aid of dramatic episodes. Her plot is as natural and inevitable as a problem in mathematics. Everything is fitted together with the most delicate contrivance, with the art that effectually conceals art. From first to last the atmosphere is exquisitely lucid, the style distinct and firm, the figures, in spite of the old-fashioned stiffness of their phrase and gait, so vital that they are more real to us than many of the people we have dined with. We feel, not that we have read a book, but that we have been magically transported into the eighteenth century, and have breathed its air and lived its life.

Like all great artists, Jane Austen is thus in a sense an historian as well as an artist. Her picture of life and manners in the close of the eighteenth century is not less vivid than the picture drawn by Defoe and Fielding of the life and manners of the earlier part of the century, and as a contribution to our historical knowledge is probably much truer, because it is more widely representative. It is often deplored that professional historians, who are capable enough of describing the pageantries of a court, the contests of politicians, the sumptuous lives of the rich, or even the miserable conditions of life among the disinherited and the criminal, appear incapable of producing any accurate picture of the *average* kind of life lived by those distinguished by neither great wealth nor great poverty, by neither uncommon learning nor uncommon ignorance. Jane Austen gives us incidentally just the sort of details about the lives of average people which the historian omits and the sociologist demands. We can leave to the historian the Napoleonic drama which was played out amid the terror and applause of Europe in the closing years of the eighteenth century. If there is no echo of its trampling hosts in the pages of Jane Austen, there is something equally valuable to us who survey the whole period with infinite curiosity; there is a picture of England itself, the England of the dull average, from whose stubborn pride was evolved the force that brought the drama to a close. Yet it is an England that seems so far away as to appear almost unrecognisable. The heroines of Jane Austen's pages travel by post-chaise, think fifty miles a prodigious journey, and an excursion to Derbyshire a serious adventure. Gracechurch Street is a locality where a wealthy merchant may fitly reside; but the proud Darcy, who has an estate in Derbyshire, would never think of penetrating so plebeian a neighbourhood. Clergymen speak with bated breath and whispering humbleness of their patrons, and livings are left by will to family favourites. People have a way of talking like copybooks; and the proprieties, especially in relation to women, are defined and strict. It is looked upon as a monstrous thing that Elizabeth Bennet should walk three miles on a country road, and her critics exclaim:

To walk three miles, or whatever it is, above her ankles in dirt, and alone, quite alone! What could she mean by it? It seems to me to show an abominable sort of conceited independence, a most country-town indifference to decorum. She really looked almost wild!

And how far away does that world seem which talked of this alarming indiscretion with the didactic gravity of this sentence:

I admire the activity of your benevolence, but every impulse of feeling should be guided by reason; and, in my opinion, exertion should always be in proportion to what is required.

It may perhaps be an inducement to many who profess themselves unable to read Jane Austen to be reminded that she is one of the truest humorists and keenest wits who ever handled the English language. Her pages sparkle with touches of wit and irony, so keen and just that they are a perpetual delight to any one who is even moderately equipped with the literary sense. Is there, in the whole range of English fiction, an absurder figure than Mr. Collins, in " Pride and Prejudice "? He is a clergyman, and this is how he speaks of his patroness:

Lady Catherine was reckoned proud by many people, he knew, but he had never seen anything but affability in her. She had always spoken to him as she would to any other gentleman; she made not the smallest objection to his joining in the society of the neighbourhood, nor to his leaving his parish occasionally for a week or two to visit his relations.

He expresses to Lady Catherine his regret that the delicate state of her daughter's health prevents her entering society, which event

has deprived the British Court of its brightest ornament. Her ladyship seemed pleased with the idea; and you may imagine that I am happy on every occasion to offer these delicate compliments which are always acceptable to ladies.

The denseness of Mr. Collins is as great as his snobbishness. When he is asked if these delicate little compliments which are " acceptable to ladies " proceed from the impulse of the moment, or are the result of previous study, he gravely replies that

they arise chiefly from what is passing at the time; and although I sometimes amuse myself with suggesting and arranging such elegant little compliments as may be adapted to ordinary occasions, I always wish to give them as unstudied an air as possible.

When he offers marriage to Elizabeth and is rejected, he coolly responds that she should remember that in spite of her manifold attractions it is by no means certain that another offer of marriage will be made her.

As I must therefore conclude that you are not serious in your rejection of me, I shall choose to attribute it to your wish of increasing my love by suspense, *according to the usual practice of elegant females.*

The lady to whom he proposes three days later is by no means an " elegant female," but that is of no consequence, since he is under strict orders from Lady Catherine to marry at once, and his holiday, granted for that purpose, terminates on Saturday. This lady— Miss Lucas—

perceived him from an upper window as he walked toward the house, and instantly set out to meet him *accidentally* in the lane.

She is eager to marry him at once, because

the stupidity with which he was favoured by nature must guard his courtship from any charm that could make a woman wish for its continuance.

When this strange pair are married, Lady Catherine is graciously pleased to show great interest in them, and even to ask them to dinner when she has no other company. Nay, more—

now and then they are honoured with a call from her lady-ship, and nothing that was passing in the room escaped her ob-servation during these visits. She examined into their em-ployments, looked at their work, and advised them to do it differently; found fault with the arrangement of the furniture, or detected the household in negligence; and if she accepted any refreshment, seemed to do it only for the sake of finding out that Mrs. Collins' joints of meat were too large for her family.

Surely in such pictures as these there is not merely truth and life, but that saving salt of humour which, more than anything else, preserves the literature of a past age from oblivion.

The comparison between Jane Austen and Shake-speare, suggested by both Macaulay and Mr. Goldwin Smith, is ingenious, and, within the limits drawn by these great critics, just; but Thackeray affords us a closer comparison. The spirit of Jane Austen is en-tirely the spirit of Thackeray.

There is the same criticism of life; the hatred of shams, and the quick irony that pierces and exposes them; the delightful turns of expression, the caustic word which is not readily forgotten, and the humour, half genial and half sardonic, by which the facts of life are illumined. The only difference is that, while Thackeray was really angry with snobs, Jane Austen is too conscious of their absurdities to be irritated over them. Thackeray can be very bitter; but Jane Austen gives her most caustic criticisms a flavour of humour which robs them of ill-nature. When it becomes a question of pathos, Thackeray out-distances Jane Aus-ten completely; but probably that is due simply to the fact that in 1850 writers did not deem it necessary to disguise their tenderer feelings, and in 1811 they did.

A woman who carefully concealed the fact that she was a writer, and wished only to be loved and trusted for her womanliness, would not be likely to uncover the depths of her heart even in books. Jane Austen was trained in the tradition that regarded any display of deep feeling as unwomanly, and the real reticence and modesty of her nature made the expression of pathos as difficult as it was undesirable. But on her humour she put no restraint save that of kindliness, and keen as is her irony it is impossible to accuse her of cynicism. In this also she resembles Thackeray, who concealed beneath the assumed savageness of the satirist the softest and most human of hearts.

But it would be a gross error to suppose that Jane Austen is incapable of pathos or fine sentiment. Who can create a true comedy of life without at times touching those deeper springs of romance and passion that underlie even the humblest existence?

Narrow as were the limits which Jane Austen set for herself, there are, nevertheless, moments of fine intensity, when her feelings master her method—as, for example, when she speaks of the love-musings of Anne Elliot, as she walks the streets of Bath, and says that they were enough almost " to spread purification and perfume all the way." For herself, she was content to live a life that never knew the agitations of passion. Her recompense was in the steadiness and firmness of those home-ties which held her fast to the quiet hearts that loved her and knew her worth. The tenderest unselfishness characterised her life from beginning to end. When she was very ill, and near death, she would not use the sofa—sofas in those days were rare—because she was afraid if she did so her mother might scruple to use it. She made shift with a couple of chairs, and persuaded her mother that they were more comfortable. It is a little touch, but a tender and pathetic one, and it shows the woman. In one of her last letters she says, " God bless you, my dear E——. If ever you are ill, may you be as tenderly nursed as I have been." And she goes on to say that she feels utterly unworthy of so much love. When the end came, one of her attendants asked her if she wanted anything. " Nothing but death," she replied, and these were her last words. She was buried quietly in Winchester Cathedral, and in the " Annual Register " for the year there is no mention of her death. To-day every summer brings numerous pilgrims to her grave, and her latest and most brilliant critic has said, " On her was bestowed, though in a humble form, the gift which has been bestowed on Homer, Shakespeare, Cervantes, Scott, and a few others—the gift of creative power."

V

THE WAVERLEY NOVELS

Walter Scott, born August 15th, 1771, in Edinburgh. "Waverley," published July, 1814; "Guy Mannering," February, 1815; "The Antiquary," May, 1816; "The Black Dwarf" and "Old Mortality," December, 1816; "Rob Roy" and "The Heart of Midlothian," 1818; "The Bride of Lammermoor" and "The Legend of Montrose," 1819; "Ivanhoe," "The Monastery" and "The Abbot," 1820; "Kenilworth" and "The Pirate," 1821; "The Fortunes of Nigel," 1822; "Peveril of the Peak," "Quentin Durward," and "St. Ronan's Well," 1823; "Red Gauntlet," 1824; "The Betrothed" and "The Talisman," 1825; "Woodstock," 1826; "The Two Drovers," "The Highland Widow," "The Surgeon's Daughter," and "The Fair Maid of Perth," 1828; "Anne of Geierstein," 1828; "Count Robert of Paris" and "Castle Dangerous," 1831. Scott acknowledged the authorship of the "Waverley Novels" in 1826. He died in 1832.

IN Lockhart's " Life of Scott " there is a vivid and picturesque description of Scott's removal from Ashestiel to Abbotsford in 1812, drawn by the hand of the master himself. Scott tells us that his neighbours

have been delighted with the procession of my furniture, in which old swords, bows, targets, and lances have made a very conspicuous show. A family of turkeys was accommodated within the helmet of some *preux chevalier* of ancient border fame ; and the very cows, for aught I know, were bearing banners and muskets. I assure your ladyship that this caravan, attended by a dozen ragged, rosy peasant children, carrying fishing-rods and spears, and leading ponies, grey-hounds, and spaniels, would, as it crossed the Tweed, have furnished no bad subject for the pencil, and really reminded me of one of the gypsy groups of Callott upon their march.

In another letter he tells us:

Our flitting and removal from Ashestiel baffled all description; we had twenty-five cartloads of the veriest trash in nature, besides dogs, pigs, ponies, poultry, cows, calves, bare-headed wenches, and bare-breeched boys.

In this spirited sketch the temperament of Scott is clearly revealed. We realise at once that he was infected with the same enthusiasm for mediævalism that was the most positive feature of Walpole's character, and that he had a real passion for country life, as authentic as that which distinguished Rousseau. Great men, and even the greatest, inherit tendencies as well as create them; and although there was in Scott a certain massive manliness and good sense, an almost distinctive sanity as it were, yet the double strain of Walpole and Rousseau met in him. Scott's passion for accumulating " old swords, bows, targets, and lances " is indistinguishable from Walpole's elaborate connoisseurship except that it has a manlier basis. Strawberry Hill and Abbotsford are creations of the same craze for mediævalism—each a parody, each an imposture, each a fanaticism. As for Rousseau, the most genuine thing about him was his real delight in Nature, and his real preference for country life. When he tells us that he is never conscious of true felicity except in the quiet of rural scenery, he speaks with an enthusiasm which creates conviction. Scott, when he says he thinks he should have died if he had not seen the heather once a year, speaks much as Rousseau did. His love for Abbotsford was quite as much love for its quiet scenery as for the expensive Gothic toy he had erected there. It was from this double tendency that the Waverley Novels were to be created. Feudalism and Nature are the two notes which Scott strikes with extraordinary effect. The man who was to write the Waverley Novels could not be better depicted than in this vivid sketch of the flitting from Ashestiel to Abbotsford; the ancient helmet with the family of turkeys in it describes his temperament and is the symbol of his genius.

Readers of Scott's Life will at once admit the truth of these observations. He had no interest in the rise of industrialism which marked the beginning of the nineteenth century, and for the corresponding rise of democracy he had a positive aversion. The feudal ideal of life not only appealed to his imagination, but expressed his convictions. The part in life he most desired to play was that of the head or chieftain of a clan, surrounded by many retainers, united in his service by a genuine loyalty. The building of Abbotsford, that tragic folly as it proved to be, was, after all, the legitimate expression of the same ideal. It was an attempt to revive the old patriarchal dignity of a feudal household. There is this fundamental difference to be observed between the historical fictions of Scott and the historical novels of all other English authors—they were the real expression of his own nature, not a laboured effort to depict the past. From childhood his mind had been steeped in the old border poetry and romance. There was not a ruined tower nor a solitary border glen with whose legend he was not acquainted.

The past throbbed in his blood. It was a perfectly natural thing that he should seek to gather retainers round him, and that he should build Abbotsford. It was equally a natural and inevitable thing that, when he had once conceived the idea of writing prose fiction, he should write romantic fiction.

This is a point to be insisted on, because it explains the immense superiority of Scott as a writer of the historical novel. There are many English writers who have produced fine historical novels, comparable with, and even superior to, the best of Scott. Charles Reade has done so in his " Cloister and the Hearth." Thackeray in his " Esmond," Shorthouse in his " John Inglesant." Taken separately and on their own merits, either of these novels may be ranked with the best of Scott, and there are many of us who, if we had the courage to be quite truthful, would assert that Scott has never equalled either Reade's or Thackeray's masterpieces. But there is this essential difference—great as these works are, yet they are manifestly the result of immense labour and erudition. They do not represent the real bent of their author's genius. They are excursions into a strange land of art, executed with consummate skill and genius, which surprise us in the same way that we should be surprised if Isaac Newton had gone upon the stage and acted Hamlet, or Shakespeare had published an essay on logarithms. In spite of all the wonderful merits of " Esmond," the real Thackeray is expressed in " Vanity Fair," and the same thing is true of Reade's " Hard Cash " in relation to " The Cloister and the Hearth." Such books are *tours de force*. They simply serve to show us that a man of genius, by dint of labour, may write almost any kind of book he likes, and write it not only well, but much better than some other man who has made this particular kind of book his specialty. But Scott writes the historical novel simply because there is no other kind of novel which he could write. He had no need to cram his subject, as Reade did, by enormous labours in the Bodleian before he wrote " The Cloister and the Hearth "; it is native to him. He writes not only with fulness of knowledge on any given period, but with that instinctive rightness of touch which comes from immersion in the spirit of the period. He may occasionally fail in accuracy as Reade could not have failed, but he never fails in that higher kind of truth which gives a firm artistic reality to past history. In a word, he brings much more than learning, much more than patient investigation, to his task—he brings his entire personality; and this is the reason why his superiority remains unchallenged.

The building of Abbotsford, which has been so much condemned by practical men as the one unpractical thing in Scott's life, is in itself a striking proof of this criticism. Many men of letters have had curious private tastes; one collects pipes, another stamps, another (a Zola, for example) old furniture. One does not find, however, that Zola's love for mediæval furniture meant that he was a mediævalist. It was a pleasant pastime, a mild extravagance; when he built a house it was an ordinary modern house, and when he took up his pen he was still a realist. Scott's case was wholly different. He is not to be ranked with the dilettante who takes up the search for old oak and armour as a pastime, and still less with the suddenly enriched man of letters who wishes to build himself a lordly pleasure-house, and get to himself honour as a social magnate. Abbotsford was a passion, not a pastime. No more sagacious and practical man than Scott ever lived, so far as the ordinary affairs of life were concerned; but on one side of his character he was as mad as Don Quixote. The moment he breathed the air of old romance his business sagacity deserted him, and he was off upon his Rosinante to the fields of quite incredible adventure. Not to recognise this strain of Quixote in Scott is not to know him at all. It is the strain which produced his novels. Abbotsford is the most valuable commentary upon the novels that exists. It is the proof, we may say, that the writing of romance was not a trade with Scott, but a fundamental necessity of his character and genius.

It is one of the most pleasant traditions of Scott's authorship that no one would have guessed that he was an author by observation of his daily life. He wrote rapidly, and with such perfect ease, that in his best period his literary work was less a labour than a pastime to him. No one saw him in his study, and, for obvious reasons connected with the mystery with which he chose to veil the authorship of the Waverley Novels, no one heard him discuss his books. The man known to the world, and to the crowd of guests who shared the lavish hospitality of Abbotsford, was essentially the man we see migrating from Ashestiel, surrounded by admiring dependents, interested in all the details of country life, and apparently absorbed in the practical management of his estate. We must not, however, allow ourselves to be imposed upon by this picture of Scott as a gentleman at ease. However Scott came by his erudition, there is no doubt of the erudition. He sometimes wrote carelessly because he wrote in haste, but he never wrote ignorantly. His antiquarian knowledge was profound. He knew not merely the general features of any period he chose to describe, but he was familiar with its smallest details. His passion for detail is so great that it often becomes pedantic. He is apt to overload his narrative with information which is of much more interest to the antiquarian than the general reader. In most of his books the commencement is heavy and tedious simply because he is at pains to picture the conditions of the period in which the story is cast. But it is this very wealth of detail which in the long run is Scott's strongest weapon, for it gives a solidity of workmanship and produces an impression of truth which few historical novels possess. His genius is evident in nothing so much as this, that it is able to move freely under what a man of less imaginative power would have found a suffocating weight of antiquarian lore, and he rarely fails to fuse this mass of material into vital form.

It has often been said that Scott fails as a writer through his lack of literary art. He writes well, with a sort of good-natured ease, and in a sound pedestrian fashion, but he does not write brilliantly. This is perfectly true, in the sense that there are few purple patches in his writings. He has little gift of epigram; there are few passages of his novels over which the mind lingers for the mere delight communicated by their perfection of literary form, and he scarcely ever utters a thought which illumines the depth of things. His fiction in this respect is like his poetry; the charm of each is naturalness. Yet it must not be forgotten that Scott's prose often rises into real eloquence. Such a passage occurs in " The Abbot," and it is a fair sample of a kind of philosophy common to the man who has never reflected very deeply upon the nature of life, and yet has a quick eye for much that lies upon its surface. After a really vivid and striking picture of the various personages who compose the age of which he writes, Scott concludes:

In short, it was that gay and splendid confusion, in which the eye of youth sees all that is brave and brilliant, and that of experience much that is doubtful, deceitful, false, and hollow; hopes that will never be gratified; promises which will never be fulfilled; pride in the guise of humility; and insolence in that of frank and generous bounty.

Many similar passages which have glow and real colour might be quoted, and they should be sufficient to prove that Scott was not so deficient in the art of fine writing as those who value the happy turning of a phrase more than the consistent picture of an epoch would have us imagine.

The main fault of Scott does not lie in this direction, but rather in his defects as a story-teller and his lack of psychological interest. It is a kind of heresy to accuse the greatest of romancists of incapacity to tell a story well, and yet what reader of average intelligence will not corroborate the charge? Scott has not, for instance, the art, common to scores of inferior novelists, of fixing the attention of the reader with the first chapter of his novel. He is often so prolix and so dull that we despair of ever coming to the story, and are tempted to skip the first half-dozen chapters in order to arrive at it. The absence of plot is nearly always notable. It is clear that he begins to write without any

very positive idea of the path he means to take. He
himself has confessed so much in the Introductory
Epistle to " The Fortunes of Nigel."

I have repeatedly [he says] laid down my future work to
scale, divided it into volumes and chapters, and endeavoured to
construct a story which I meant should evolve itself gradually
and strikingly, maintain suspense, and stimulate curiosity; and
which, finally, should terminate in a striking catastrophe. But
I think there is a demon who seats himself on the feather of
my pen when I begin to write, and leads it astray from the purpose. Characters expand under my hand; incidents are multiplied; the story lingers, while my materials increase; my
regular mansion turns out a Gothic anomaly, and the work is
closed long before I have attained the purpose I proposed.

No criticism could be truer than this. With Scott
it very often turns out that the real interest of the
book settles round some subsidiary character, and not
round the character which was manifestly designed for
primacy. The love story of Waverley is forgotten
because the mind of Scott has become fascinated with
the romance of the Highland clans in 1745. Julia
Mannering, who was manifestly cast for a leading part
in the story of " Guy Mannering," is quite eclipsed by
Meg Merrilees. The ostensible purpose of " The Heart
of Midlothian " appears to be a vivid picture of the
Porteous Riots. The real story of the book is the
story of Jeannie Deans. We can scarcely grumble,
for nothing that Scott has done is so full of real power
and pathos ; but we may safely wager that when Scott
began the book he had no idea of making Jeannie Deans
its central figure. " The Heart of Midlothian " also
illustrates another great defect of Scott as a story-teller
—his frequent inability to end upon the true dramatic

note. The interest of "The Heart of Midlothian" is exhausted when Jeannie Deans has won her sister's pardon; all that follows is padding. It is true that some of the greatest of Scott's novels are free from these defects. "The Bride of Lammermoor" is an admirably constructed story, and in "Kenilworth" the thread of dramatic interest is never dropped for a moment. That Scott did succeed as a story-teller in these instances suggests that his failure in many other instances arose rather from haste and carelessness than incapacity. He poured his books out so rapidly that he never gave himself time to meditate upon them. His interest in them was energetic rather than intense. And perhaps also he was so sure of his audience, and of his own power to interest his audience before he had done, that he thought it of little consequence to spend much thought upon his plot, when he was conscious of how splendid was the material with which he had to deal.

The absence of psychological interest in Scott is a point more difficult of statement. It may very easily be put in such a form as to be a gross misstatement. Briefly, what is meant, is this: that while Scott can grasp and state with rare perspicacity the visible outlines of a character, he has little gift for analysing its finer subtleties. His characters live—there is no mistake about that; they are as truly the creatures of genius as the creatures of Shakespeare, but it is in an entirely different way. James I. lives, but it is not as Hamlet lives. Jeannie Deans lives, but it is not as Ophelia lives. The Marguerite of Goethe's "Faust" lives; but what shall we say of Flora MacIvor? Shakespeare and Goethe have created types, Scott only persons. Ophelia and Marguerite represent humanity; Jeannie Deans represents only a very excellent specimen of peasant heroism. Not only so, but the very personages whom Scott most clearly designs for hero and heroine are often, and almost uniformly, the least interesting personages in his books. Nigel is a terribly dull young man, whose adventures are only interesting because they serve as an introduction to the Court of James I., the pride and state of Buckingham, and the melancholy of Charles. Quentin Durward is little better; he is merely a note of introduction to Louis XI. Scott's women are frequently unsuccessful, and perhaps the most severe test of a novelist's art is its power of creating women, because for such a task a very rare degree of psychological insight is required. Scott can give us the outside of his heroine, much as Macaulay gives us the outside of history or biography. He can describe her dress and manners, with a most vivid art, just as Macaulay describes the habits and appearance of Dr. Johnson. But he does not unlock the intimacies of personality any more than Macaulay does. Singularly enough he comes nearest to this highest form of art in his subsidiary characters. He does possess a real insight into the souls of abnormal, grotesque, or very humble persons. But in the main this is a gift which Scott lacks. He sees the pageant of life, but not its mystery; tells us how men act, but not how they feel. Shakespeare did both, and hence the soul of Hamlet is better known to us than his history. If Scott had painted Hamlet, we should have known his history, but not his soul.

VI

SCOTT'S GREATNESS

IT is characteristic of Scott's genius that his greatest successes are attained when he has to deal with the largest canvas. Give him a truly great scene to describe, such as the appearance of Elizabeth amid the revels of Kenilworth, and he is at his best. Nowhere, out of Shakespeare's historical dramas, can we find such a series of splendid figures, drawn from the life, and energetic with great passions and ambitions. Quentin Durward may be intrinsically unimpressive, and Nigel may be the most wooden of heroes, but how full of vital force are the figures of Louis XI. and James I. Take such a passage as this as an example. It describes James I. as Nigel found him, when he was unexpectedly introduced to the king's closet:

The scene of confusion amid which he found the king seated was no bad picture of the state and quality of James's own mind. There was much that was rich and costly in cabinet pictures and valuable ornament; but they were arranged in a slovenly manner, covered with dust, and lost half their value, or at least their effect, from the manner in which they were presented to the eye. The table was loaded with huge folios, amongst which lay light books of jest and ribaldry; and, amongst notes of unmistakably long orations and essays on king-craft, were mingled miserable roundels and ballads of the "Royal Prentice," as he styled himself, in the art of poetry, and schemes for the general pacification of Europe, with a list of the names of the king's hounds, and remedies against canine madness. . . . Over his green doublet he wore a sad-coloured nightgown, out of the pocket of which peeped his hunting-horn. His high-crowned grey hat lay on the floor, covered with dust, but encircled with a carcanet of large balas rubies. . . . But such inconsistencies of dress and appointment were mere outward types of those which existed in the royal character. He was deeply learned, without possessing useful knowledge; sagacious in many individual instances, without having real wisdom; . . . fond of his dignity, while he was perpetually degrading it by undue familiarity; capable of much public labour, yet often neglecting it for the meanest amusement; a wit, though a pedant; and a scholar, though fond of the conversation of the ignorant and uneducated. . . . He was laborious in trifles, and a trifler where serious labour was required; devout in his sentiments, and yet too often profane in his language; just and beneficent by nature, he yet gave way to the iniquities and oppressions of others. He was penurious respecting money which he had to give from his own hand, and yet inconsiderately and unboundedly profuse of that which he did not see. In a word, those good qualities which displayed themselves in particular cases and occasions were not of a nature sufficiently firm and comprehensive to regulate his general conduct; and showing themselves as they occasionally did, only entitled James to the character bestowed on him by Sully—that he was the wisest fool in Christendom.

This is in itself an admirable and just description of James, done in the style which Macaulay afterwards made so popular. But it is much more than that—it is a collection of various clues to character in James, from which Scott works out a piece of truly creative art. The subsequent scene in Greenwich Park, when the king suspects Nigel of an attempt upon his person, and in the extremity of his cowardice imagines himself wounded, is a masterpiece of characterisation. The weakness, vanity, pedantry, awkwardness, and fundamental good-nature of James reveal themselves in every act and word of the alarmed king. Scott himself feels, and makes us feel, the curious mixture of affection and contempt with which he was regarded. When Scott is dealing with ordinary mortals he often writes in an ordinary way, and betrays by the lethargy of his style his lack of interest in them. But give him some great historical figure, such as a James I., a Louis XI., or an Elizabeth, and his genius is at once stimulated to a supreme effort. His art, as he truly says, is incapable of the fine miniature work of a Jane Austen; but give him a big brush and a broad canvas, and he has no equal.

It is in scenes like this that we are willing to admit that kinship with Shakespeare which has often been claimed for Scott. Carlyle's comment upon this claim, that " Shakespeare works from the heart outwards, Scott works from the skin inwards, never getting near the heart of men," is well known; but it has no more than that measure of truth which is required to preserve a paradox from absurdity. In writing such a sentence it is probable that Carlyle was thinking of the supreme imaginative figures of Shakespeare, such as Hamlet and Othello, Ophelia and Desdemona; but such a comparison is unfair to Scott. A much fairer comparison would be between the historic figures of Shakespeare and the historic figures of Scott, because here the material is similar and there is coincidence of aim. Shakespeare himself used two entirely different forms of art—in the one giving form and substance to the bodiless creatures of his mind, in the other attempting the vivid presentation of entirely human creatures, more or less known already by the part they played in history. The only just comparison between Shakespeare and Scott must be confined to their common use of the latter form of art. We cannot compare Ophelia and Jeannie Deans; we may compare Shakespeare's Wolsey with Scott's Charles Edward, Shakespeare's Henry VIII. with Scott's James I., and Shakespeare's Queen Katherine with Scott's Elizabeth. And in such a comparison Scott has little to lose. He is doing in another way just what Shakespeare does; he is attempting the vivification of history. He is dealing, as Shakespeare deals, with a mass of more or less authenticated legends that cluster round a great personage. The work of each is the interpretation of a character concerning which much is already known. It is not invention that is needed, but creative imagination working upon ascertained material. This kind of imagination Scott has in a degree scarcely inferior to Shakespeare. When we put the historical plays of Shakespeare and the historical romances of Scott side by side, we become conscious of a real kinship in their spirit, and an equal creative power in their representation of central figures; and this is the only kind of parallel which can or should be permitted.

Scott's greatest triumphs are achieved in the depiction of great historic personages and scenes, but it must not be forgotten that he has a firm grasp upon life as a whole, and a wide sympathy with all sorts and conditions of men. His imagination is peculiarly susceptible " to the influence of great achievements and prolonged success in wide-spreading affairs "; but he was enough of a poet, and enough of a Scotsman, to have an almost equal sympathy with the simplest and humblest forms of life. Mr. Bagehot has pointed out, with equal truth and felicity, that Scott is singularly skilful in his delineation of the poor.

He avoids the error of Dickens, who vulgarised the poor, making them " poor talkers, poor livers, and in all ways poor people to read about"; he avoids also the error of sentimental novelists, who clothe the poor with the glamour of Arcadia. Scott's poor folk are genuine poor folk, shrewd, manly, sensible, generous, avaricious, proud, humble, selfish, and heroic. " His poor people are never coarse and never vulgar; their lineaments have the rude traits which a life of conflict will inevitably leave on the minds and manners of those who are to lead it; their notions have the narrowness which is inseparable from a contracted experience; their knowledge is not more extended than their restricted means of attaining it would render possible. Almost alone among novelists Scott has given a thorough, minute, lifelike description of poor people, which is at the same time genial and pleasing."

In achieving these results Scott was no doubt greatly helped by the fact that he was a Scotsman, and that he had strong feudal sympathies. In spite of all the stiffness of Scotch character and Scotch respect for rank there has always been much more of genuine democratic feeling in Scotland than in England. The rich and poor live together in a more genuine social bond. The strong self-respect which exists in each makes intimate intercourse possible, without the suspicion of condescension on the one side or of subservience on the other. Scott's lifelong friendship for his humble retainer, Tom Purdie, is an excellent example of this spirit. It was a genuine friendship, scarcely possible in any other country than Scotland.

The dying spirit of the clan, which Scott sought to revive, had many disadvantages; but it had this supreme advantage—that it created a real community of life between persons of entirely different social position, which was destined to disappear when wealth became the sole claim to social honour. Scott, in spite of his high Tory politics, was a genuine democrat in spirit, and really loved the common people. Hence he was admitted to their intimacy, and he depicted them with both sympathy and knowledge. And he had also, as every man of real creative genius must have, a vivid interest in humanity at large. He has himself told us that he never found himself in the company of the stupidest of companions in a post-chaise without finding that, in the course of conversation, he had some ideas suggested to him which he would have been sorry to have been denied. It is to these causes that the wide popularity of Scott may be traced. He makes friends with all men through his books, as he did in his life, by virtue of his geniality, his shrewd good sense, his warm appreciation of all that is best in human nature, his comprehension of its hidden valours, and his sympathy with its frailties.

The popularity which is based upon such qualities as these is a popularity which is likely to endure. During Scott's lifetime this popularity was quite uncon-tested; and he enjoyed an immunity from criticism which was of no advantage to him. Nor did he possess the gift of self-criticism. There is much truth in Carlyle's criticism that Scott's is " extempore writing," and that " something very perfect of its kind might have come from Scott, nor was it a low kind; nay, who knows how high, with studious self-concentration, he might have gone?" Carlyle was perhaps arguing from his own difficulty of production, or was thinking of the infinite patience by which Goethe built up his "Wilhelm Meister," when he thus criticised Scott. But who shall preach to genius, which is accustomed to take its own way, and is always ready to plead that no other way is possible to it? No doubt Scott might have produced far more perfect work had he possessed more of the spirit of self-criticism and self-concentration. He worked too hastily to do his best, and writing was much more of a trade with him than a vocation. The real object he had in view was not the satisfaction of his artistic conscience in the production of perfect work, but the satisfaction of his romantic dreams in the creation of Abbotsford; and such a motive is bound to be vitiating. We can plainly trace its effect in all his later work. We find faults of prolixity, slovenliness, and haste, which are trying to a temper educated in more exigent ideals of art. It needs a good deal of native resolution to struggle through the cloudiness of Scott's verbiage, the dulness of his preliminaries, the confusion of his plots. We feel sometimes that he grew tired of a book long before he finished it, and so do we. We find it hard to forgive him his habit of introducing some apparently pointless episode, such as the story of the Lady Hermione in "The Fortunes of Nigel," just at a point where his narrative has begun to acquire epic force and movement. We suspect him, not without reason, of a deliberate attempt to pad his story with matter which he knows is irrelevant. There is, in fact, a certain Scotch heaviness apparent in his books; he resembles the best of Scotch preachers, who are the dullest of orators when they are uninspired, and the fieriest when they are inspired.

But when we have said all the hard and all the just things we may about Scott, the fact remains that, in spite of Carlyle's advice, it is exceedingly doubtful if any amount of concentration would have enabled Scott to write in any other way, or any better. An extempore style of writing may be bad, yet by its means Scott produced so great a masterpiece as " The Bride of Lammermoor " in six weeks. It may be wrong to write for money, yet it is pretty certain that Shakespeare had the main chance well in view, even when he wrote " Hamlet," and he followed it so well that he died a prosperous burgher of Stratford-on-Avon. We have fallen in love to-day with the introspective novel; but Scott had never heard of it, and could not have produced it if he had. We like novels that explain philosophy or attack religion; Scott was content to tell a story, and let philosophy and religion look after themselves. He was simply a large-hearted and humane man of the world; an out-of-doors man who cared for his horses and his dogs a good deal more than he cared for the praise of his critics; a lover of life and of his kind, who took life generously and heartily; a man of instinctive virtue, of genial sanity, of great depth and sweetness of disposition, of quiet but authentic heroism in the hour of trial; one of the truly great men of the world, because he was in so much a child, and kept the child-like heart of love and simplicity, of natural piety and joy, to the last. He wrote according to his nature, and being by nature great, in spite of all his faults, he has written in a great way, and has left behind him a beloved and imperishable memory.

VII

WILLIAM MAKEPEACE THACKERAY

Born July 18th, 1811, in Calcutta. Published "The Paris Sketchbook," 1840; "The Yellowplush Papers," 1841; began publication of "Vanity Fair" in monthly numbers, 1847; "Pendennis," 1848; "Esmond," 1852; "The Newcomes," 1853; Editor of "The Cornhill Magazine," 1860. Died on Christmas Eve, 1863, at Palace Green, Kensington.

WALTER SCOTT died, worn out with heroic labours, in the autumn of 1832. He retained to the last his great popularity, in spite of the manifest failure of his later novels. It was only to be expected that he should have had many imitators, the chief of whom was Mr. G. P. R. James, whose first successful novel, "Richelieu," was published in 1825, and the best of whom, Mr. Harrison Ainsworth, attained a reputation which was undiminished almost half a century after Scott's death. John Galt, the author of "The Ayrshire Legatees" and "The Annals of Our Parish," must also be ranked with the disciples of Scott as a painter of Scottish life. Galt has only been equalled by Scott himself in the combined skill and humour with which he has described the foibles of the humble Scottish folk, and his fame would have stood much higher had his career been less unfortunate and his life less brief. The immediate influence of

Scott upon his contemporaries is visible in the works of these writers, but nevertheless for some time before Scott's death there were signs of changing taste in the public. The fame of Bulwer Lytton was achieved with the publication of " Falkland," in 1827, five years before Scott's death. In 1836, four years after Scott's death, appeared " Sketches by Boz," by Charles Dickens. In the same year in which Scott died Thackeray came of age, and in 1837 may be said to have begun the career of definite authorship by the publication of " The History of Samuel Titmarsh," in " Frazer's Magazine."

Fame has, upon the whole, been kindest to the last of these three writers. Thackeray has taken his unquestioned place as a classic, supported by the unanimous voice of criticism, and the somewhat reluctant, but nevertheless growing appreciation of the public. In the case of Dickens a distinction may be drawn between fame and popularity. The popular and the critical voices must be combined to produce fame. So far as the popular voice is concerned, no writer, not even Scott himself, has ever secured such an overwhelming plebiscite of praise; but hitherto, for various reasons, which may be considered later, criticism has been much divided on his merits. With Bulwer Lytton a worse thing has happened. After being hailed as a man of supreme genius by the critics of his own generation, he has been treated as an impostor by the critics of our own, and his novels, which once achieved boundless popularity, are now practically forgotten. The careers of these writers so closely coincide, that their greatest books were challenging attention at one time, which may be roughly defined as extending from the death of Scott, in 1832, to the death of Dickens, in 1870.

In contrast with Scott several things are at once apparent about Thackeray. The first is that he was a man of the world in a sense in which Scott was not. Scott was racy of his own soil, and remained so to the last. Thackeray was, by the very nature of his life as well as by temper, cosmopolitan. He had been educated in the proud traditions of an English gentleman; had early been brought into contact with the wider life of his race; was an artist and a club-man, touching on one side the life of Bohemia, and on the other the life of Mayfair; was travelled, cultured, and widely read, and was in all things the child of cities. Being thus a man of the world, it was inevitable that the material of his novels should be different from Scott's. Again, it must be noted that Thackeray brought fiction back to modern reality, from the study of the past to the study of the present. Not that Thackeray had not a very real kinship with Scott in his love of the past. He knew certain periods of history with a critical accuracy which Scott never attained. His "Esmond" is among the greatest, if not the greatest, of all historical novels in the English language. But even "Esmond" is penetrated by the modern spirit. Thackeray may write brilliantly of the past, but it is always with the pen of the man who lives in the present. He is also the founder of what may be called philosophic fiction. Scott, and indeed all his predecessors, had been content simply to tell a tale or to depict the movement of events in their relation to character. Here and there passages of reflection occur, but they express little more than the trite commonplaces of morality. Thackeray, on the contrary, has a definite philosophy to expound. He holds a certain view of life, which he regards as essential, and whether he is writing of the times of Marlborough or Wellington his art is constantly dominated by his philosophy, and the message he has to declare is distinctive. In all these respects Thackeray differs entirely from Scott. He introduces a new spirit into English fiction, and impels its development upon new lines. Scott really brings to a climax and splendid close the older school of fiction, although he has little in common with it; Thackeray—and with him Dickens must be reckoned a co-partner—inaugurates the new school.

There is another point to be noticed, which is even more significant. Thackeray's fiction is the intimate product of his temperament. This is not quite the same thing as saying that it expresses his philosophy of life; what is meant is rather that Thackeray's fiction has a personal element, in which the expression of his own character counts for more than the expression of his philosophy. It would be difficult to form an idea of the personal character of Fielding or Smollett from their books; and we have already remarked that Jane Austen gives us no hint of her own thoughts and opinions in all her voluminous writings. The same thing is equally true of Scott. No one, after reading the Waverley Novels from beginning to end, could form any correct idea of what manner of man their author was. He stands detached from his writings, himself unknown and unwilling to be known. Thus, for example, no one would suspect, in reading the later novels of Scott, that he was a less happy or fortunate man than when he wrote the earlier novels. An immense misfortune has beaten him to the ground, but there is no hint of it in his writings. He goes on writing in the same way, with some diminution of energy and spirit no doubt, but with no change of temper. The man in all things stands distinct from his writings, and the last thing of which Scott would have dreamed would have been to make his novels the channel of personal confession.

Thackeray's novels, on the contrary, are one prolonged personal confession. He creates characters, invents situations, narrates events, but behind all there is the subtle and pervasive element of his own personality. We are interested in Becky Sharp and Beatrix Esmond; we are equally interested in Thackeray. We follow their adventures with delight, but we wait with equal delight for Thackeray's comments upon them. We look into their hearts, but all the time we know that we are engaged in looking into the heart of Thackeray. This is a new element in fiction, closely akin to the new element which is vaguely described as the " personal note " introduced into the poetry of Byron. Although poetry is in the nature of things the most personal form of literature, yet there is a marked difference between the poetry of the early eighteenth century and the poetry of the nineteenth century, in the slightness of the personal note in the one, and the fulness of that note in the other. Pope and Gray tell us little of themselves; Byron and Shelly tell us everything. The poetry of Pope may be judged as literature alone; but one cannot judge the poetry of Byron and Shelly in this way, because the personal pathos and tragedy of the careers of the two poets are continually insistent on our memory. This new sensitiveness, this impulse of self-revelation which Byron introduced into poetry, Thackeray introduces into fiction; and we see this tendency in much of later nineteenth-century prose, such as Hazlitt's; still more in its greatest poetry, such as Browning's, and in almost all its greatest fiction, which has been produced under an impulse of self-confession, and is a veritable literature of temperament.

It becomes, therefore, a matter of importance to know what manner of man Thackeray was, since the right understanding of his work is impossible without the right understanding of the man. The masculine quality of his intellect needs no exposition. Lord Houghton, in the noble memorial verses which he wrote on Thackeray's death, rightly singles out this quality for praise, when he compares him with Dryden and Fielding: "Fielding without the manner's dross." Lord Houghton does not perceive so clearly that there was in Thackeray an exquisite sensitiveness, quite wanting in Dryden and Fielding. In all that concerns style Thackeray is masculine enough, but in the greater matter of the spirit he displays a sensitiveness almost morbid in its capability of pain. There is a very touching passage in " Vanity Fair " in which Thackeray speaks of the lonely and bitter childhood of William Dobbin, and goes on to ask, " Who amongst us is there who does not recollect similar hours of bitter, bitter, childish grief? Who feels injustice; who shrinks before a slight; who has a sense of wrong so acute, and so glowing a gratitude for kindness, as a generous boy? " One cannot but suspect an element of autobiography in this passage. There is much in Thackeray's writings which gives us the impression that his heart was badly bruised in childhood. No man had a friendlier nature, none a finer capacity for making friends, and yet there was a certain loneliness in Thackeray's life. Perhaps it was in the main that loneliness of individuality of which he himself has spoken, when he says that "the giants live apart"; but it was also the loneliness peculiar to highly sensitive natures, which have a distrust of life, based upon an insistent sense of the unsatisfactoriness and the frequent cruelty of life. It is not that Thackeray does not enjoy life at times, and does not often write as a man who enjoys it. It is not that he is destitute of courage to live life boldly; he is a writer who has a really fortifying message to those who shrink from the battle of life. But he cannot help writing as a man who has survived all youthful illusions about life. He is none the worse for the process, because he has kept his courage, and the heart of a little child, and his faith in "the ultimate decency of things." But henceforth, even in the gayest scenes, he is uneasily conscious of painful things which are visible to no one else. Through his most boisterous burlesque—and no man ever wrote burlesque so well—there throbs the ground note of sadness. From first to last the sermon he preaches is from the text of his greatest book, " Vanitas Vanitatum omnia Vanitas."

Many instances of this extreme sensitiveness of Thackeray to the tragic elements of human life will suggest themselves. It very often comes upon the reader as a surprise, because there is nothing in the immediate context of the story to suggest it. We expect the note of tragedy in " Macbeth "; but Thackeray makes us aware of it in the servants' hall. It is to the tragedy of common things that Thackeray is most sensitive, hearing always behind the decent shows of life "the still sad music of humanity." Take, for example, this passage:

Between me and those fellow-creatures of mine who are sitting in the room below, how strange and wonderful is the partition! We meet at every hour of daylight, and are indebted to each other for a hundred offices of duty and comfort of life; and we live together for years and don't know each other. John's voice to me is quite different to John's voice when he addresses his mates below. If I met Hannah in the street with her bonnet on, I doubt whether I should know her. And all these good people, with whom I may live for years and years, have cares, interests, dear friends and relatives, mayhap schemes, passions, longing hopes, tragedies of their own, from which a carpet and a few planks and beams utterly separate me. When we were at the seaside, and poor Ellen used to look so pale, and run after the postman's bell, and seize a letter in a great scrawling hand, and read it, and cry in a corner, how should we know that the poor little thing's heart was breaking? She fetched the water, and she smoothed the ribbons, and she laid out the dresses, and brought the early cup of tea in the morning, just as if she had no cares to keep her awake.

And then he goes on to tell the story of his manservant Henry, who waited at table through a tedious dinner, and at last, when every guest was attended to, said meekly, "If you please, sir, may I go home?"

He had received word that his house was on fire; and, having seen through his dinner, he wished to go and look after his children and little sticks of furniture.

That is all. It is not Thackeray's manner to enter upon any pathetic dilation of the scene—he lets it work its own inevitable effect. But who does not see at once that to a man with this supersensitiveness of nature life could not but be painful? The pain he suffered is what Mrs. Humphry Ward has called "the horrible pain of sympathy"; and, we may add, the noble pain too.

The sensitiveness of Thackeray is responsible for the spirit of irony which pervades his writings. He is full of sentiment, but ashamed of sentiment; he wishes to confess himself fully, but he shrinks from possible ridicule; he constantly gives us the impression of a man who is afraid to let himself go. Hence he falls back upon irony, which is the defence of the shy and sensitive man. His heart is full of soft feeling, of magnanimity, tenderness, nobleness, but he knows how these qualities are regarded by the rough world, and he has reason to dread the world's criticism. What can he do in self-defence but adopt the tone of the world? How can he better guard himself from the impertinence of the world's scrutiny than by making believe that he also is a true child of Vanity Fair? And he makes believe too successfully for his credit. He will talk as though all men were liars, as though tenderness were an unknown quality in human relations and magnanimity an extinct virtue, as though greed and grab and Mammon and the service of the golden calf were the chief forces at work in society. He overdoes his part purposely, trusting to the wise discernment of his reader to recognise the imposition and the reason for it. He reserves for such discerning readers his whispered asides, in which the real man speaks. They will see "the fire of unshed tears" in his eyes while he jests; they will hear the thrilling note of pain through his brilliant banter. There is in his heart a little black pool of pain which is apt to over-flow, and poison all the channels of his life—they will perceive it. He is conscious of a certain hysteric tend-ency to weep against his will, because the awful tragedy of life at times overcomes him—they will un-derstand it. No doubt the discerning reader does understand, but all readers are not discerning. The stupid people are very numerous, and nothing is so in-comprehensible to a stupid man as irony. Hence it happens that Thackeray's irony is constantly misunder-stood. He is thought to be in earnest when he jests, and jesting when he is in earnest. For the last thing a man who is neither shy nor sensitive is capable of un-derstanding is that the shy man is shy about his most sacred beliefs, often belying them in his words; and that the sensitive man goes in fear of his sensitive-ness, often making haste to laugh for fear that he should weep.

The result of this common misunderstanding of Thackeray's ironical method is that he has been ac-cused of cynicism. The accusation has obtained too much credence to be brusquely ignored. What is a cynic? One of our dramatists has replied with the brilliant definition that "a cynic is a man who knows the price of everything and the value of nothing." In this sense Thackeray was certainly no cynic. No man knew better the value of the best things in life, such as virtue, honour, love, courage, and magnanimity. If he also knew that there are other qualities in human na-ture which often have their price in Vanity Fair, he only knew what every moralist and every man of the world knows but too well. Swift was an unquestion-able cynic, because he had no belief in the radical goodness of human nature. He saw no good thing in man, and quite honestly believed him to be the vilest and most detestable of all animals. Will any one venture to say that Thackeray manifests anything like the same hatred and repugnance toward human nature which Swift displays? Thackeray's own essay on Swift is a significant answer. "What had this man done?" he writes, "what secret remorse was rankling at his heart? What fever was boiling in him, that he should see all the world bloodshot? A weary heart gets no gladness out of sunshine: a selfish man is sceptical about friendship, a man with no ear doesn't care for music." In an earlier passage of the same essay Thackeray denounces Swift for that very cynicism which refused all reverence for human nature. He accuses him of being himself nothing better than a Yahoo: "a monster gibbering shrieks, and gnashing imprecations against mankind—tearing down all shreds of modesty, past all sense of manliness and shame; filthy in word, filthy in thought, furious, raging, obscene." It was no cynic who could write thus of the supreme cynic of English literature. Thackeray has no particle of sympathy with the main thesis of all cynicism, which is the utter pettiness, meanness, and imbecility of mankind. Yet there must be some ground for the charge of cynicism made against him. It is not an accusation made by stupid people only; Mr. Frederic Harrison has made it. The stupid man may be bewildered by irony, and misinterpret it; we can hardly suppose a really brilliant critic like Mr. Harrison so dull as to mistake Thackeray's exposition of a base man's view of life for his own view. How is it then that the charge has come to be made, and to be so generally believed? I think the answer is found in the kind of material which Thackeray employed in the creation of his fictions. He constituted himself the censor of his age. He had, of necessity, to bring himself into contact with much that was most corrupt in that age. He has exposed that corruption so thoroughly that the impression has been created that he took pleasure in his task, and did it with a gusto. His work of censor has been forgotten; what has been recollected is the obvious fact that the world he paints abounds in men and women who display the meanest qualities, and are actuated by the meanest passions of human nature.

VIII

CHARACTERISTICS OF THACKERAY

THE great characteristic of Thackeray is, then, his assumption of his part of the satirist and censor of morals. That he does go about his work as censor with gusto no one will deny. He is conscious that he wields the keenest of weapons, and he has the same kind of pleasure in its use that a great surgeon has in the delicate and finely tempered instruments of his art. He lays bare the secrecies of the soul with a subtle skill which cannot but afford artistic pleasure to himself; and the more intricate the operation, the more secret the disease, the more deftly concealed the sordidness or essential meanness of the soul submitted to his moral surgery, the keener is his pleasure in the triumph of his art. All this is natural; perhaps it is natural, too, that he should appear to us more at home in dissecting the foibles, follies, and meannesses of human nature than in discovering its magnanimities. There can be no doubt that upon the whole his bad people are better done than his good folk; they are more vital and complete, and therefore more impressive. Colonel Newcome is one of the noblest characters in fiction; but noble as he is, his nobility too often verges on a simplicity which lessens our respect for him. Amelia, with all her virtues, is silly, and Dobbin is a good deal of a fool. But where are there any

characters in fiction drawn with such superb art as
Becky Sharp and Beatrix Esmond? Becky Sharp is
the supreme creation of modern fiction. We see her
under variety of circumstance, and in all she is absolutely consistent and artistically impressive. Her cunning, daring, greed, her fundamental good-nature, her
contempt of principle, her wonderful skill in acting
any part that serves her ends, her quickness and subtlety of mind—all are rendered with a sort of dreadful
truth. It is as though her creator flung a search-light
into the innermost recesses of her nature, and showed
us the crawling vileness of the woman. We follow
her, repelled and yet fascinated, from first to last. Of
course this is a great triumph for the literary artist.
And, in extenuation, we ought to remember two
things: first, that the character of Becky Sharp is absolutely consistent with the scheme of the book; and,
secondly, that all great artists have found it easier to
make an impression with a bad character than with a
good one. The last observation is self-evident. There
is no student of Shakespeare who will not admit that
Iago is a more powerfully sketched character than
Othello, and that Lady Macbeth is much more impressive than Desdemona. There are few novels in which
the villain and the sinner do not hold the stage; even
George Eliot, with all her will to put ethics before art,
cannot help making Hetty Sorrel more fascinating
than Dinah Morris, and Tito Melema more interesting
than Romola. It is almost of the nature of things that
it should be so. We know all about goodness, but we
know little of the subtleties of sin, and they excite our
utmost curiosity. Such a theme calls out all the
psychological power of the true artist. It affords him

the raw material of tragedy. And thus, in spite of himself, it often happens that, as an author develops his book, such a character as Becky Sharp's fascinates his own mind, gradually usurps the stage, and from a moral point of view throws the whole picture out of perspective.

We must also remember the scheme and plan of such a book as " Vanity Fair." The very title of the book is its own apologia. It does not pretend to present us with an adequate picture of life as a whole, but of one section of it only. It is, as Mr. Frederic Harrison has justly called it, " a long comedy of roguery, meanness, selfishness, and affectation. Rakes, ruffians, bullies, fortune-hunters, adventurers, women who sell themselves, and men who cheat and cringe, pass before us in one incessant procession, crushing the weak and making fools of the good. Such, says our author, is the way of Vanity Fair—which we are warned to loathe and shun." We may admit that it is not pleasant; but is it true? Was Thackeray, writing when he did, and living in the world that then existed, justified in so scathing a piece of satire? It is quite beside the mark to say that we do not like satire. It is equally beside the mark to say that we have never known such a world as this. The thing to be remembered is that in all ages the satirist of manners has been of the utmost service to society in exposing its follies and lashing its vices. It is the work of the great satirist to apply the caustic to the ulcers of society; and if we are to let our dislike of satire overrule our judgment, we shall not only record our votes against a Juvenal and a Swift, but equally against the whole line of Hebrew prophets.

Again, it is a recognised rule of literature that we must make allowance for books according to the age in which they were written. We make this allowance in the case of Shakespeare and Fielding; the life they knew was often brutal, manners were coarse, and speech outspoken, and we admit that books written at such a time could not but reflect the nature of their age. Thackeray claims, and has a right to claim, the same literary charity. He professed to know by heart a certain corner of the world, and he described it as it was. It is no concern of ours whether we like the description or not; what we should ask is, Is it correct, is Becky Sharp a true picture of the scheming and unprincipled woman of keen brain and loose morals, and is this indeed Vanity Fair?

To that question any dispassionate critic is bound to reply in the affirmative. The vital force with which Becky Sharp seizes on the mind is a proof of the truth of the conception, and the same remark applies to the whole book. It is an almost absolute rule that no book makes a great impression on the general mind that is not substantially true to life. Failing in that, it fails in everything. It is passed on to the limbo of the artificial and fantastic, and is quickly forgotten.

But the larger question is, Does such a book enlist our sympathies on the side of vice or virtue? The whole debate on the claims of realism of which we hear so much to-day ought to turn—though often it is very far from doing so—on the answer to this question. We have a right, and a just right, to expect morality in the creations of art. There is much nonsense talked on the legitimacy and illegitimacy of novelists writing with a purpose. But all great artists are bound to have a purpose in their writing. Could Hamlet, could Macbeth, could Othello, have come into existence without some deliberate purpose in the mind of Shakespeare, some intention to use a dramatic motive for moral ends? Each play of Shakespeare's has its purpose deliberately written on it. It is written in accord with supreme moral instincts, and is thus what a play was often called in the dawn of dramatic art—"a morality." It is the same with novels, which in our age have taken the place held by the drama in Elizabeth's day. They are not, and cannot be, mere irresponsible and unrelated transcripts of life. To put it at the very lowest, they are written from some point of view; they express the writer's sense of what human life is like; and thus they unconsciously express also his moral ideas—or the absence of them. The chief matter about a novel, then, is not so much what it is composed of; what elements of life and what transcripts of human character are included in it; whether it deals with high life or low life, picturing for the most part men of character and virtue, or, on the other hand, rogues and profligates,—the chief question is, Does it finally and irresistibly enlist our sympathies on the side of goodness or evil, of virtue or vice?

In Thackeray's case the answer to this question is quite beyond cavil. Not only has he no sympathy with vice, but he is quite pitiless toward it. He has much less charity even than George Eliot, who has a way of hinting that the vices of her characters are hereditary, and therefore indelible, and may be fairly regarded with pity. Thackeray, on the contrary, is not merely merciless in his analysis of evil, but he constantly steps aside from the platform of pure art to occupy the pulpit of the hortatory moralist. In all his books the moralist shares the honours with the artist, and that man must be possessed of a very curious temperament who can read Thackeray without a sense of moral invigoration. No doubt Thackeray does show us a terrible " comedy of roguery, meanness, and selfishness "; quite as certainly he makes us loathe and shun the vices which he dissects with such pitiless elaboration.

But Thackeray does much more than scourge vice; throughout his books there runs a genuine vein of religion. A perfectly just claim might be made for him that he is the most religious of all English novelists, because he touches more constantly, more subtly and profoundly, than any other novelist those chords of sweet and reverent feeling which compose the religious sentiment.

Thackeray's religion is conventional in type, but it is entirely free from the insincerities of conventionalism. His ideal of religion is the ideal of the average Englishman of culture—a religion grave, sober, reticent, careful of decorum, averse to enthusiasm, respectful of usage, and in the main built upon solid virtues rather than speculative dogmas. It is true that he not infrequently introduces some type of religiosity that he may ridicule it. Sir Pitt Crawley, with his narrow puritanism, is an instance; so is Lady Emily Sheepshanks, of whose famous tract, " The Washerwoman of Finchley Common," we hear somewhat too much. The unforgettable descriptions of the pompous obsequies over old Sir Pitt, and of Becky Sharp after her downfall, going to church with great regularity, and becoming known as the patron of good works, are touched with a much bitterer and more deserved irony. But it is not in such passages that we should look for the expression of Thackeray's religion; that religion finds its real expression in the tenderness and the devoutness with which he speaks of the mysteries and discipline of life. How exquisite, for example, is the picture he draws of the widowed Amelia and her child:

Every night and every morning he and she—(in that awful and touching communion, which I think must bring a thrill to the heart of every man who witnessed or remembers it)—the mother and her little boy—prayed to Our Father together, the mother pleading with all her gentle heart, the child lisping after her as she spoke. And each time they prayed to God to bless dear papa, as if he were alive, and in the room with them.

Amelia Sedley is, as Thackeray frankly tells us, a weak creature, but he reveres her for her pious and humble heart. Old Sedley is also weak, but he meets death with quiet fortitude, and Thackeray supplies the true comment on his misfortunes when he says, " Well, well,—a carriage and three thousand a year is not the summit of the reward nor the end of God's judgment of men." The same reading of life appears in Colonel Newcome, who grows in all the graces of the heart under the discipline of sorrow, and keeps through all his misfortunes the simple faith of a little child.

Thackeray appears to paint these weak and unfortunate people for the express purpose of showing us how true a stay a humble faith in God is amid the vicissitudes of life. He says many bitter things of the fortunate, but there is only kindness in his lips when he speaks of the unfortunate. Towards the end of his own life he writes that as he walked through the streets of Edinburgh his heart was "strangely softened." The heart of Thackeray often knew that gracious mood; and when these devout gusts of tenderness pass over him, and memory, sympathy, and faith unseal the fountains of his emotion, no English novelist writes with so manly a pathos and piety, and none moves us so deeply. Perhaps it was of this very walk that Dr. John Brown has given us so vivid a description. Dr. Brown tells us that, at the north-west end of Corstmorphine Hill, there rose black against the pure radiance of the evening sky a wooden crane, and that, as they gazed at it, Thackeray gave utterance in a tremulous, gentle, and rapid voice to what all were feeling, in the word "Calvary." "All that evening he was very gentle and serious, speaking, as he seldom did, of divine things, of death, of sin, of eternity, of salvation; expressing his simple faith in God, and in his Saviour." The story is entirely characteristic. Behind all the assumed levity of Thackeray, and at the root of all his irony, there was a profound religious nature, and there is no book of his that does not contain many wise and beautiful passages which are the true expression of a pious heart.

It is from this rare union in Thackeray of a masculine intellect with a deeply pious and tender heart that his gift of pathos is derived. The power of pathos, so often associated with a certain weak sentimentalism, a certain femininity of temperament, is associated in Thackeray with the strongest masculine qualities, and is all the more impressive because it is governed by the natural reticence of the masculine temperament. We can imagine what the feminine novelist, who is as often a man as a woman, would have made of the death of George Osborn at Waterloo—the pages of rhetoric, the notes of exclamation, and the effusion of sentiment: Thackeray contents himself with two sentences:

> No more firing was heard at Brussels—the pursuit rolled miles away. Darkness came down on the field and city; and Amelia was praying for George, who was lying on his face, dead, with a bullet through his heart.

There is no striving after effect, no laborious accumulation of detail; the pathos of Thackeray is quite effortless, but as potent as Nature herself. It comes nearer the supreme art of Shakespeare than any other writer has done; it is like Shakespeare's pathos—the pathos of the packed phrase, the pathos of the brief poignant word, which goes to the root of things.

The pathos of Thackeray is certainly quite different in quality from the pathos of any other novelist, and is at the very pole of what passes for pathos in his great rival, Dickens. Is there any man of mature years who finds himself still affected to tears by the death of Little Nell? Is there any reader of average critical instinct who does not perceive the artificiality of the entire death-scene of Paul Dombey? One need not go so far as to say that these scenes strike the note of mock pathos—they do not; they are truly pathetic after their fashion, but it is an artificial, a melodramatic fashion. Compare with them the death of Colonel Newcome; or the less hackneyed account of the death of Samuel Titmarsh's first child:

> We were to leave our lodgings on Monday morning, but on Saturday evening the child was seized with convulsions, and

all Sunday the mother watched and prayed for it; but it pleased God to take the innocent infant from us, and on Sunday, at midnight, it lay a corpse on its mother's bosom. Amen! We have other children happy and well, now round about us, and from the father's heart the memory of this little thing has almost faded; but I do believe that every day of her life the mother thinks of her first-born that was with her for so short a while; . . . and she wears still at her neck a little, little lock of golden hair, which she took from the head of the infant as he lay smiling in his coffin. It has happened to me to forget the child's birthday, but to her never!

No elaboration, no attempt to wring the heart; the whole description is so plain as to be almost bald; yet who does not feel its overwhelming tenderness, and who of us, laboriously trying from time to time to describe some crisis of human sorrow, does not envy this power of achieving so fine a result by such simple means?

The same element of ease and unaffected naturalness which distinguishes the pathos of Thackeray is apparent in his humour and in his entire art. He is never guilty of forcing the note. He never mistakes farce for humour. He can see the oddities of human character, but in rendering them he avoids the temptation to the grotesque. There is a certain balance of mind in Thackeray, an old-fashioned dignity of character, very rare in imaginative writers. He prefers to move among ordinary people, describing them with easy wit; they are quite sufficient to stimulate his imagination. There is not a single person in " Vanity Fair " who is not a perfectly normal type, and the majority are commonplace. Sedley and old Osborn are ordinary men of commerce. The distinguishing note of Dobbin and Amelia is that they are undistinguished. The Crawleys are a dull race, and Rawdon Crawley is the dullest of them all. Even Lord Steyne and Rebecca Sharp are quite recognisable types. If we turn, by way of contrast, to the pages of Dickens or Victor Hugo or Balzac, we find that very often the reverse is true. The temptation to the grotesque is potent with each. The modesty of nature is constantly exceeded in order to produce striking effects. Pecksniff is not a man—he is a vice. Creatures like Jean Valjean of Hugo or the Vautrin of Balzac are personifications of a theory; they are something more, and something less than human. They are the creatures of genius, no doubt; but it is a kind of genius that lacks lucidity, balance, justness, and reasoned apprehension. But in Thackeray's genius the most remarkable quality is this very justness of apprehension. It is the product, in part at least, of strong intelligence and wide culture. He possessed the critical spirit in a degree that is rare among novelists. He had more than genuine historical knowledge of certain periods—he had the historical instinct. His "Lectures on the Four Georges" and the "English Humorists" are a proof of both. His masterly description of Marlborough in "Esmond" is unequalled by any similar description in the pages of professed historians. His own novels are, in fact, histories. They are colloquial histories, done with a rapid pen and a full mind. They are the outpouring of a man of trained intelligence and wide knowledge, who is so sure of the inherent interest of his material that he is relatively careless about the art of construction and situation. Thus, while they are really the creations of a very fine and delicate art, they appear artless;

while they abound in fine situations, they depend for interest less upon situation than any other novels in the language; and while they are supreme works of imagination, we are less conscious of their imaginative genius than of their critical penetration, their reasoned wisdom, their rare intelligence.

This predominance of the critical spirit in Thackeray, this constant sway of intelligence over imagination, produced a curious temper of detachment between the man and his work. He uses the right word for his creatures when he speaks of them as " puppets ": " Come, children, let us shut up the box and the puppets, for our play is played out." We read of Dickens becoming so interested in his creatures that he wept and laughed over them; and Stevenson complains that his heroes have a disastrous knack of turning their backs on him, and walking bodily off the stage, to his unutterable dismay. It is safe to say that Thackeray experienced none of these sensations. He makes no complaint, as many novelists have done, that his creatures " will not come right," and to some extent his art suffered by this lack of self-absorption in it. He is apt to write about his characters instead of letting them reveal themselves. Welcome as his frequent disquisition is for its wit and irony and tenderness, yet it is sometimes a hindrance to his narrative. What can we say, but that it is Thackeray's method—a peculiar and unique method, which he alone can justify? Puppets his creatures are, yet so firmly handled, so convincingly contrived, that it is only when their author bids us step behind the curtain that we perceive the string that moves them. For the most part the illusion is complete. Nothing can be liker life than the great scenes in which George Osborn takes farewell of his wife before Waterloo, or the yet greater scene in which Becky's intrigue with Lord Steyne is detected by her husband. It is the most vital praise that can be given to Thackeray, that in spite of a method which is radically bad he makes it the instrument of superb triumph. He becomes the artist while remaining the moralist. He excites our strongest interest in his drama, while he himself regards it with a kind of distant commiseration. He leaves us thrilling to his play, in spite of his ironical pains to assure us that the heroine is painted, and the hero but a sorry creature off the stage. In a lesser writer such liberties would be resented; if we do not complain of them in Thackeray, but rather enjoy them, it is because the genius of the writer is so great that we become unconscious of the eccentricities of its expression.

A word may be added on Thackeray's place as a writer. Thackeray is one of the greatest masters of style in English literature. The greatness of his style lies in its simplicity, its ease, its unaffected eloquence, its nervous strength. He wrote rapidly, but never carelessly. Through all the twenty-six volumes of his writings there is not a page which is not technically perfect. He had an instinct for the subtleties of language, trained by long acquaintance with Queen Anne literature. His writing has that quality which is rarest in good writing—it is good writing, but not fine writing. He has no need and no wish to contort language in order to achieve brilliance; he avoids the " purple patch "; but his style never fails to flow with an equal melody, which delights the ear without astonishing it. The last thing to be said of Thackeray, then, is not the least thing—it is that he is a great writer as well as a great novelist, which is a rare achievement. Others have known how to tell a story as well as he, and indeed many lesser men have been better story-tellers; but no English novelist has employed in the telling of his tale a style of such dignity, such purity and strength and real distinction.

IX

CHARLES DICKENS

Born at Landport, Portsmouth, February 7th, 1812. First original paper, " A Dinner at Poplar Walk," published in " The Monthly Magazine," December, 1833; " Sketches by Boz," 1836; " Pickwick Papers," first number issued in March, 1836; " Oliver Twist," 1838; " Nicholas Nickleby," 1839; " The Old Curiosity Shop," 1840; " Barnaby Rudge," 1841; " American Notes," 1842; " Martin Chuzzlewit," 1843; " The Christmas Carol," 1843; " Dombey and Son," 1846; " David Copperfield," 1849; " Bleak House," 1852; " Hard Times," 1854; " Little Dorrit," 1855; " A Tale of Two Cities," 1859; " The Uncommercial Traveller," 1861; " Great Expectations," 1861; " Our Mutual Friend," 1864; " The Mystery of Edwin Drood " (unfinished). Died at Gad's Hill, June 6th, 1870.

THE course of English fiction, in so far as we have hitherto been able to trace it, has been marked by very little that resembles scientific development. Beyond tracing certain relations between its parts, and certain derivative impulses, the principle of evolution is but feebly present, and only the pedantry of criticism will be much concerned about the matter. It will content the critic, who is more interested in the quality of art than the study of its origins, to remark the culmination of romantic fiction in Scott, the rise of domestic fiction in Jane Austen, and the appearance of a new kind of realism in Thackeray. If any general term can be employed to define the particular place of Dickens in fiction, we may say that he is a democratic novelist. In a sense scarcely applicable to any other novelist, he was a man of the people and wrote for the people. He had a real depth and intensity of popular sympathy, of which we find but occasional evidence in either Scott or Thackeray. In the course of his career he was attracted by many forms of art—the historical or pseudo-historical, for example, as illustrated in " Barnaby Rudge " and " A Tale of Two Cities "; but the driving force of his genius was at all times a passionate sympathy with democracy. He is the spokesman of the masses; he writes for them, and lives by their praise; he is understood of the common people, and delights in kinship with them; and he may thus claim to have been the creator of the democratic novel.

The early life and associations of Dickens are responsible for this outstanding feature of his genius. He owed nothing to gentle birth or early culture, as Scott and Thackeray did. He was educated at no public school and was a graduate of no university. A certain scorn of classical education is visible in his earlier books; Mr. Feeder, B.A., and Dr. Blimber, with his incessant prosing about the Romans, are the types he gives us of the instructors of youth. He makes no apology whatever for his ignorance of art. He rather prided himself upon it. When in mid-life he visited Italy and looked upon those supreme creations of art, of which a truly great man had once said, " We are the shadows, and these the realities," he saw little in them that did not excite his ridicule. He had no respect for any kind of rank, and little understanding of the finer qualities developed in fine natures by its social obligations. These and many similar limitations and defects are clear enough in his writings; but they are the defects of his qualities. They certainly will be passed over lightly by any generous critic, who remembers the narrowness and deprivation of Dickens's early life. The thing to be wondered at, the thing to be grateful for, is that Dickens kept so sweet a temper, that he was so little soured by the flagellations of unjust fate, and that against his democratic passion, which unquestionably worked strongly and successfully in the social regeneration of his time, nothing worse can be charged than some narrowness of view and some defects of taste.

It is, in truth, little less than miraculous that with so precarious an equipment Dickens should have won his way to fame at all. When the elder Dickens was asked where his son had been educated, he replied with true Micawber cheerfulness, " Ha, ha! he may be said to have educated himself." The son, in looking back on the same circumstance, has another comment. " It is wonderful to me," he says, " how I could have been so easily cast away. It is wonderful to me that no one had compassion enough on me—a child of singular abilities, quick, eager, delicate, and soon hurt, bodily or mentally—to suggest that something might have been spared, as certainly it might have been, to place me at any common school." It is difficult to acquit the parents of Dickens of something like criminal callousness or carelessness in this matter. The elder Dickens unfortunately belonged to that shiftless class which his son described as having " come to regard insolvency as the normal state of mankind, and the payment of debts as a disease that occasionally broke out." Dickens has often been blamed for some lack of filial reverence in caricaturing his father as Micawber; those who read the story of his childhood will agree that he took but a light revenge for a course of neglect and humiliation which he never should have endured. How deeply the whole matter rankled in his heart we may judge from the pathetic circumstance that the worst humiliations of his childhood were concealed from his wife until long after marriage, and he could never bring himself to speak about them to his own children.

Let us try to conceive the situation: a delicate and sensitive child virtually orphaned; reared amid scenes of dubious morality and shiftless waste; cast upon the world with as little compunction as Rousseau displayed in the disposal of his offspring; unacquainted with any wise example either of virtue or religion, and deriving any sanction of right conduct which he was able to attain from native intuition and natural impulse; a bright imaginative boy condemned to the life of a miserable drudge, doing the most menial work among the most uncongenial associates, and doing this work at an age when most children are busy at their games. It is hard to conceive a childhood more sad or more deplorable; yet he has told us that his parents were as entirely satisfied with his condition as though he had been a youth of twenty, " distinguished at a grammar school, and going to Cambridge." He has also told us that, for all the care exercised over him by those whose duty to him was the clearest, he might have been a little vagabond or a little thief. It was no exaggeration. The child had no home; his father was in prison for debt, and the only holiday from sordid toil he knew at one time was to spend Sunday in the prison with his father. He had no friends; he lived a lonely life in a great city, from his weekly wage of eight shillings providing himself with food and lodging as he could. But the solitary child had a precocious manliness about him as pathetic as it was extraordinary. He endured his hardships gallantly, and in a spirit of true heroism. And he had what was rarer than fortitude—a certain sunniness of nature, which remained undarkened by misery, and was proof against the bitterness instilled by his misfortune. His light-heartedness, his cheerful optimism, his humour, were derived from his father; they were the only legacy that ever came to him from that least parental of all parents. It is not wonderful that such experiences should have developed to the highest point an impassioned sympathy with the poor; the singular thing is that he kept his geniality. It is another illustration of that curious paradox which may be observed so frequently in human life, that the people most acquainted with grief are the optimists, and the people who know least about it are the pessimists.

To the familiar beatitudes endorsed by human experience another should be added: Blessed is humour, for he who can laugh at life shall be spared the bitterest tears of life. Humour, which is in its essence kindly, kept the discarded child from despair; and there was added to this gift of humour an extraordinary power of observation, which provided him with interest even in his darkest days. It is impossible to imagine the moment when Dickens was not interested in human life. In later life, when he moved along the lighted ways of fame, he naturally felt, with some bitterness, his early disadvantages; but it is probable that even as a drudge in a blacking factory he was too busy observing the curious life around him to make much complaint. He was silently engaged in studying the pathos and farce of decayed gentility—its pride, its shifts, its sorrows, its ambitions. Extravagant traits of character, touches of the grotesque and pathetic in the creatures with whom he was associated, were treasured in his memory, and were produced in later years with marvellous fidelity. No man presented a more sensitive surface to life, and yet by some strange alchemy the pictures printed most indelibly on his memory were not sordid. Contrast, for example, the way in which Tolstoi paints a Russian prison, and the picture Dickens draws of the Marshalsea. Tolstoi puts into the foreground objects which it is brutalising and degrading even to remember; he forces his reluctant reader to look on the worst kind of foulness; he leaves no element of filth or squalor to implication, but insists upon its categorical exposure. Dickens, on the contrary, though he had the keenest cause of hatred and abhorrence for the old Marshalsea prison, can bring himself to speak of it in a kindly temper. "People are not bad because they come there," he writes in " Little Dorrit." " I have known numbers of good, persevering, honest people come there through misfortune. They are almost all kindhearted to one another." The difference between these two great writers is one of temperament. The absence of humour in Tolstoi makes him a pessimist; its presence in Dickens makes him an optimist. Each speaks the truth, the one in bitterness, the other in love; but the larger truth is with Dickens, as the larger truth must always be with the man of genial vision. Humour is essential to sanity; no sane and entirely lucid vision of life is possible without it. It is, in fact, a species of grace by which men are saved, and the thing from which it saves them is the pit of pessimism.

Dickens was saved from pessimism by his humour; he also found deliverance from the worst pressure of early adversity by a genuine love of imaginative literature. He has given us a list of his early reading: it includes the works of Smollett, Fielding, and Goldsmith, "Don Quixote," "Gil Blas," "The Arabian Nights," "The Spectator," "The Tatler," and a volume of Mrs. Newbold's "Farces." He draws an interesting picture of himself as "not a very robust child, sitting in by-places near Rochester Castle, with a head full of Partridge, Strap, Tom Piper, and Sancho Panza." It was a fortunate accident which provided the boy with such reading; it was still more fortunate for him that his taste was so far formed by these great authors when he entered on his term of London drudgery that he was able to find in them a refuge from the outward miseries of his life. His outward life was the life of the street urchin; his inner life, the life of the imaginative artist. In his lonely London garret he kept glorious company, and was least alone when most solitary. By virtue of imagination he could shut the door at will upon the world, and we may be sure that the outer life seemed less real to him than the inner life. It was so throughout his career; and the child with head full of Partridge and Sancho Panza was father of the man who wept and laughed with excitement over the creatures of his own novels.

It has often been remarked that in mature life Dickens read little; that "few really great men can have had so narrow an intellectual scope"; that even in the most lenient use of the phrase he was not at any time a cultured man; but there was a sense in which he did not need books, because he habitually lived in a romance-world of his own. One is not sure after all whether the kindliest circumstance could have provided him with a better means of education than he discovered for himself. A stricter scheme of culture might have meant a diminished vigour of imagination. If he had but a few books, they were all great books; and it might be said of him, as it was said of Abraham Lincoln, that "the poverty of his library was the wealth of his life." He himself has been at pains to tell us that little as Fielding and Smollett seemed suited for the reading of a child, yet whatever there was of evil in their pages was not there for him. What did exist for him was robust and noble English, matchless skill in the analysis of character and the delineation of manners, keen insight, manly sympathy, jovial laughter, a world where the creatures were no mere puppets in a show, but authentic human beings, overflowing with genuine vitality and energy. Much as Dickens regretted his lack of schooling, it may be doubted if any school would have permitted him a scheme of reading so inspiring and so catholic, for the thing least studied and oftenest contemned in public schools is English literature, and particularly that special form of literature from which Dickens learned his art as novelist.

Not only was "the intellectual scope" of Dickens narrow, but the very nature of his life narrowed also his range of observation. His power of observation was intense rather than wide. He is pre-eminently the novelist of cities; or, it would be correcter to say, of a city—the great metropolis where his life was spent, and which no man ever loved more heartily. He would have endorsed with eagerness the opinion of old Samuel Johnson that there is no place like London to live in. He loved, like Johnson, to stand amid the great tide of life which flows through Fleet Street, and preferred the knowledge of men to the knowledge of nature. But for that very reason the sphere of his observation was severely limited. He knew the Cockney thoroughly. He could reproduce perfectly his mispronunciations, his odd narrowness of view, his alert shiftiness, his smartness, his power of repartee. He loved the by-ways of the great city, and found in them infinite food for tragedy and mirth. Probably no man ever knew London so well. Like Sam Weller, his knowledge of London was "extensive and peculiar." His most exhilarating amusement was to walk for hours in its crowded streets, and to penetrate in semi-disguise its obscurer haunts, where the well-dressed Londoner is never seen save by accident, and then is only too eager to escape from the possible perils of his environment.

But when Dickens penetrated the splendid squares of the aristocracy, and still more when he ventured into the silence of the country lanes and the sleepy streets of the villages and hamlets of England, he was out of his element. His fine lords and ladies have no authentic vitality about them, and his village scenes have the air of elaborate stage-pictures. The first impressions are always the deepest, and the first impressions of Dickens's life were of squalid poverty, of poor men's shifts and poor men's uncomplaining heroism, of the half-humourous, half-pathetic adventures of men down on their luck—Micawbers who were always waiting for something to turn up, and debtors who managed to keep a " stiff hupper lip " even in the Fleet prison. Many of the landmarks of Dickens's London have already disappeared, and others are rapidly disappearing. The very language in which his Cockneys conversed has changed, and has vanished with the old coaches, the old hostelries, and the old chop-houses. So much is this the case that it has even been said that in fifty years' time Dickens's works will have become unintelligible to the average Englishman. This is, however, a prophecy which is likely to prove a most gratuitous form of human error, for great books live, not by their form alone, but often in spite of it; and if Burns can survive in spite of a dialect which Scotsmen no longer speak, and imperfectly comprehend, it is not likely that any change in the local conditions of life will render Dickens obsolete.

This extraordinary power of observation in Dickens is the cardinal quality of his art. It is so vivacious, so sensitive, so ceaselessly active, that it may rank as the distinctive quality. How much he sees, and how vividly, is revealed even in his dullest page to a degree that would be remarkable in the pages of many other writers who have a claim to brilliance. Take, for example, the picture of the Plornish family at home in Bleeding Heart Yard in " Little Dorrit." " Little Dorrit " is far from being his best book, and the Plornish family is little more than a thumb-nail sketch, but nothing could be more lifelike. Here is a brief category of things he sees, and makes us see. A hand painted on the wall (depicted with " a ring and a most elaborate nail of genteel form ") points the way to the apartment where the Plornish family reside. The door was opened by " a woman with a child in her arms, whose unoccupied hand was hastily rearranging the upper part of her dress. This was Mrs. Plornish, and this maternal action was the action of Mrs. Plornish during a large part of her waking existence." To the question whether Mr. Plornish is at home, she replies, " Well, sir, not to deceive you, he's gone to look for a job." " Not to deceive you " was her method of speech. She is most gratified when Clennam takes his hat off, because few people think it worth while to remove their hats in a poor man's house; " but people think more of it than people think." Plornish, being a man of slow speech, leaves the conversation to his wife, repeating the last parts of her sentences after her " as if he were making responses at church." " Me and Plornish says, ' No, Miss Dorrit, no ill-convenience ' " (Plornish repeated " no ill-convenience "), and so forth. When Mrs. Plornish is not speaking, she is " hushing the baby from side to side, and laying her chin upon the little hand," and feigning " to bite the fingers of the little hand as she kissed it." How truly all this is observed! Every touch in the picture counts, and is done with a sort of pre-Raphaelite accuracy. There is no trick of speech or manner that escapes the observation of Dickens; the little group stand focussed for an instant in a ray of light so intense that once seen they can never be forgotten. And this gift never fails Dickens; it gives vitality to his lightest sketch, truth and vivacity to his most careless page, and is the element from which is born a creative art unmatched by even the greatest of his rivals.

Among the books which delighted his childhood, " The Arabian Nights " will be noticed; and Mr. Gissing has observed that Dickens makes more allusions to this book in his novels than to any other book or author. The fact is suggestive, for it indicates another tendency of Dickens's genius—the tendency to fancifulness, to romance, to the grotesque. His chief faults are the result of this tendency, and they are faults which he himself did not perceive, and therefore made no effort to restrain. A writer of fiction usually chooses one of two methods—the method of plain veracity, or the method of fanciful romance: Dickens uses both. In such a study as the Plornishes all is veracious, for all is truly observed. Can we say the same thing of Little Nell or Oliver Twist or Em'ly, or even Bill Sikes? Pip and Joe Gargery are truly observed; but who does not feel that Miss Havisham is a purely fanciful figure, having not the least resemblance to reality? We can readily bring ourselves to believe in the existence of Oliver Twist, but that he should have remained so preternaturally innocent amid the scenes of infamy where his early lot is cast is quite incredible. Sikes the burglar is real enough in the moment of his great crime; but Sikes shouting to the infuriated crowd, "Wolves tear your throats!" is a mere stage-villain, using language which no hunted murderer ever did or ever could use. One can imagine that there sat on the shoulder of Dickens an irresponsible Puck or Ariel of pure fancifulness, perpetually misleading him. Passages of the most thorough observation alternate with passages of impossible romance. At one moment life is seen with the most lucid sanity of vision, the next moment it is a phantasmagoria. He is not content with plain narrative for long—the genii of "The Arabian Nights" are sure to intrude themselves. The normal and the typical are constantly thrust aside to make way for the abnormal and the erratic. His books often remind us of those curious mirrors which are hung outside the doors of certain eating-houses, which reflect the face of the passer-by as either preposterously thin or ludicrously fat. And yet all the time Dickens retains his power of holding a perfectly undeflected mirror up to nature; he can observe life with a minute truth of detail if he likes; the error is clearly not of power, but of perversity. He so wills it, and his better gift of accurate observation is constantly displaced by his lower gift of fancifulness, without the least perception on his part of confusion in form, method, and ideal.

Had Dickens kept the two methods distinct, there would have been no cause for complaint. The fairy tale and the realistic novel are both perfectly admissible and accepted forms of art. It is when the effort is made to unite the two that the lucidity of art is lost. What reader of " Great Expectations," that most delightful of all his books, has not wished Miss Havisham out of it, or at least wished that she were other than she is? All that goes on beneath Joe Gargery's humble roof delights us by its simple truth; all that happens in the darkened rooms of Satis House offends us by its manifest untruth. We can even accept the convict part of the story as not incredible, although it is melodramatic; but Miss Havisham belongs to the land of nightmare. The influence of this tendency to the unreal and fantastic upon Dickens's genius was unfortunately a growing tendency, and was injurious to his art in every way. He came to delight in the grotesque for its own sake. It became increasingly difficult for him to describe any character without exaggeration. He worked in crude colours, neglecting and scorning the finer gradations of enduring art. The habit of caricature grew upon him, and, as was natural, the power of genuine portrait-painting decayed, for the one is destructive of the other.

It is not only the fancifulness of " The Arabian Nights " which colours the genius of Dickens—there is also an eager taste for melodrama. His earliest passion was for the stage. He showed himself in later life an accomplished actor, and it may be said that with few exceptions his books were written with a constant eye to stage-effect. Hence he is constantly guilty of over-emphasis or purposed exaggeration in his characters. Probably this is the reason why it is not always easy for people who read Dickens with extreme pleasure in youth to return to him with anything like the same degree of pleasure in mature life. The growth of observation and the philosophic temper in themselves has taught them that there is little in actual human life or essential human nature quite like the delineations of Dickens. The frequent lack of firm and lucid outline, of fundamental sincerity and truth, in his characters is perceived. His rogue is always too much of a rogue; his simpleton comes too near to imbecility. It is plainly contrary to nature that Pickwick should have been so utterly a noodle, and Pecksniff so preposterous a hypocrite. About too many of the characters of Dickens there lingers the odour of the footlights, the sense of something inherently false and meretricious. We know the moment Pecksniff appears what he will say and do, and we know that he will never, by any chance, surprise us with a touch of nature. We know these things by the sure instinct which instructs the lover of transpontine drama that the villain of the piece will never deviate into momentary virtue, nor the virtuous and afflicted heroine be guilty of a single act of weakness. That this is not the method of the greatest imaginative writers scarcely needs saying. The art of Shakespeare and Fielding is so subtly tempered that there is the perfect illusion of reality. The creatures of their pens may be sublime or comic, but in neither case do they overstep the modesty of nature. But Dickens makes no effort and no pretence of keeping within the modesty of nature. He uses all the tricks and artifices of the stage to attract and sustain attention—making much of a deformity of either mind or body, obtruding the abnormal, treasuring and making much of odd sayings, and repeating them at every turn until they become the catchwords for laughter and applause. That he is a humorist none will question, but his method belongs rather to broad farce than to humour; and one is not sure whether he would not be more correctly described as a great master of farce than a great humorist—the greatest lord of farce who ever lived.

X

THE GREATNESS OF DICKENS

SO far we have studied the deficiencies of Dickens;
we may now turn to the more congenial task of
studying his greatness. It must not be assumed
that the theatrical element in the genius of Dickens
implies any lack of sincerity in his character. He was
as sincerely theatrical in his method of portraying life
as he was sincerely upright in living it. It was the
extreme vividness of his own perceptions that led him
to over-emphasize all he felt and saw. In his case the
epigram that "the style is the man" finds an unusual
degree of warrant. Just as he writes jerkily, yet with
a wonderful vividness, so he saw life, as it were, by a
series of electric flashes. A higher power of intense
imagination few men have had. Give him a piece of
real drama, and it lives. In this singular power of
intensity nothing in English fiction can surpass the
murder of Nancy or the death of Bill Sikes in "Oliver
Twist." We are not surprised to find that it greatly
exhausted him to read these scenes; he read them as
an actor. And in saying this we unconsciously discover the secret of his power.

Dickens had by nature the temperament of the actor
in its highest perfection, and with all its limitations.
That temperate sanity of view which surveys a great
drama as a whole he did not possess; but his whole
soul was in his part. He built it up sometimes by

touches which are felt to be meretricious, oftener by really great strokes of art. After a while we forget the meretricious, just as we become reconciled to the strut of a supreme actor when his art absorbs us. And it is quite certain that the actor himself has forgotten it. He is so fascinated by the vital reality of the thing he simulates that all power of self-criticism is dead. The least power of self-criticism would have showed him the shocking pathos of three-fourths of his death-bed scenes, and the occasional absurdity of his horrors, such as the death of Krook by spontaneous combustion. We did not see it once—when the spell of Dickens was first strong upon us; but we rarely fail to see it later on. But Dickens did not see it at all. " The garish lights " of the world's great stage were in his eyes; its applause rang in his ears. It was all real to him; and in the intoxication of boundless praise from a multitude as much under the spell of his vivid imagination as he himself was, there was no one just enough or wise enough to point out the errors which we all can recognise to-day.

Writing as a supreme master of farce—the Shakespeare of farce, we might say—it was natural that he should fall into the occasional error of vulgarity. Taste is something that can never be really acquired: either a man has it or he has it not. Dickens certainly did not possess it, and it is probably a good thing for us that he did not. A Dickens brought up with care, duly drilled in the etiquette which is supposed to constitute good form, and mellowed by the traditional spirit of a great university, might still have been a great author, but he would not have been the Dickens we know. He would no doubt have written better

English, but he would have written worse books. He certainly would not have chosen his themes from the most sordid and tragic annals of great cities. As it was, the one school Dickens knew was the London streets. He might have said that he was educated in the University of London in the same sense that Browning said he was educated in the University of Italy. He was unhappy out of London. He could find inspiration nowhere else. He discovers that the genius which flowed freely in London will hardly stir at all in Genoa, and he has to come back to London before he can do his work with ease. He had, as we have seen, a preference for the seamy and sordid side of life; it was that which he knew best. He fails when he tries to paint a prosperous merchant, he fails still more egregiously when he tries to paint a lord; but his Wellers, poor Joes, and Wilfers, his loungers at inn-doors, lawyer's clerks in shabby coats, bailiffs, ruffians, tide-waiters, and Bohemians of the dingy and mangy order, are all perfect. They are all vulgar creatures, and now and then they are depicted with a vulgar touch. Manners and customs of forty years ago were more vulgar than they are now, and much must be allowed for this. Besides which it must be remembered that farce itself always borders on vulgarity, and it is asking too much of "a special correspondent for posterity," as Mr. Bagehot has called Dickens, who makes it his chief aim to paint low life in the London of the fifties, that he shall never by any chance touch his picture with a breadth which is more after the manner of Hogarth than Du Maurier.

"Here is a writer," says Mr. Frederic Harrison, "who is realistic if ever any writer was, in the sense of having closely observed the lowest strata of city life, who has drawn the most miserable outcasts, the most abandoned men and women in the dregs of society, who has invented many dreadful scenes of passion, lust, seduction, and debauchery, and yet in forty works and more you will not find a page which a mother need withhold from her grown daughter." It was the same characteristic which struck Thackeray when he spoke of " the sweet and unsullied page " of his great rival. There is also a certain high-mindedness which holds him and us above any defiling contact with the most defiling themes. Of how many novelists can this be said? Where else is there a writer who has descended so deep into the underground world of a great city, the dim and populous infernos of lust and crime, and yet has brought us back to the daylight with nothing but pity in our hearts, and not a single impure image in our minds?

But much more than this may be said. Not only are we none the worse for these incursions into the sordid and tragic, but we are positively the better. Fagin and the Artful Dodger, Nancy and Bill Sikes, are not pleasant associates, but they do us no harm. For Dickens had much more than purity—which is, after all, but a negative quality—he had intense powers of pity and sympathy. There is a certain benignity about him, a radiant humanity. I suppose that no English writer of any period has ever been so widely loved, and this personal affection which he excited is a testimony to his benignity. Admiration for a book is often very far from implying love for its author; but from the first Dickens was loved. Hosts of the common people felt that they had in him a champion, if not a deliverer—a friend who understood their woe, if he could do little to ameliorate it. Even so cautious and cold a critic as Jeffrey completely loses his head, and shouts blessings on the man who has made him weep delicious tears. In fact, the works of Dickens were never truly criticised; if they had been, he might have learned how to better both his method and style. He was received with almost frantic joy, and the demonstration never sensibly diminished during his life. Men felt incapable of criticising a writer who had moved them so deeply. And as we reread his books we begin to understand the reason of it all. He may err in taste and err in art, but he never errs in sympathy. He depicts even his Nancy, vulgar drab as she is, in such a way that our hearts ache for her. With the exception of his deliberate hypocrites, who are always overdrawn, and therefore not convincing, he rarely touches any character without showing us something that may be loved or pitied in it. He fails most palpably when he sets himself to be deliberately pathetic. Then we hear the pump going hard behind the tears, and we come near to mockery. He is hardly to be blamed for it; the public he wrote for saw nothing maudlin in it, and certainly he saw nothing. He obeyed the standard he had set up, and it was a standard which every one in his day approved. But in the sympathy that surprises us by felicitous touches he never fails; it was a boundless element bathing all his books. There is certainly no writer who approaches him in this benignity of spirit, which invokes and claims personal affection in the reader.

One result of this intense sympathy we all acknowledge. It stands to the eternal honour of Dickens that he did much to infuse a more humane spirit into the general life of the people. It was his pen that abolished the debtor's prison, public executions, and the worst abuses of the parochial and private school systems—to speak only of reforms that are generally acknowledged as his handiwork. If there were any means of arriving at an accurate estimate, we should certainly find that he did much more than this. It is impossible to say how much of human kindliness has been invoked by such a story as the "Christmas Carol." The hardest man who reads it, even though he be a veritable Scrooge, cannot help asking himself who is his neighbour, and diligently inquiring until he finds a Tiny Tim in need of a Christmas dinner. The most callous man who has read the death of poor Joe can scarcely help looking at the tattered crossing-sweeper of the London streets with a softer glance. To accomplish these results was to perform the highest offices of both religion and benevolence. Satire and irony alone can never attain such results. They sting, they wound, they arouse indignation or vituperation, but they do not arouse general outbursts of sympathy. It needs love to do these things, and Dickens was pre-eminently a lover of his fellow-men. Nor is it possible to regret the disabilities of his early life when we remember these things. No man who had not known the miseries he had known could ever have written as he did. For him, as for every man of genius who has profoundly moved us, it is true that "he learned in suffering what he taught in song." The poor and the harassed, the people of no account who know sordid struggles and mean anxieties, will always love Dickens, and the house which has no other books will have his. Above all things, he was a novelist of the people—far more so than Scott or Fielding or Thackeray, or any other writer with whom he may be compared. To reach the people the pen need not be superfine, but it is certain that it must be held by a hand that has a kindly heart behind it. If sometimes the •fastidious may reproach such a writer with vulgarity, is it not a very light charge, not worth consideration, when we remember the affection, pity, and sympathy he has excited and stimulated into active forces which have penetrated the whole mass of society with the spirit of a most serviceable humaneness?

It is impossible for us to-day to understand the kind of feeling with which Dickens was regarded by his contemporaries. It was a cult, a passion, an adoration, a fanaticism. Every one recalls the story of the old gentleman on his death-bed who thanked God for the likelihood of living till the next number of " Pickwick " came out. Not so familiar, but equally significant, is the story of the man who rode several miles at midnight that he might awaken his friend with the great and welcome news, " Carker's dead! " The method Dickens adopted of publishing his books in monthly parts would have been fatal to any writer who was not a great creative artist. It was a method not without serious disadvantage to his art. It was responsible for much of the over-emphasis in his characters to which allusion has been made. Between the fourth and fourteenth parts of " Martin Chuzzlewit, " Pecksniff might have been forgotten, if his hypocrisy had not been restated with every mention of his name. It had the worse disadvantage of making him extremely sensitive to the approval or disapproval of the public, and this led him to make efforts to attract and please the public at the expense of his art. He deliberately alters the plan of " Martin Chuzzlewit " because he is alarmed at the poor sales of its early numbers, and he speaks of himself as suffering the " horrors of a fever " when the financial results of the " Christmas Carol " sink below his expectations. For the sake of his own art, its composure, its freedom, its completeness, he would have been wise had he never hit upon the device of periodic publication; but how much does it say for his immense creative genius that it was able to fill his stage with figures so vital and fascinating that tens of thousands of people waited eagerly for the monthly curtain to be raised. We read the new novels of to-day, and after a fashion we discuss them; but who waits for their appearance in a fever of expectation, who weeps and laughs over them, who is kindled into vigorous love or hatred of night to inform a friend of anything that happens in them, who is kindled into vigorous love or hatred of their personages, and what modern novel could survive the dismemberment of monthly publication? Dickens achieved these miracles. Yes, he peopled the imagination of his countrymen with the creatures of his art. He created a personal bond between himself and his reader, unique in the entire history of literature. When, in later life, he appeared as the public interpreter of his own books, he was received with the most frantic demonstrations of affection. Never had any writer such a hold upon his readers—never again can such a phenomenon be anticipated; for that land is fortunate which can boast once in many centuries the birth and triumph of a writer who can unite the genius to be loved and the genius to create, as they were united in the life of Dickens.

For the last and greatest thing to be observed in Dickens is the enormous range of his creative genius. When criticism has uttered its last word about his faults, the elements of caricature, farce and grotesque exaggeration in his characters, the greatest word of all remains to be spoken—they live. From what other novels could we select a dozen persons so intimately true and vital, so clearly defined and real that the statesman, the preacher, the journalist, the man in the street hearing or uttering their names is at once understood and can be in no doubt as to their significance?

Such a tribute cannot be paid to Fielding or Jane Austen, to Scott or to Thackeray; Shakespeare is the only other artist in English literature who can lay claim to it. Or to propose a yet severer test: what other writer has created figures so vital and so lucid, that his books may be read at the same time by the boy of twelve and the man of fifty, to the equal delight of each? Only a few books in any literature survive this test—in our own literature " The Pilgrim's Progress " and " Robinson Crusoe," for example; but there is scarcely one of Dickens's books of which it is not true that persons of all ages and all classes own their charm. And where else is there such ease and fulness of creative power? At the touch of his pen the very stones of the street raise up children to art. The mere bulk of his books is extraordinary, the greater of them being equal in matter to three or four modern novels. The number and the variety of his characters are still more astounding. The modern novel is often little more than an enlarged anecdote, in which two or three or perhaps half-a-dozen persons keep the drama moving. A story of Dickens is not an anecdote, but a history. The actors and personages in it are numbered by the score. His stage has not a few but a throng of actors on it. And yet in all this throng there is not one that is not clearly individualised—not one who does not speak and act in a way intimately his own—not one who is not recognised and recollected by the mere mention of his name; and there are many who represent with such accurate detail definite defects and qualities, distinct tendencies, virtues, vices, follies, tragedies, humours, and eccentricities that they have become the symbols and parables of things that happen in the universal life of man. The writer of whom these things is true is secure of fame. His genius has inwoven itself into the life of his race, and is a part of its tradition.

> He is a portion of the loveliness
> Which once he made more lovely; he doth bear
> His part, while the one Spirit's plastic stress
> Sweeps through the dull, dense world, compelling there
> All new successions to the forms they wear.

Tastes may change, new gods be set up in the market-place, new reputations rise and wane, but the time can never come when the great creative artist is dethroned and finally forgotten. It is as a great creative artist Dickens takes his place with the immortals; and so long as men live not by bread alone, but by the food of the imagination—so long as men know how to laugh at pure absurdity, to revel in the jovial fun of high spirits and audacious youth, to thrill and sadden at the tragedies of life, to feel pity, mirth, and love—so long will the writings of Charles Dickens live; and his satire on things evil will serve the cause of virtue, his message of benignity will continue to enlarge the scope of human sympathy, and his vigorous humanity will reinforce the inherent altruism of mankind to a yet wider and completer social service.

XI

THE BRONTËS

Charlotte Brontë, born at Thornton, Yorkshire, April 21st, 1816. Emily Brontë, born at Haworth, Yorkshire, 1818; Anne Brontë, 1820. Poems by the three sisters published 1846. "Jane Eyre," published 1847; "Shirley," 1849; "Villette," 1853; "Wuthering Heights," by Emily Brontë, published after her death. Emily Brontë died 1848; Anne Brontë, 1849; Charlotte Brontë, March 31st, 1855.

IT is late in the day to find anything new to say of the Brontës, yet there are still things which may be said with profit. One thinks of them with the astonishment and pity which Wordsworth felt for

> Chatterton, the marvellous Boy,
> The sleepless soul that perished in his pride.

And the imagination associates them with Chatterton because there is a certain vital resemblance, which, however, it is fair to add, only the imagination can perceive. Each presents the fascinating spectacle of a new force springing up suddenly, and with volcanic energy, in a place the least likely, and under circumstances the most nearly impossible. For there is nothing so elusive, so capricious and uncalculated in its movements, as that great hidden stream of literary energy which flows under the surface of things, and flings up its geyser-fountain from time to time in the unvisited solitudes of humanity, in regions beyond the

124

critical chart and compass. Chatterton, Burns, Carlyle, and if we go back far enough, Shakespeare too, all afford illustrations of this law of caprice in literary energy. The "lord of languages," the master of creative art, often enough is born in places which seem to lie remote, beyond the realm of letters. Through generations of passionate or tranquil lives the force has been slowly accumulating which at last takes memorable shape, and blossoms into what we call genius. It is like the disease in the oyster which makes the pearl; myriads of healthy bivalves pass unnoticed, till at last some curious assimilation in the blind life produces something wholly different, the lustrous gem for which men search with eager hands. Where did the genius come from that suddenly dropped its pearl in the drunken chorister's house at Bristol, or in the lonely, rain-swept parsonage of Haworth? And none can answer; but when we put such questions, we become conscious of that which in the main we all forget—the mystery of life.

Charlotte Brontë lives by three great stories, " Jane Eyre," " Shirley," and " Villette." Emily Brontë lives by a story which in some of its elements is a still greater literary performance, " Wuthering Heights." Anne Brontë is remembered only by her comradeship with her greater sisters, and the patient, submissive tragedy of her life, as Branwell is remembered by the sordid tragedy of his. We are irresistibly reminded of how strongly the personal equation enters into literature when we consider the now familiar history of these disastrous lives. We never forget the Bay of Spezzia when we read Shelley, nor the long fight with death in Rome when we read Keats, nor the lonely end at Missolonghi when we read Byron. How much the fame of each of these poets owes to the story of their lives it is impossible to determine, but it is clear that the personal equation colours all and counts for much. It is so in the very nature of things with a poet, because his work is of all literary performance the most intimately personal, the warm expression of his heart. The same thing is true of Charlotte and Emily Brontë. Each wrote in prose, but it was a poet's prose. It was in neither case literary craftsmanship alone, but strong and vivid personal passion, which made their work memorable. They were children of the wind and moor, full of wild, untameable energy, hating the conventions of life, at battle with the order of life, among the very first to strike that resonant note of revolt against the artificial limitations of a woman's world which is heard everywhere in our literature of to-day. Emily's genius was violent, tragic, perturbed—a boiling mountain stream thundering down lonely hills, and chafing itself into dispersion on its way. Charlotte's genius was of a calmer order, and had more of sanity in it; but in her soul the same untameable tumult clamoured. Energy is the distinguishing note in each. All that they wrote was strong with passion, with an indignation like Swift's, but more spiritual, because feminine; less bitter, but more impetuous; destitute of savage brutality, but steeped in the same immense mournfulness. It is this genuine virility of passion which has kept their work from decay, not less than its great imaginative power and literary perfection.

The stream that pours through narrow channels has not the most volume, but it often has a greater occasional depth, and displays more astonishing beauties than the stream which is a great flood moving majestically to the sea. The life of the Brontës was such a stream. We can neither estimate aright the greatness nor the limitations of their work without remembering the limitations of their life. It is almost vain to visit Haworth and the Brontë country to-day to discover the material out of which these strange sisters wrought their romances, because all is altered. The old church has gone. The grey, unsocial-looking parsonage is enlarged, and looks almost habitable. A long, many-windowed, red-brick Georgian house is pointed out to you as the residence of Charlotte's Mr. Helstone; a desolate grange, once moated, with low, iron-studded doorways, and weather-worn, mullioned windows, as the stage on which another of her scenes was enacted. The Black Bull of Haworth where Branwell drank himself to death is still there, and the steep, unlovely street; but the valleys are full to-day of the smoke of factories, and the old order has given place to new. One unalterable feature of the landscape still remains, the wild moors, which begin almost at the door of the parsonage, and stretch for miles in lonely wastes of purple, and black coombs, and steep ravines, filled with the perpetual sound of water and soughing winds. It is not every parsonage in a manufacturing district that can open its back doors immediately upon the freedom and unsullied air of the moors, and truth to tell there are many worse parsonages than that in which Charlotte and Emily Brontë were reared. For souls such as theirs, such a scene must have had many compensations. If they were shut away in an obscure corner of the world, they were also secreted in the lap of Nature. If they saw little of men and women who were capable of stimulating minds like theirs into a new glow of thought and impulse, they were of that shy and seclusive order to whom social life is a burdensome impertinence rather than a pleasure. And if they were forced to know, in intimate association, men and women of rude and rough natures, yet it must be remembered that there is no race of a more marked individuality and strength of nature than this people of the Yorkshire dales.

In happier, or perhaps we should say different, circumstances, Charlotte and Emily Brontë might have written books of a kindlier humanity and more comprehensive vision, but " Jane Eyre " and " Wuthering Heights " had never been written. Indeed, we may doubt if, apart from the environment of that tragic life at Haworth, they would have written anything; for, supreme artists as they are in the craft of literature, neither of the sisters was of the order which delights in the art of literature for its own sake. Of literary sympathy they had little. We do not hear of them as taking any pleasure in the study of literature in any broad or comprehensive sense. They had none of that sensuousness of literary passion which feels a fine phrase strike through the mind like the glow of wine. They were framed upon severer lines, and their sensitiveness was of the tragic order. The first book they published was poetry, and here, if anywhere, we might expect to find the softer glow of fancy; but as with all the other books, it is a hard mountain seriousness which forms the bottom strata, and the fancy is nothing more than an occasional gleam of splendour travelling over moorland solitudes. Thus it happens that these four books of the two sisters are of the order which we call to-day " human documents." They are not the performance of writers who simply have a mild ambition to make books, but of passionate hearts agonising to express themselves. To these prisoned spirits there was no other means of expression. That common boon of human intercourse, of which the humblest household may make free, was virtually denied them. Old Patrick Brontë, when his house was full of young children, always dined alone, and he retained the habit all his life. Like his daughters, his chief joy was in long solitary walks upon the moors. He never asked how they spent their time, and apparently never cared. He did not share their confidence even in literary matters. The only praise he uttered when " Jane Eyre " was put into his hands was that it was better than likely; and we can fancy that it was difficult for the old stoic to wring out even this grudged praise from his closed heart. The sisters themselves toiled in silence at their tasks, and never interfered with each other. There seems to have been some radical difficulty of communion between the members of this tragic house. They went upon their " separate and sad " ways without speech—proud, indomitable, uncommunicative. It was not until they took the pen in their hands that their hearts were opened; then all the suppressed passion which was consuming them found vent, and what neither could say to other they proclaimed in a voice of a torrent to the world.

One of the first things that strikes the visitor to Haworth is, that, in spite of the sombre severity of Mrs. Gaskell's picture, there was no inherent reason why this parsonage on the moors should not have been visited by human cheerfulness and gaiety. Rude as the people were, they were warm-hearted, and, as Charlotte Brontë's own letters witness, not without an excellent capacity for friendship. The place was not more lonely than Cowper's Olney, and the neighbours far less boorish. It is possible to imagine this lonely stone house upon the hill a centre of radiant domesticity in spite of its contiguity to the grey graveyard and the houseless moor. The fact is, that the reasons for that cloud of depression which hung over the whole life of the sisters must be found elsewhere. Again it is the figure of Swift which is recalled by a study of the whole picture. In this Irish Patrick Brontë there throbbed something of the fierce pride, the immitigable flame of anger and resentment against the world, the mad impulse and violence of temper, only held down by the vigilance of an unconquerable will, which tortured the life of Swift into insanity. He was a dumb Swift, too—striding about the moors in moody anger, and unable to find utterance. And he bequeathed himself especially to Charlotte and Emily; only to them was vouchsafed the power of speech he lacked. If ever there was a woman cast in the tragic mould, it was Emily Brontë. She and her dog Keeper stand distinct before us as types of a certain half-noble, half-savage untameableness. For her the wildness of the moors was perfectly attuned to the wildness of her imagination—the only thing in all the world with which she harmonised. What was that consuming resentment which burned alike in Swift and Patrick Brontë and his two daughters? It sprang from the same source in each—the conflict of great powers with the solid hindrance of mean impediments, from a torturing vision of things coveted but denied, from an overmastering sense that the world was not justly administered. Nowhere could such temperaments have found happiness. It was in the power of circumstance to deepen the gloom, perhaps to have lightened it, but never to have dispersed it. With the keenest, even the bitterest sense of what love might be, they were not fashioned for love. With an immense power of loving, and a sovereign sense that without love life was a thing altogether hideous, they neither of them found the love that could master them, and melt the rich ore of their natures into noble forms. With a professed faith, which they stated the more vehemently the more insecure they felt about it, they were practically faithless. It was with them as with Cowper; they " at the cross of hope, with hopeless hands " were clinging. So that, sad as it is, and almost cynical, yet perhaps the truest word which is capable of doing most to solve the mystery is Mr. Leslie Stephen's: " They afford one more exemplification of the common theory, that great art is produced by taking an exceptionally delicate nature, and mangling it slowly under the grinding wheels of the world."

From these mingled forces of heredity and environment there resulted two things which powerfully affected the life and art of the sisters. The first was the temper in which they regarded life—a temper of passionate stoicism. They early learned the truth that any real help must be found in themselves. If they had any element of rejoicing, it was that they possessed unconquerable souls. They summoned themselves for battle against the world, and fought indomitably to the end. Emily Brontë insisting upon doing her daily house-work when she was visibly dying; Charlotte putting aside her rejected manuscripts, and quietly beginning another book; poor Branwell crawling out of bed that he may die standing, and defiant of death,—all show the same spirit. Old Patrick Brontë had taught them stoicism to some purpose. With Death and Poverty always hungering on their track, they never turn from their course; like those who fling their treasures to the wolves, they do but drive the faster through the storm. Death is always knocking at the door of Haworth parsonage, but they write on unmoved. They feel themselves the inheritors of calamity; they expect nothing of the world, but they are resolved that the world shall never find them suppliant. They ask no favour, neither will they give any. They know nothing even of dependence on each other; each moves in the orbit of her own completeness. They will not beg of each other, nor crave sympathy, nor own weakness each to each; the steel armour of pride they wear holds them upright, and has no supple hinges at the knee. Charlotte has expressed it all with infinite vehemence in " Shirley " when she writes :

Take the matter as you find it: ask no questions, utter no remonstrances; it is your best wisdom. You expected bread, and you have got a stone; break your teeth on it, and don't shriek because your nerves are martyrised; do not doubt that your mental stomach—if you have such a thing—is strong as an ostrich's—the stone will digest. You held out your hand for an egg, and fate put into it a scorpion. Show no consternation; close your fingers firmly upon the gift; let it sting through the palm. Never mind: in time, after your hand and arm have swelled and quivered long with torture, the squeezed scorpion will die, and you will have learned the great lesson how to endure without a sob. For the whole remnant of your life, if you survive the test,—some, it is said, die under it,— you will be stronger, wiser, less sensitive. . . . Nature is an excellent friend in such cases, sealing the lips, interdicting utterance, commanding a placid dissimulation—a dissimulation often wearing an easy and gay mien at first, settling down to sorrow and paleness in time, then passing away, and leaving a convenient stoicism, not the less fortifying because it is half bitter.

Matthew Arnold has said the same thing of Emily, painting in great phrases her indomitable soul, when he writes of her—

> Whose soul
> Knew no fellow for might,
> Passion, vehemence, grief,
> Daring, since Byron died,
> That world-famed son of fire—she who sank
> Baffled, unknown, self-consumed:
> Whose too-bold dying song
> Shook like a clarion-blast my soul.

The second result of heredity and environment is seen in the art of the sisters. It lacks suavity, comprehensiveness, breadth. It has no luminous outlook over wide fields of life. It is not catholic—an art which charms and persuades all kinds and conditions of men. It moves within the narrowest compass, it rarely passes into the firmament of the universal, it finds its material solely in this remote dale, and the passions and scant external experiences of their isolated lives. But this does not imply any detraction of the art; it rather makes it appear the more wonderful. What was there to write about in the obscure people of Haworth? What was there that could interest the world in the small perturbations of a needy governess? One might as well ask, What was there for Burns to write about in a mouse or a daisy, Shelley in a skylark, Wordsworth in the small celandine or the daffodils beside a nearly nameless lake? It is the seeing eye which is needed; to such an eye the miracle of the world is folded in the humblest fragment of it. Charlotte Brontë knew Haworth and herself; Emily Brontë knew the moors and the rugged men who moved across them; they wrote of what they knew, and with such fine art that we know them also. It is not the highest art; the highest combines, from many sketches of individuals, some catholic type of man or woman which sums up a recognised element, or elements, of humanity. Charlotte Brontë does not do this. She paints a portrait with inimitable insight and fidelity. She expresses her own nature with subtlety and passion in all her heroines. In so far she is subdued by the material she works in, like the dyer's hand of Shakespeare's sonnet; but it is that very circumstance which makes her work so remarkable. That one so utterly remote from the great currents of life could construct such books as these out of such scenes as lay at her door, and such thoughts as burned within herself, is one of the marvels of literature. It goes to prove what has been often said in many various ways, that there are the elements of romance in the humblest life if only we knew how to distinguish them, as there are in the dewdrop forces which, if liberated, might wreck a world.

When we turn to the work of the Brontës, the task of criticism is made difficult by two circumstances, one of which has been already mentioned: viz., the strength of the personal equation in their literary performance; and, secondly, the progress which the art of fiction has made since their day. When " Jane Eyre " was published there was a general outcry about its moral laxity of tone, and one reviewer went so far as to hint that no woman who was not an alien from her sex could have written it. We have grown accustomed to so much stronger meat since those days that " Jane Eyre " seems to us a comparatively innocent confection. When Mrs. Carlyle once met George Eliot, she cried with vivacious astonishment, " She, an improper female!" It is much in the same way that we laugh quizzically at the denunciations which were levelled at the little governess of Haworth when we read " Jane Eyre." So far from being improper, it is the puritanism of the stiff little figure of Jane Eyre which lends humour to the whole conception. The nearer Jane comes to temptation, the more rigid does she grow. She never loses her self-respect for a moment, and in the utmost throes of passion she is still so much of a proper person that she addresses Rochester as " sir." Judged only as a story, " Jane Eyre " is a book which does not well bear second or third reading. It lacks dramatic vitality. There is an hysteric theatricality about it which offends the sober judgment. Rochester is not a really masculine creature; he is just the sort of person who might be imagined by a lonely and passionate woman who knew little of men. And yet, curiously enough, the book as a whole belongs to the category of realistic fiction. It is realistic in the sense that it records the actual thoughts and passions of a woman who is intensely alive, in all their crude turbulence and nakedness, and it does this in spite of a plot which is flimsy and melo-dramatic, and which has no basis in any facts of life as they were known to the writer. The real charm of the book is its style. It is written with superb vehemence; it is full of a sort of flashing energy of phrase; it uses words like weapons, each striking and ringing like a clash of swords in some great combat; it is full of noble thoughts nobly expressed; and it warms us by its living passion even when it wholly fails to convince us by its plot. It is by such qualities it made its fame, and it is by such qualities it has re-tained it. Much of the book sounds to us to-day strained, stilted, and old-fashioned, and hence the effort that is needed to reread it; but when we do begin to read it, we are amply repaid by its power of ex-pression, and at times almost forget its defects of art.

Probably Charlotte Brontë herself would have con-curred in this judgment of her first book, for in her subsequent writings these errors are rigorously avoided. "Shirley" is from first to last a piece of admirable fiction. It is a study of life taken from her own doorstep, fresh, vivid, and convincing—a piece of excellent impressionism, and at the same time a speci-men of highly wrought and finished art. Here she is dealing with the life she really knows. There is no mistaking the three curates; they are portraits from the life. Her nearest approach to humour is here, and there is a healthy vivacity about the writing which we miss in the other books. For a time the cloud is lifted from her life. The book reminds us of some brief interval of midday sunlight on the moors, be-tween the morning gloom and evening sombreness, when every ridge of the folding hills is touched with bright colour, and the air is warmly fragrant, and there is the actual song of cheerful birds above the solitary waste, where silence and mystery are familiar and habitual. We can fancy that she herself wrote it in the buoyant mood begotten of her first success. At last the tide of misfortune seemed to have turned, and larger horizons had opened to the prisoned soul. When we reach " Villette," the cloud has fallen again. Once more the hills are dimmed and blurred, and the rain is sweeping down their scarred valleys, and the wind of misfortune is crying desolately on the un-peopled moors. The rare geniality of a nature usually sombre and reticent is always delightful, and it is this sort of geniality which we find and enjoy in reading " Shirley." We catch a passing glimpse of what Charlotte Brontë might have been had her life been more fortunate. Once, when the three sisters were walking on the moor with a friend, a sudden burst of light filled the sky, and, looking up, they saw a beauti-ful parhelion. The three girls stood close together on a little ridge of heather, silent and delighted with this rare vision of three suns in the changeful sky. " That is you," said their friend; " you are the three suns." It was only a passing vision, a fair premonitor of evil weather, and we can fancy that long before night came the storm was once more vehement upon the rainy moorland. " Shirley " marks the brief parhelion of Charlotte Brontë's life. For a little while the sun has warmed her and made her radiant, and the evil weather was to follow.

Any one who cares to know how a novel is created cannot do better than study the structure of " Shirley."

In a rare and extremely interesting book, "The Risings of the Luddites," by Frank Peel, published at Heckmondwike in 1888, may be found the history out of which Charlotte Brontë took a great part of the plot of "Shirley." She would be familiar from childhood with these wild stories of wild doings in the Yorkshire dales. The attack upon the mill, which is described with such admirable art in "Shirley," is little more than a narrative of the actual facts as related in Mr. Peel's book. With this for a background, and the people she knew as artist's models, Charlotte Brontë had ample material for a great story. And a great story the book is. It is drama, not melodrama. It has few of the improbabilities, the girlish crudities, which spoil "Jane Eyre." It is wrought with a firm hand and infinite spirit. She knew perfectly and thoroughly the types of characters which she describes. They live for us because they lived for her. Of course the book would not be Charlotte Brontë's unless there were moments when the narrative is suspended, and pages of profound thought and reflection, exquisitely expressed, lead us aside from the main stream of action. But who can regret this when he remembers such an inspired passage as that on Eve?

Nature is now at her evening prayers; she is kneeling before those red hills. I see her prostrate on the great steps of her altar, praying for a fair night for mariners at sea, for travellers in deserts, for lambs on moors and unfledged birds in woods. Caroline, I see her! and I will tell you what she is like; she is like what Eve was when she and Adam stood alone on earth. . . . I saw—I now see—a woman-Titan: her robe of blue air spreads to the outskirts of the heath, where yonder flock is grazing; a veil white as an avalanche sweeps from her head to her feet, and arabesques of lightning flame on its borders. Under her breast I see her zone, purple like that horizon; through its blush shines the star of evening. Her steady eyes I cannot picture; they are clear—they are deep as lakes—they are lifted and full of worship—they tremble with the softness of love and the lustre of prayer. Her forehead has the expanse of a cloud, and is paler than the early moon, risen long before dark gathers: she reclines her bosom on the ridge of Stillboro' moor; her mighty hands are joined beneath it. So kneeling, face to face she speaks with God. That Eve is Jehovah's daughter, as Adam was His son.

There is, perhaps, a suspicion, not amounting to evidence, that such a passage as this was written with a sense that it was a bit of fine writing, but it may at least be said that, rhetorical as it is, it accords perfectly with the character of Shirley. A great deal might be written, and profitably written, on Shirley's character, for it is one of the finest and strongest in the whole realm of fiction. Charlotte Brontë meant it to be an idealisation of her sister Emily; and in the passion for Nature, the free and independent spirit, the more than masculine indomitableness of will and resentment of conventions, it is easy to recognise Emily. In none of her other writings is there such a sense of masterly ease, such freedom and breadth of touch. There are, no doubt, scenes in "Villette" which strike a deeper note of passion, and, taken by themselves, are more memorable. No one who has once read "Villette" is ever likely to forget the scene at the theatre, with its vivid and overwhelming description of Rachel's acting—not merely one of the finest pieces of dramatic criticism ever written, but one of the most powerful pieces of imaginative writing in the language. Nor is the self-torture of the sick girl in the long, ghostly, deserted dormitory, and her wanderings in the city, through which " the wind thundered strong and horizontal from north-west to south-east," and her brief solace at the confessional, a picture that can be readily obliterated. If we had to choose half a dozen of the greatest scenes from Charlotte Brontë's works, probably two-thirds would be drawn from " Villette," for nowhere is her imagination so alive, so eager and intense, as in this last product of her genius. But if we had to choose the one book which as a whole does the highest justice to her powers, many of us would prefer " Shirley." There is a certain unstrained freshness in " Shirley " which is delightful after many readings; there is a glow of geniality which keeps it sweet; there is a naturalness and ease of depiction to which only the greatest artists can attain; and there is that unmistakable sureness of handling which reveals to us that in this case Charlotte Brontë was in love with her subject, and wrote it with delight, and with a vivid sense of its truth and reality.

In no other book are the pictures of Nature finished with so easy and skilled a touch. There are scores of such vignettes as these in the book:

I know how the heath would look on such a day—purple-black: a deeper shade of the sky-tint, and that would be livid. Yes—quite livid, with brassy edges to the clouds, and here and there a white gleam, more ghastly than the livid tinge, which, as you looked at it, you momentarily expected would kindle into blinding lightning.

The storm did not break till evening. The hills seemed rolled in a sullen mist; and when the rain fell in whitening sheets, suddenly they were blotted from the prospect; they were washed from the world.

On Nunnwood slept the shadow of a cloud: the distant hills

were dappled, the horizon was shaded and tinted like mother-of-pearl; silvery blues, soft purples, evanescent greens, and rose shades, all melting into fleeces of white cloud, pure as azure snow, allured the eye as with a remote glimpse of heaven's foundations. The air blowing on the brow was fresh and sweet and bracing.

And of " Shirley " itself we may say that the atmosphere which bathes it is " fresh and sweet and bracing." Perhaps that is why we love it best; it gives us the most pleasure.

Of Emily Brontë and the one solitary memorial of her genius, " Wuthering Heights," it is hard to speak in language which does not seem uncritical and exaggerated. " Wuthering Heights " is one of those books about which only two feelings are possible—hearty dislike, or intolerant admiration. If a man does not feel the greatness of the book, it is a vain task to attempt his conversion—if it does not appeal to him, it is because he lacks the sense to which the book appeals. It is not his fault, it is his misfortune. It can hardly be expected that a man who is wholly destitute of or feebly endowed with the poetic fibre, whose ideal of natural beauty is placid streams and green pastures, who knows nothing of the violent and savage passions which lie imperfectly curbed under civilised exteriors, should in the least understand a book which is violent, visionary, daring, unrestrained, a wild prose-poem rather than a novel, a thing instinct with dangerous, vehement passion, less a book than the stormy crying and defiance of a soul at hand-grips with fate, and fighting a losing battle without hope. And what we are pleased to call " the reading world " did not understand it, nor do they understand it yet.

To no writer are the touching lines of Mrs. Meynell more applicable:

And if e're you should come down to the village or the town,
With the cold rain for your garland, and the wind for your
    renown,
You will stand upon the thresholds with a face of dumb desire,
        Nor be known by any fire.

Charlotte Brontë had just a sufficient touch of wordly shrewdness and restraint to harness her genius to a task that knew its limits. But Emily Brontë wore no fetter of either prudence or custom. She was the child of the storm and lonely moorland—the cold rain her garland, the wind for her renown. Is it not she who has pictured the soul in heaven crying disconsolately for the lost earth, and at length, flung forth by the indignant angels, waking on the cold moorland, and weeping for joy to pluck the familiar heather once more? One knows not what wild thoughts passed through that great brain, and shook that unconquerable soul. But in "Wuthering Heights" the truest image of Emily Brontë is to be found. There is a Titanic greatness about the book; its large outlines, fading into uncomprehended shadows, at once stimulate and oppress the imagination. The very heart of Nature beats in it, the very force of Nature throbs through it. Its thoughts and images move between the poles of tragic intensity and appalling vagueness. We feel the book to be something almost unearthly—a thing wrought by wizardry, and capable of communicating a strange delight to those who once fall beneath its spell. In its passion for Nature it is unequalled. It is the intimate child of Nature, but Nature in her wildest moods. What such an artist as Emily Brontë might have accomplished had her life been prolonged it is impossible to say; but " Wuthering Heights " gives us the impression of a genius which might have wrought with unrivalled power in the realm of tragic art. That any amount of posthumous praise will ever reconcile the average mind to so stormy a genius as hers seems unlikely, but such praise is at least justified by the verdict of so discriminating a critic as Matthew Arnold, who links her name with Byron's, and can find her no other " fellow for might." It is justified also by the immeasurable attraction she has had for all who have sought to understand her, and the influence which her one book has exercised upon all who are capable of appreciating it. " Jane Eyre " will die, and even " Shirley " and " Villette " may be forgotten; it seems likely that " Wuthering Heights," inchoate and fragmentary as it is, will survive them all. It will live with the " Hyperion " of John Keats, as one of the most astonishing torsos of literature.

" She died in the time of promise," wrote Charlotte of her great sister in her touching memoir. " I am tired of being enclosed here," wrote Emily in " Wuthering Heights," in what reads like a prevision of her own fate. " You are sorry for me—very soon that will be altered: I shall be sorry for you. I shall be incomparably above and beyond you all." For Charlotte remained the harder task of living and enduring to the end. How she accomplished that task, with what pious stoicism and courage, how when the sun once more shone upon her in a happy marriage it was almost instantly withdrawn in final darkness, all readers of her biography will know. Was Mrs. Browning thinking of Charlotte Brontë when she wrote in " Aurora Leigh? "—

> How dreary 'tis for women to sit still
> On winter nights by solitary fires
> And hear the nations praising them far off!
> Too far! Ay, praising our quick sense of love,
> Our very heart of passionate womanhood,
> Which could not beat so in the veins unless
> Being present also in the unkissed lips
> And eyes undried, because there's none to ask
> The reason they grew moist.

There is clearly none to whom the words have a more obvious and pathetic application. The hosannas of the world reached Charlotte Brontë only through the darkness of Calvary.

XII

GEORGE ELIOT

George Eliot, or Mary Ann Evans, born at Griff, Warwickshire, November 22nd, 1819. Translated Strauss's "Leben Jesu," 1844. Published "Scenes from Clerical Life," 1856; "Adam Bede," 1859; "The Mill on the Floss," 1860; "Silas Marner," 1861; "Romola," 1863; "Felix Holt," 1866; "Middlemarch," 1872; "Daniel Deronda," 1876. Died December 22nd, 1880.

WITH George Eliot, as with Dickens, there has been of late years a steady set-back of fame, and something like an organised system of depreciation among critical authorities. Even Mr. Frederic Harrison, who writes as George Eliot's friend, and displays a genuine anxiety to make the best possible case for her, admits his incapacity to re-read "Romola," and to recall "the indefinite lingering plot, or the precise relations to each other of the curiously uninteresting families who talk scandal and fuss about in Middlemarch town." Once regarded as a Colossus, we are now bidden to believe that George Eliot was merely a woman of very energetic and industrious mind, who by dint of enormous toil made herself a novelist, but was never an artist. But this is manifestly untrue. An artist George Eliot was, and at times a very great artist. The place of Mrs. Poyser in English fiction is as assured as the place of Sam Weller; and this is to say that she has accomplished the highest work of an artist in creating types and persons who are real to us. What is probably meant by the statement that George Eliot was not an artist is that she was rarely an artist only; too often she spoiled her art by the weight of learning, pedantry, and philosophy with which she overlaid it. And this is true. For a period of four years in her life George Eliot wrote with consummate art. These were the years during which she produced " Scenes from Clerical Life " (1858) ; " Adam Bede " (1859) ; " The Mill on the Floss " (1860) ; and " Silas Marner " (1861). " Romola," with all its splendid merits, marks her decadence as an artist, and betrays exhaustion. In " Middlemarch " this decadence is still more pronounced, and it is complete in the utterly tedious " Daniel Deronda."

The reason of this decadence is plain, and has been already indicated. It is that George Eliot took herself too seriously as a teacher to maintain for any long period the true freshness and spontaneity of the artist. We are quite sure that. when Dickens wrote the " Pickwick Papers " he had no idea whatever but that of thoroughly enjoying himself, and of communicating his enjoyment to his readers In a less degree we are conscious of the same temper in the early writings of George Eliot. In the hours when she can forget that she is a very learned woman, capable of throwing theologians and philosophers in the arena of " The Westminster," she writes perfectly, with that exquisite pleasure in her own creations which is the chief joy of the artist. But from the first we are conscious of a wide difference between her and Dickens, or any other of her great contemporaries.

Even when she depicts the simple humours of the countryside she makes us understand that behind it all there is a very definite and subtly argued philosophy of life. Probably no writer of fiction has ever had so reasoned and philosophic a conception of life. No one has brought to the task of fiction so serious a mind. No one has taken so high and solemn a view of the moral issues of art. But in the end the pedant extirpated the artist. If George Eliot had had a happier life; if she had known less of books, and had never muddled her mind with philosophy and theology; if she had begun to write twenty years earlier, with the idea that the true function of fiction was to depict life, and had simply set herself to dramatise what she saw in the serio-comedy of human action, without too nice an attention to philosophical analysis, she would have been a far greater writer. As it was, she began to write novels long after most novelists have become famous. It was upon the whole a sort of miracle that a mind stuffed so full of dull pedantries could ever have addressed itself to such a task at all. For the four years which I have named she broke fairly free from the traditions of all her previous intellectual activity. Then the old mould gripped her mind again, and she relapsed into blue-stockingism. The miraculous period was over, and henceforth her books presented the curious spectacle of artistic genius struggling hard, and in vain, against an ingrained ponderousness of mind.

An acute thinker, a keen if somewhat ponderous critic, a review-writer of power and promise—such was George Eliot at thirty-seven, and such she might have remained but for the slow crystallisation of other forces in her nature, and the accident which revealed her true vocation. Contrast her with any other great novelist of whom we have authentic record. In most cases the story-telling faculty has been remarkable even in childhood. It was so with Jane Austen, with the Brontës, with Dickens, with almost any great novelist who can be named. Scott, indeed, does not begin to write novels till he is of a mature age; but then Scott was always a romancist, a lover of ballad and incident, and, as a romantic poet, had already prepared himself in the best possible way for the writing of fiction. But until George Eliot wrote " Scenes from Clerical Life," she had shown neither love nor aptitude for fiction. She had spent her life in laborious scholarship, in the pursuit of the highest ends of abstract thinking, in a passion for knowledge not less real, but far more intelligent, than her own Mr. Casaubon's. If Herbert Spencer or Darwin or Matthew Arnold had suddenly, at forty, become a novelist, it would hardly have been more astonishing. When her books began to be talked of, the Brays, who had known her most intimately, were the last to guess the secret of their authorship. Massive and deep they knew her mind to be, but these were the last qualities they would have dreamed of as necessary to fiction. Nine persons out of ten would have agreed with them; and probably, of all the persons who knew George Eliot, there was only one who recognised her true bent, and was not surprised at her success.

That one person was Mr. G. H. Lewes; and it is generally admitted that it was upon his suggestion she attempted fiction. It says much for his prescience that he should have discerned the true nature of her genius so accurately. But he had opportunities of discernment denied to others, and knew, better than any other could know, the passionate sentiment which throbbed behind her intellectual subtlety, the fineness of her imagination, the fervour of her affections, the greatness of her heart. With the caution and precision of a philosophic thinker she combined the intensity of a woman's nature in its essential womanliness. In spite of all her great range of learning, she was the merest woman in her surrender to the emotions. And she also had the clearest faculty of observation. This was not the mere reporter's faculty of picking up phrases, catching the outlines of things, rapidly seizing the points of a scene or a character, but something slower, deeper, and more enduring. It had already recorded indelibly all the sensations of her girlhood— the infinitely subtle and complex nature of its emotions, the errors of its raw immaturity, the baffling variations of its temper. It allowed nothing in the tragedy of the soul to escape it, and little in the aspects of the outer life. Why not interpret all this? asked Mr. Lewes. Why not utilise all this profound depth of emotion, which drains away in waste, as well as the merely logical and intellectual faculties, in the production of books? She did so, but with timidity and distrust. The result was that, when she began to write novels, it was at once apparent that a new force had arisen in literature. At thirty-seven the caustic reviewer was suddenly changed into the ardent romancist; but it was a species of romance altogether original in the history of fiction. It had humour, pathos, wit, but it had something more and something different. It had also a masculine grip, a complete and often a half-paraded mastery of the newest scientific and philosophic thought; and although no positive effort was made to inculcate either the one or the other, yet in every line there was conveyed the profound conclusions of a great and serious thinker.

How far the elaborate learning and philosophic training of George Eliot helped her as a novelist is a nice question, and capable of much argument. One or two conclusions, however, are obvious on a candid examination of her works. The chief is, that in many important respects she never mastered what may be called the craft of novel-making. There is a certain lumbering stiffness of movement, which is apparent in all her books. When she is dealing with things which are within her own experience, she is admirable, unapproachable. Nothing can excel, in general fineness and harmony of effect, the opening sections of " Adam Bede " and " The Mill on the Floss." She knew the countryside, and its humours, with absolute completeness. It is not, perhaps, the technical completeness of Thomas Hardy; but while she is quite as observant as Hardy in recording phrase and manner, she has a more spiritual insight than he in analysing the deeper springs of character. The Bedes, the Tullivers, the Gleggs, and Bob Jakin and Mrs. Poyser are living people; she had known them, and knew the slow rusticities in which they lived, and every tree and meadow of the prospects they looked upon day by day. As long as she moves in this atmosphere, her art is perfect; and, perhaps, the most astonishing thing about that art is, that without any sort of preliminary attempt she was able to produce, at the first sweep of her pen, scenes which cannot be improved, chapter after chapter which, in finish and completion, leaves nothing to be desired.

But in all her books it is easy to draw the line between what is really spiritualised biography—autobiography very often—and invention. She creates the theatre of the soul, she projects upon it immortal figures, she clothes them with the light of a searching and profound imagination. Nothing in the inner tragedy is missed: the very whisperings and by-play of the soul are accurately reported. But in the arrangement and marshalling of the outward drama—that is to say, in the invention of the story itself—she is awkward and weak. Nothing can be more commonplace and banal than the reprieve scene in "Adam Bede." It is the sort of thing which the schoolgirl always puts into her first novel. Nor did ever great novel have more inadequate ending than "The Mill on the Floss." If you ask for philosophic insight, for the keenest analysis of spiritual emotion, for the finest and most sympathetic painting of country manners, you can have them, and in their perfection, for these lay well within the knowledge of George Eliot. If you ask for plot, you cannot have it. Of dramatic instinct she is nearly destitute. Her mind cannot unbend: it has little flexibility. It has enormous powers of imagination, and therefore of creativeness, but no invention. In mere invention she is out-distanced not merely by many first-rate but by scores of third and fourth-rate novelists.

The same defects and qualities appear even more conspicuously in "Romola." She has told us that she began it a young woman, and it left her an old one. What that significant confession really means is, that it cost her an immense effort, and that the book was accomplished by a sheer dead-lift. But there was no such draining of energy in her early books, and for a good reason. She wrote of her Bedes and Tullivers with a sort of effortless joy in her work, with the ease and precision of unhindered creativeness. The work is perfect because it is spontaneous, and because she knew her element and the limit of her power. But "Romola" was dependent almost wholly on the one quality she lacked—invention. It was useless to cram the subject: she could not weld it into coherence. We never once see Florence adequately as we read, nor have we any vivid insight into Florentine life and character. What we do see, and what we never forget, is the subtle analysis of two complicated characters—Tito's and Romola's. Once more it is the spiritual tragedy that makes her book great and memorable, and it is of sufficient intensity and grandeur to dwarf into insignificance the outward aspects of the story. By the caprice of the artist the scene is laid in Florence, but her protagonists are of the same race as Maggie Tulliver and Will Ladislaw. One might even go further and say that the book professes to be about Florence, but it is really about the heart of George Eliot, and is another version of her own spiritual tragedy, with the Duomo and St. Mark's faintly washed in by way of background.

The more one considers these things, the more likely is he to arrive at definite ideas concerning the real nature of George Eliot's genius, and perhaps to conclude that her prime force was, after all, spiritual. It was by accident that she wrote novels; it was, as we have seen, merely the application of great powers in an unexpected direction, and, as it turned out, with success. But essentially she was a Methodist who had lost her creed, a mystic without faith, an austere and separated soul with an ethical mission to fulfil, but deflected by the complexities of her genius into an unusual manner of fulfilling it. Surely, when we think of it, never was a person less designed for the rôle of popular novelist, and we can quite understand her speaking in depreciation of her books. Her real interests remained throughout her life what they were when she first began to write—strictly intellectual. The world she loved best to dwell in was the world of abstract thought. So far as her own character went, she had no humour, no keen pleasure in life, no geniality. One of her closest friends said that he had never once known her to make a humorous remark. She told another friend that she counted it a bitter injury and injustice to have been born. Gloom rested over her life—a gloom that was sometimes softened and suffused by some reflected light, but it never lifted. Her letters are of a deadly dulness. The impression they give is of a slow, massive, and powerful intellect—subtle and acute enough, but without elasticity. There is no vivacity, no genial by-play—nothing indeed of those qualities which have made the letters of many much inferior persons delightful reading. Loved she was by those whom she admitted to her intimacy, honoured by many more who knew the grander side of her character and the great range of her ability; but all who knew her testify to the gloom that lay upon her life—at times the noble gloom of the great and serious thinker, at others of the bitter pessimist.

On the other hand, the very seriousness of George

Eliot's conception of life gives an ethical value to her writings which is rarely found in fiction. If in early life we read " Adam Bede " for the mere sake of the poignantly pathetic story of human life which it unfolds, we are likely to read it many times in later life for the sake of the ethical message which it contains. Gradually we begin to see that there is not a single character of George Eliot's that does not stand for some ethical idea. The Bedes, and Mrs. Poyser, and Hetty Sorrel, and Maggie Tulliver, and Godfrey Cass, all represent an ethical idea. They stand entirely outside the category of the Pickwicks and the Pumblechooks. We feel that they were meant to teach something. They preach sermons to us, and it is evident that their author intended them to do so. Upon the whole, one would be inclined to say that George Eliot's characters could never have taken so deep a hold on the mind, could never have impressed us so powerfully and continuously, if they had not also been so many ethical ideas, miraculously incarnated in flesh and blood, and with so subtle an art that all kinds of readers can appreciate them, quite apart from any ethical passion in the reader, or in spite of the entire absence of such a passion.

Looked at from this point of view—and it is probably the point of view that George Eliot herself would have wished us to take—how intense and enduring is the ethical force of her books! Take but one aspect— an outstanding aspect, which no one can miss—her treatment of the sexual problem. Holding the opinions she did, and remembering the character of her own life, it would not have surprised us if she had taken a view of marriage which is common enough among many of the revolted women of to-day. But no one could write less like a revolted woman than George Eliot. She lays down as a first principle of society that there shall be no consummation of love without marriage, and no marriage without love. The finest chapter in " The Mill on the Floss " is given up to the elaboration of this principle. Maggie Tulliver nowhere reaches such a height of character as in the scene where she pleads with Stephen Guest, not only against him, but against herself. Every one will recall the passage:

"Many things [says Maggie] are difficult and dark to me; but I can see one thing quite clearly—that I must not, cannot, seek my own happiness by sacrificing others. Love is natural; but surely pity and faithfulness and memory are natural too. And they would live in me still, and punish me if I did not obey them. I should be haunted by the suffering I had caused. Our love would be poisoned. Don't urge me; help me—help me, *because* I love you!"

The same note is struck again later on when Maggie has been entrapped into her elopement with Stephen. She pleads that her will has never consented, and that it is impossible she can ever consent to snatching happiness by the betrayal of others. The last thing the noble soul should seek in life is personal happiness, especially happiness that is bought by the misery of those who have trusted in us. It is by such acts as these that society is broken up, and the mutual faith that holds its units together is lost. To those who read between the lines there is surely in this passionate contention the confession of George Eliot's own soul. So far from urging others to do as she has done, she puts all the force of her conscience and genius into the argument against herself. There is something that is at once noble and pathetic in this. It has the effect of a personal recantation. Her ultimate conscience speaks, as Balaam's did, and it blesses that which, philosophically, she might have wished to curse.

One effect of George Eliot's spiritual apprehension of life is seen in her sense of its disciplinary nature. This is another note which she is never tired of striking. When she pictures Maggie Tulliver reading with awakened soul the yellow pages of Thomas à Kempis, it is that she may learn the old lesson so constantly reiterated by Carlyle: "Love not pleasure, love God: this is the everlasting Yea." The true dignity of man is found in his power of self-renunciation. If he be a mere bundle of voracious appetites, what is he better than the beast? But the very presence of appetites in man is the divine hint that he is meant to bridle and overcome them. It does not matter what he loses in the process; his gain is always more than his loss. Here George Eliot, philosophic pessimist as she often was, and professed antagonist to Christianity, comes very near the old monkish treatment of human nature. She has nothing to say on behalf of the gratification of natural appetite. Compare with her, in this respect, the impassioned plea for liberty of appetite in "Jane Eyre." Charlotte Brontë exemplified, as Mr. Russell succinctly puts it, genius and ignorance, just as George Eliot exemplified genius and knowledge. It is true that Charlotte Brontë shrank from the conclusions of her thesis, and vehemently repudiated them; but the nature of the thesis is plain. George Eliot, with her much wider range of ideas and knowledge of life, takes the lofty ground that the discipline of life entails upon us first of all the discipline of the passions. Her heart warms toward a St. Theresa because she is the very type of suffering endured for the ideal, and she makes Theresa the subject of her noble proem to " Middlemarch." This tendency to monkish philosophy and ideals in George Eliot is very curious, the more so when we consider her antagonism to Christianity. It is quite conceivable that a very little would have turned her at one period of her life into a good Catholic. This " very little " never happened, however; but in her insistence on the disciplinary character of life she has got at the heart of the Catholic ideal, and expresses it with an austere emphasis worthy of an anchorite.

The same tendency is seen, under another form, in her treatment of humble life. She loves to paint persons whose lot in life in insignificant, but whose spirit is high. Nowhere has she accomplished this with so much effect as in Adam Bede. Adam is the complete realisation of Carlyle's peasant-saint—perhaps we ought to say artisan-saint. In other respects also the conception bears the mark of Carlyle, notably in the dignity with which honest work is clothed. A bishop once said that probably Adam Bede was the nearest portraiture of what the human life of Christ in Nazareth was like that is possible to human art—and it would be difficult to offer a higher compliment to George Eliot's genius. But the fundamental idea that underlies Adam Bede is found in many other of the personages of George Eliot's drama. Tom Tulliver is another variation of the same type. She wishes us to see that honest work always ennobles character.

The character of Tom is far from being a noble one, but it acquires a certain dignity from its patience, resoluteness, and sense of duty. If Stephen Guest and Philip Wakem had been more strenuously engaged they would both have been happier men. Even Maggie, whom she loves, falls into most of her troubles through a certain vagueness and indolence of nature. Vice is the product of unoccupied minds. Virtue grows of itself in energetic natures. Arthur Donnithorne falls into his fatal passion for Hetty Sorrel mainly for want of something better to do. Hetty Sorrel is betrayed by her vagueness of mind, which indulges itself in all sorts of vain and foolish dreams. Adam Bede stands out in contrast with both as the type of the healthily balanced nature, disciplined and strengthened by the pressure of daily work and practical aims, which leave no room for idle reverie.

Clear through all the drama rings one note, like the monotonous boom of some bell of bronze—the divineness of duty. George Eliot is never so impressive as when she is showing us the tragedies which spring from neglected duties. The sole residuum of her early evangelical faith was this reverence for duty. Perhaps it was in one way the reaction of her evangelicalism.

Having thrown away the idea of grace, of men and women being saved by a diviner power, and with scarcely any action of their own, she naturally went to the other extreme, and urged that the only salvation for man was the salvation he wrought out for himself in his strict adherence to the highest ethical standards which he knew. No one will say that this was not something that was worth teaching, and that needed to be taught forty years ago much more than it does now. It is quite possible to teach the doctrine of grace in such a way that it debilitates the will. There was a time—and George Eliot lived in that time—when such teaching was common. Anything that seemed to savour of man doing anything to save himself was counted heretical. Mr. Froude once said that he had never in his life heard a sermon on the Ten Commandments or the duty of plain honesty. George Eliot, bred in the most orthodox evangelicalism, probably might have said the same. When she passed out of evangelicalism, it was to find herself in an austere world, where faith counted for nothing, and duties for everything. She uttered this belief in every book she wrote. She made it her mission to impress men with the power that lay in themselves to make their lives worthy. We may supply the neglected element in her teaching if we will, and say that it is still true that works without grace are vain; but it is also true that faith without works is dead, and this dogma George Eliot taught with all the force of her conviction, and often with most commanding eloquence.

As a consequence of this conviction it was also natural that she should perpetually insist on the irreparable consequences of human error. She allows no way of escape for the sinner. She insists that there is no forgiveness of sins in nature. She does this often in a way that can only be regarded as pitiless. Too often she speaks as though men and women were merely the puppets of irresistible tendencies. She says in effect: " See, in this man there is a piece of diseased moral tissue. It is quite certain that it will grow worse, and the ulcer will spread. Medicine and surgery are alike useless. In three months he will be dead, and I will show you the process by which dissolution is achieved." No wonder many people called her a fatalist, and felt her novels to be unspeakably depressing. Where was that fine romantic necromancy which always contrived that all things should come right in the end? Where was the genial interference on behalf of human nature, so common among novelists, who always exercised a species of grace on behalf of their heroes, and manumitted the punishment they had richly deserved? Certainly not in George Eliot. If it had not been for her humour, her vital sympathies and deep pity, the play of her compassion and generosity of feeling, her books would have been the most dismal imaginable. She did her best to conceal the iron logic of her reasoning under such feelings, and, upon the whole, she was so successful that the reader was enabled to forget it in the pure artistic pleasure which she afforded him. But the iron logic is there all the same. She weighs character to its finest grain. If she sets nought down in malice, she certainly extenuates nothing. She insists that as men sow so shall they reap. No divine power is so clear to her as the goddess called Nemesis. None is so awful, so unrelenting, so invariable, in her dealings with men. The appropriate frontispiece for every book she wrote would be the scales and the sword.

Nowhere does this moral intensity appear so clearly and forcibly as in the characters of Tito Melema and Godfrey Cass. She takes infinite pains to show us that Tito was not a bad man. He had a perfectly genuine appreciation of all that was fine and noble and high-spirited in human conduct. But he was never the sort of man to distress himself about being good. Brought to close quarters with the austere virtue of Romola, he is chilled to the bone. She bids him breathe too rare an atmosphere, which he cannot endure. He asks for a warmer and more luxurious atmosphere. He is essentially of a pleasure-loving and luxurious nature. He is by no means the sort of man to step deliberately into evil; he is too fastidious in his tastes, and too anxious to keep the fair show of virtue. But he slides into it, and, having once begun to fall, falls rapidly. His first act of perfidy to his wife is the beginning of a long line of perfidies. In the end he becomes a contemptible wretch, whose dismal doom is justly merited.

In Godfrey Cass the same moral is enforced, but in another form. Godfrey has a happy knack of forgetting that wild oats spring up. When once his miserable wife seems safely dead, he forgets that she ever existed. He feels that he has purged his fault, and that upon the whole he should be pitied for all that he has suffered. He is ready now to live a life of perfect virtue, and does so. But he has yet to learn that our actions are like children—we may strangle them, but we cannot be as though they had not been. The slow-footed Nemesis is on his track all the time. It all comes home to him in the bitter moment when the child he had disowned through so many years now disowns him, and he cries:

There's debts we can't pay like money-debts, by paying extra for the years that have slipped by. While I've been putting off and putting off, the trees have been growing—it's too late now. Marner was in the right in what he said about a

man's turning away a blessing from his door; it falls to some-
body else. I wanted to pass for childless once, Nancy—I shall
pass for childless now against my wish.

There are few pages in George Eliot's writings so
simply pathetic as this. Without an effort she rises
at the same time into tragic greatness. And it is in
reading such passages as these over again, after a lapse
of years, that we perceive how truly George Eliot was
a teacher, and was even greater as a teacher than an
artist. Perhaps it is this fact that truly differentiates
her from all other novelists—a moral intensity which,
while acting occasionally to the detriment of her art,
at the same time invests it with an enduring dignity,
and is the real source of all its noblest achievement.

And one thing more may be added. Just as George
Eliot, in spite of her own breach of social conventions, maintains these very conventions in all her writings with an almost passionate earnestness, so, in
spite of her renunciation of Christianity, the spirit of
Christianity asserts itself unmistakably in her books.
Dinah Morris preaching on the village green is one
of the immortal pictures of literature. No page so
pious, pathetic, and spiritual is to be found in the writings of any novelist of the Victorian era. The fact
was that the evangelicalism rejected by her mature
intellect was never dislodged from her heart. She
was an eminently spiritual woman, and no errors of
creed or conduct had the effect of destroying this spiritual element in her nature. She loved St. Theresa
because she was conscious of intimate sympathies with
her, and she wrote with impassioned tenderness the
prayers put into the lips of Dinah Morris, because they
were her own prayers, and she also was all compact

of piety and divine yearning as Dinah was. A man, when he rejects the Christian faith, usually does so with thoroughness; but in woman the faiths of the heart outlast the denials of the mind. Thus by a noble inconsistency, at once profoundly touching and striking, George Eliot, positivist and semi-pessimist as she openly declared herself to be, remained a Christian in heart; and in the fulness of her fame was still pretty much the same woman who had prayed before the Cross in the quiet Warwickshire village as a girl, and had sought with tears and penitential outpourings the conversion of her soul. The true George Eliot is not the woman who dispensed the unsatisfying bread of positivism to admiring disciples in St. John's Wood— she is Dinah Morris wrestling with God for the soul of Hetty Sorrel, and Maggie Tulliver thrilling in spirit to the devout passion of Thomas à Kempis.

The hour has not yet come for any true life of George Eliot to be written; but enough is known of what the real nature of that life was to excite both reverence and pity. Few women have ever suffered more, or more unjustly; and if her face is sad and sombre, and the tone of her writings mournful, there is ample explanation. But one thing may be safely prophesied—that whatever revelations may be in store for the world, they will serve only to reveal the fine magnanimity of her character, and increase the general reverence for her genius. She was great alike in mind and nature, and her place in literature is among the small band of creative artists whose names are immortal, and whose supremacy is disputed only by the rivalries of egoism, challenged only by the vanity of envy.

XIII

CHARLES READE

Charles Reade, born at Ipsden, Oxfordshire, June 8th, 1811. Fellow of Magdalen College, 1835. Published "Peg Woffington," 1852; "Christie Johnstone," 1853; "Never Too Late to Mend," 1856; "The Cloister and the Hearth," 1861; "Hard Cash," 1863; "Griffith Gaunt," 1866; "Put Yourself in His Place," 1870. Died at Shepherd's Bush, April 11th, 1884.

THE position of Charles Reade in English fiction is both curious and anomalous. Fame has dealt grudgingly with him. The voice of criticism, which has been uproarious in praise of many lesser men, has never spoken of him except in accents of qualification and hesitation. That he possessed rare and astonishing powers of intellect; that he brought to all the work of his pen a gigantic diligence in the accumulation of facts; that he was impetuous, generous, sensitive, lovable, pugnacious, beyond the measure of the artistic temperament in its most striking instances of eccentricity; that he exercised an influence on the social movements of his time more direct and powerful than that of any of his contemporaries in fiction, save Dickens; that he was brilliant, versatile, epigrammatic, a master of melodrama, a writer possessing great gifts of invention and imagination, with a power of catching the popular ear as remarkable as that of any writer of his time,—all this is admitted, and yet criticism speaks as though unconvinced of his merits. His fame continues to excite contention. His name is never uttered before the tribunal of the immortals without demur.

For this strange condition of things Reade is himself in part responsible.

He regarded himself as primarily a dramatist, deliberately placing on his tombstone the word "dramatist" before the word "novelist." The dream of his life was to write a successful play; he himself has told us that he devoted eighteen years to the study of dramatic art, with the total result that he earned thereby about half a crown a week. His chief friends to the end of his days were actors and actresses, playwrights and stage-managers, rather than men of letters. His novels were an after-thought rather than the deliberate choice and exercise of his genius. Thus his most popular book, "Never Too Late to Mend," is based on his drama called "Gold," and that, in turn, was suggested by a play which he saw in a Paris play-house. "Christie Johnstone" was meant to walk the boards before she appeared on the soberer stage of fiction, and "Peg Woffington" was derived from the once famous play "Masks and Faces," in which he collaborated with Tom Taylor. There can be little doubt that had he achieved immediate fame as a playwright the world would never have heard of him as a novelist. The question, therefore, naturally arises whether a man who was so slow to recognize the scope of his own genius really possessed that imperative gift which distinguishes the creative poet and the imaginative writer; for, in spite of many instances of deferred powers, such as Scott's and George Eliot's, the great novelist is usually sure of his vocation from the beginning.

Much must be allowed also for the extraordinary power which Reade had of exciting enmities. A man well born, meant for high position in the Church, a Vice-Chancellor of Magdalen College, tingling to his finger-tips with a sense of superiority, proud, pugnacious, resentful of criticism, and never able to submit to the give and take of practical struggle, Reade was continually creating difficulties for himself, from which not even genius could wholly extricate him. He fell into the error of all pugnacious and sensitive men— he believed the world was in conspiracy against him. The critics are, one and all, fools and blockheads. The actors' world in which he moved is full of rogues and cheats. He is mercilessly robbed of the fruit of his toil, and fills the world with his outcries. When he is hit, he hits back without compunction. A volume might be filled with his controversial letters, and it would form one of the most racy and humorous volumes in the world—also one of the most vituperative. To one of his antagonists he writes: " Sir, you have ventured to contradict me on a question with regard to which I am profoundly learned, where you are as ignorant as dirt." When a certain lord coveted the house in which Reade resided at Albert Gate, he retorted by erecting a huge sign-board in front of the house, bearing the legend " Naboth's Vineyard." It would have been contrary to the course of nature if a man of so swift and impetuous a temper had not made enemies, but Reade never imagined that the fault was with himself even in the most minor degree. The best that can be said on these matters is that Reade was generally right in his contentions, but right or wrong he loved contention, one suspects, for its own sake. He was a born fighter, and his fight was usually against conventions. The man who spends his days in combat with blockheads must necessarily incur misapprehensions that render the sober appreciation of his genius among his contemporaries a matter of extreme difficulty.

There is another side of the question which impinges on the realm of art. The art of the dramatist, as we have seen, differs fundamentally from the art of the novelist. The dramatist works upon a canvas where every stroke must tell. He must secure an immediate effect. He must over-emphasise the characters in order to secure this effect. The novelist, on the contrary, works out the development of his characters by slow and delicate processes. We do not comprehend the egoism of Sir Willoughby Pattern, or the deliberate selfishness of Tito Melema, until we are half-way through their histories. The novelist shows us character in its growth, while the dramatist deals with it in its completion. The novelist is seldom a good playwright, and the playwright is yet more infrequently a good novelist. Reade sought to combine both arts, making the dramatist's art the base from which he attempted the work of the novelist. The result is that his books lack repose. His characters are always over-emphasised. He must create for them striking and dramatic situations, sometimes in defiance of the probabilities of the story. His novels bear the trace of their origin; they are expanded dramas. He works too palpably towards a crisis; he is always ringing the curtain down upon a tableau. His over-emphasis is seen in the very construction and printing of his books. When he has something striking to say he uses capital letters, to the irritation of his readers. It is a trick akin to the grimace or gesticulation of the actor, who trusts to physical rather than intellectual means to impress his message on his audience. Had Reade from the first been a novelist, and a novelist only, he had been a much greater novelist. What he could do, when he was distracted by no memories of the stage, and had thrown off stage methods of construction, he has shown us in his " Cloister and the Hearth," which is not merely his greatest book, but one of the greatest books in English literature. Of the rest of his books it may be said that while they have superb characteristics of energy and invention, they all suffer more or less from those features which count for virtues in a drama, but vices in a novel.

In searching for stage effects, Reade often puts the natural effect of his fine literary art in jeopardy. He is so anxious about the climax that he discounts it by forestalling it. He allows us to see too clearly the dramatic point at which he is aiming, and we are cheated of the effect of surprise, which in poetry and fiction is the most delightful of all effects. An example of this weakness is found in the truly magnificent episode of the wanderings of Fielding and Robinson in the Australian bush, in " Never Too Late to Mend." They are being hunted by murderers; they come upon their own tracks, and find they are moving in a circle; they find at the same time that other footsteps mingle with their own trail. This latter discovery changes the whole situation. The murderers are now ahead of them instead of behind them. " What are you doing?" asks Robinson, when Fielding starts afresh upon the trail. " I am hunting the hunters," he replies. An admirable and thrilling situation, but when Reade prints the sentence in capital letters he spoils a great effect. "Those capital letters," says Mr. Christie Murray, "have long since called the attention of the reader to themselves, and the point the writer tries to emphasise is doubly lost. It has been fore-stalled, and has become an irritation. You come on it twice; you have been robbed of anticipation and sus-pense, which, just here, are the life and soul of art. You know before you ought to be allowed to guess; and, worst of all, perhaps, you feel that your intelli-gence has been affronted. Surely you had imagina-tion enough to feel the significance of the line with-out this meretricious trick to aid you." Any one can see that the tradition of the stage is responsible for this device. It is closely akin to the stage "aside," the hint of the dramatist, which is meant to express a meaning which he dares not entrust wholly to the actor. On the stage it is necessary, simply because it is difficult to make the story clear without it. But in a novel it is not necessary, because the story should explain itself.

On the other hand, Reade's long apprenticeship to dramatic art taught him many things which are in-valuable in fiction. He has the keenest eye for situa-tion. He gets to his point at once. His dialogue is terse, brisk, epigrammatic, and is sharpened into con-stant brilliance. The student, when he turns novelist, is apt to pack his narrative with pedantries, philoso-phies, and meditations, which would be admirable in an essay, but only retard the movement of a story. Many pages might be deleted from Scott and Thacke-ray and George Eliot without the slightest injury to the story—rather, indeed, to its advantage. We could ill spare these passages, it is true—we who find in them the most intimate revelation of the author's mind; but the story could spare them. They divert attention from the main issues of the drama, and while we are engaged in reflection the characters in the drama become a trifle dimmed and indistinct. To put it plainly, neither Scott nor Thackeray nor George Eliot shows more than a rudimentary knowledge of how a novel should be constructed. But it is in the art of construction that Reade excels. He hurries us breathlessly from scene to scene. If he is too fond of arranging striking tableaux, it must at least be admitted that the tableaux are striking. His stories are full of movement; they have not a dull moment, nor a moment when his invention flags. To achieve such effects no doubt something is sacrificed. His characters are usually very white or very black; he has no time to mix the more elusive colours on his palate. His drama often has something of that crude element which we call transpontine; his hero must be applauded, and his villain hissed from first to last, and after his great scenes we are conscious that he expects the affirmatory uproar of the theatre. Nevertheless, dramatic power in fiction is too rare to be lightly despised, even though it lean to transpontine forms of art. It is a great achievement to enthrall the reader, to make him burn and thrill, to excite his pity, anger, terror, praise, and hatred in scene after scene through a long book; and this Reade does, and for the power to do it he was debtor to the stage.

Of Reade more than of any other great novelist it may be said that his method is episodical. We do not remember his books by their total effect so much as by a series of brilliant episodes. The hunted hunting the hunters; the finding of the huge nugget of gold by Jacky; the captive lark singing its few faint notes to the crowd of home-sick miners; Griffith Gaunt standing in the snow; the two German printers with their clumsy printing-machines by the wayside on the road to Italy,—these and a score of similar episodes only have to be named to be instantly recalled by even the casual reader. They have the kind of distinctness and the haunting power which we usually associate with great works of pictorial art. We remember them in the same way that we remember a piece of painted drama like Lady Butler's " Roll-call," or the " Survivor of an Army." And they touch the emotions in much the same way and by the same means. They are summaries of something elemental in human nature,— fear, greed, home-sickness, adventure, loneliness, emotions known to all men, whatever their condition. A novel which hurries us from episode to episode may not be the greatest form of novel, but a novel which contains episodes so thrilling, and so catholic in their appeal, that they become indelible in the memory, have the kind of greatness which none but a pedantic critic will despise.

Fundamentally Reade was a realist, although his romantic and dramatic instincts play constant havoc with his realism. He studied life at first-hand; he had Zola's passion for " human documents"; he grudged no labour to get at facts. " That book," he said of " Never Too Late to Mend," " took four years, morning, noon, and night, out of my life. I wrote here, there, everywhere—in town, at Oxford—laying down a definite plan, from which I never departed; always determined to leave nothing to accident, nothing to guess-work." The labour which he undertook in the preparation of a book, drudging, tedious, unweariable labour in the accumulation of materials, was prodigious. Blue-books, statistics, reports, histories, magazines, journals, and police-court news were diligently read, sifted, preserved, and indexed so methodically that he knew where to find what he wanted at a moment's notice. There was excuse for his boast that he was " profoundly learned " on the subjects he wrote about, for he never wrote on any subject till he had mastered all that was to be known about it. Sir Edwin Arnold speaks with wonder of the " enormous note-books which he compiled, in the course of his various publications, with their elaborate system of reference and confirmation, and their almost encyclopædic variety and range "; and he says truly that these note-books should rank as " among the greatest curiosities of literature, and be a perennial monument of his artistic fidelity." Reade went much further than the compilation of note-books; he sought where it was possible to share the experiences he depicts. He himself had been shut up in the dark cell of a prison before he describes the torture of the unhappy Robinson. Robinson himself was a prisoner whom he met in Durham Gaol, and the merciful warder he describes died the other day in Birmingham. Reade knew perfectly well that on the controversial themes of which he wrote nothing told like the sheer weight of fact, and it is little wonder that he excited both consternation and hatred in antagonists who were not armed with his encyclopædic knowledge. Yet, with all his strong bent towards realism, he escaped the chief peril of realism—the lack of sane perspective—by virtue of his intellectual breadth. He saw the evil he exposed with an intense vividness, but he saw it in real relation to good. His was not the realism of Zola, which Stevenson describes as " romance with the small-pox; diseased anyway, and blackhearted, and fundamentally at enmity with joy "; it was rather a Biblical kind of realism, which uses very plain and strong words with prophetic force, but still retains the prophetic vision of the working out of good in the general scheme of things.

The distinction is worth noting, because it will assist us to clearness of thought in considering other forms of fiction beside Reade's. Realism is never offensive except when it is allied with radical lack of faith in human nature. We may thread the darkest labyrinths of these Infernos where men suffer abominably and unjustly, and take no harm with this clue in our hands; but without faith in human nature man loses his own soul in laying bare the ulcer of his brother's soul. The offence of Zola's art lies, after all, not so much in its material as in its spirit. A prison is one thing to Reade, and quite another thing to Zola, although the facts which each beholds are the same, because the spiritual attitude of each is so widely different. It is well to know the worst, but we should believe the best even while we know the worst, if our knowledge is not to dismay us and corrupt us. It is in this respect that Reade's realism is sanative and wholesome; he does not abuse his vision by confining it only to dark and painful things. There is a consciousness of the " ultimate decency of things," and a corresponding buoyancy of spirit in all his writings, which indicates the masculine temperament in realism, as opposed to the feminine and the hysteric.

It should be remembered also that Reade's realism was always directed to practical ends of social reformation. He not merely laid his finger on the diseased tissue in the body politic, and said, " Thou ailest here, and here," but he declared a remedy.

In 1853 the prison system of England was a system of torture carried out on professedly humanitarian principles. One authenticated case, among many revealed by the Royal Commission which sat in that year, was of a boy named Andrews, fifteen years of age, sentenced to three months' imprisonment with hard labour for petty larceny. This boy was put upon the treadmill, and, being unable to perform his task, was, by the governor's orders, put on bread-and-water diet, deprived of bed and light, and finally condemned to a strait-waistcoat and strapped to the wall. Three days later he committed suicide by hanging himself in his cell. It was the ferocious stupidity of the treatment that excited Reade's indignation. He saw, what many have seen since, that the English prison system manufactures rather than reforms criminals. Treat a man as a savage beast and you make him one. Put him to useless labour and you destroy his manhood. The first aim of the prison authorities should be not to punish but to reform the unhappy creatures over whom they have absolute power. Reade took up his parable with an eloquence, a force of conviction, a lofty passion of indignation, which stirred the public as no bare statement of fact could have done. He did more—he created vital drama from the gross material of blue-books. Although there is no concealment for an instant of the purpose with which he wrote, yet that purpose was always subordinate to art. In his hands fiction becomes a vital force in the formation of public opinion, and yet so justly tempered is his narrative that it never ceases to be a work of literary art. To unite the functions of the propagandist of ideas with those of the artist is always a task of extreme difficulty; but where many failed Reade achieved a triumphant success, and his success lies in the fact that he had the true creative instinct, the touch of flame, which welds a mass of fact into dramatic forms.

It must be counted to Reade for righteousness that he thus used his great powers for public ends. There is, however, one of his books, "The Cloister and the Hearth," in which he writes as an artist only, and it is his greatest book. A distinct purpose in a novel must always have one drawback—it limits the stage. Be the writer never so fine an artist he must obey the limits of his theme, he must stick to his text, and he must check those excursions of his imagination which divert his own mind and the attention of his readers from the cause he pleads. When Reade came to write "The Cloister and the Hearth," he was free from these limitations. His stage was nothing less than the entire Middle Ages. He was free to wander where he would, to survey men and cities, to employ all the resources of a vast erudition, to gratify his taste for art, to re-create the life and manners of one of the most fascinating periods of universal history. Every novelist should have the boldness to write one book to please himself rather than his public. It is his consolation for years of drudgery. Reade claimed his right, but with the usual result as regards the public. The book received no welcome, and came near to perishing at its birth. It appeared as a serial in "Once a Week," but was so mercilessly tampered with by the editor of that journal that Reade abruptly closed the story. Reade never forgave the editor; and when that unfortunate man was subsequently confined in a lunatic asylum, he caustically remarked that little else could be expected from a fellow who tampered with his "copy." The cause of the public indifference to the story was not far to seek. Novelists, like painters and poets, have to obey the tradition of their earliest successes. The man who paints a pig better than anything else must go on painting pigs all his life, if he means to live by his art; and similarly the novelist who has gained his success by realism indulges in romance at his peril. Reade was quite aware of this. He said rather bitterly that "the public don't care about the dead. A baby found strangled in a bonnet-box at Piccadilly Circus interests them much more than Margaret's piety or Gerard's journey to Rome." Yet fortune has declared in favour of the book which the public neglected and Reade almost regretted writing in his hour of disappointment. Fifty years ago it may have been true, as Reade said, that for one reader who read "The Cloister and the Hearth" a thousand had read "Never Too Late to Mend"; but it is no longer true. The story which offended the editor of "Once a Week," and injured the circulation of that estimable journal, has become a classic. The stone which the builders rejected has become the corner-stone in the edifice of Reade's fame.

It is a truly marvellous book. It is full of knowl-

edge of all sorts, derived not only from immediate re-
searches in the Bodleian, but from years of meditation.
It is full of wisdom, too, the ripe wisdom of a thinker
who has something authoritative to say on the nature
of human life. In mere picturesqueness, in the staging
of great and brilliant scenes, in the constant thrill of
romance, it is unrivalled. Who does not recall some of
these scenes—the humble burgher life at Tergou, the
ducal feast at Rotterdam, the flight of Gerard, the
fight in the woods, the crossing of the Rhine, the
burning of the mill—these, and a score of other episodes, painted with a masterly vivacity and extraordinary imaginative power? The life of inns, taverns,
wayside hostelries; of cloisters, palaces, and seats of
learning; the gross poverty of the poor, and the equally
gross splendour of the rich; the life of the road, full
of peril and adventure; the total absence of security
and justice in the social conditions; and through all the
rapid scenes the sense of something new stirring, the
slow upheaval of thought, the birth-throe of new intellectual life and a new age,—all this is conveyed to
the reader with inimitable spirit, with the vivid skill of
the impressionist who creates pictures in a phrase,
united with the solid erudition of the scholar. Truly
great figures emerge too; not only Gerard and Margaret, but Fra Colonna and the Pope; Perugino in his
bare lodging in Rome, and Margaret Van Eyck, guard-
ing jealously the secrets of her art. And with this
creative art in episodes and figures there goes something rarer—a reproduction of the exact atmosphere
of the period. We are able to think the thoughts of
the Middle Ages as well as see their life. The book is
vast in scope as well as exact in detail. It is in this

respect that it is most remarkable; for no other artist, not even Scott, has worked on so daring a scale. Other artists have succeeded admirably in painting a period, and making a group of figures representative of the period, but Reade paints the Middle Ages themselves, and to follow his narrative is, as Sir Conan Doyle observes, "like going through the Middle Ages with a dark lantern." And yet even this striking saying expresses but part of the matter; for if there is the vividness of a shaft of light plunging into dark places in the episodes of the book, there is also a lucid clearness in the whole, as of dawn—a broad landscape, over which is spread an equal light.

The fame of Reade will more and more come to rest upon "The Cloister and the Hearth." It gives the true measure of his powers, and it ranks as one among the very few immortal books in modern fiction. With such an achievement the most ambitious genius may be content. There is but one regret when we close the book; it is that its author should have been so ignorant of the real character of his genius, that he should have devoted half his life to dramas which are forgotten, when he might have produced works of literature which would have ranked him with the great masters. But if, as he himself said, "he flowered late," he flowered in rare fashion, for the greatest writer might be proud to own Reade's greatest work.

XIV

CHARLES KINGSLEY

Charles Kingsley was born at Holne Vicarage, Dartmoor, June 12th, 1819. Published "The Saint's Tragedy," 1848; "Alton Locke," and "Yeast," 1849; "Hypatia," 1853; "Westward Ho," 1855; "Two Years Ago," 1857; "Hereward the Wake," 1866. Appointed a Canon of Westminster and Chaplain to the Queen, 1873. Died at Eversley, January 23rd, 1875. His collected works fill twenty-eight volumes.

CHARLES KINGSLEY shares with Charles Reade a high place in the secondary order of novelists. Fundamentally Reade was the broader and greater man, and his one great novel, "The Cloister and the Hearth," gives him classic rank. Kingsley has produced nothing of the same weight, distinction, and brilliance. It is possible that Reade, upon the strength of his one masterpiece, may be remembered with the great masters, in much the same way that Blackmore will be remembered by his "Lorna Doone." Kingsley, however, has written nothing that suggests a doubt as to his ultimate place in fiction. "Westward Ho" is not comparable with "The Cloister and the Hearth" or with "Lorna Doone." "Hypatia" is upon the whole a brilliant failure. Yet it cannot be doubted that Kingsley has exerted an influence upon his age attained by neither of these novelists. It is an influence subtle and peculiar, based in part on personality, in part on the nature of his message—an influence more commonly associated with the prophet than the novelist.

The nature of the times in which Kingsley wrote, as well as the nature of the man, had much to do with this influence, which seems to a reader of the twentieth century out of all proportion to his genius. He was the product of circumstances, the interpreter of tendencies, the voice of a movement. The years during which Kingsley's best work was done were years of great perturbation of thought in England. The entire social system had become the subject of alarm and debate. There was a general uneasiness of feeling— a conviction on the part of some, and a strong suspicion on the part of many, that all was not well with the land. There was much bitter and excited debate on social conditions—little careful diagnosis, but the loud proclamation of many vague and violent remedies—a sense of impending change, exciting in equal degrees hope and fear. There was a general consciousness that the old landmarks were shifting or had shifted. Men were feeling their way to new ideals and dreaming of new combinations. It looked as though all that was traditional in faith and thought, together with all that was old in social convention, would be cast into the melting-pot, to emerge in what form God only knew. Kingsley interpreted this uneasiness, though he did little to allay it. He became the intermediary of greater minds than his own. He gave currency to the religious views of Maurice and the social gospel of Carlyle. He lifted up his voice in noble anger, and took possession of the platform of fiction as a prophet of righteousness. His books were impassioned declarations of faith and principle. At this distance of time it is difficult to discriminate how much of his fame belonged to the prophet, how much to the artist; but it is certain that his prophetic fervour gave him a strong influence over many minds not usually sensitive to the appeal of art.

The highest kind of artistic genius combines intense energy with calm equipoise; it works, as Goethe so finely said, "without haste and without rest." Judged by such a canon, Kingsley did not possess the highest kind of genius. His books were wrung out of him by an effort that told severely on his physical health. He is apt to become hysterical through excess of feeling. He often resembles the orator who strains his voice in order to secure attention, shouting a statement which would have been infinitely more effective if uttered with quiet and deliberate emphasis. He never attains the great artist's sane and gracious vision of the proportion of things. It may be said of him, as it was said of the author of "Obermann":

A fever in these pages burns,
. . .
A wounded human spirit turns
Here, on its bed of pain.

His physical restlessness was one of the characteristics much commented upon by his friends. There is the same overwrought vivacity in all his books. It is very impressive at times. It excites our wonder, it communicates its contagion, it expresses itself in bursts of eloquence that carry us away with a rush, but after a time it wearies us. We feel much as a man might feel in the company of a too declamatory friend, who never has a "flash of silence." If he would but sit down and talk quietly, if he would but lay aside now and then the prophet's mantle, if he would but recollect that it is against nature that a man should be always on the tribune; but no, even in the closest privacy he will still address us " as though we were a public meeting." In books, as in friendship, repose is the secret of enduring charm. In Kingsley's books the element of repose is altogether wanting.

The nature of Kingsley's gift may be fairly, though not quite adequately, measured by one of his earliest books, " Yeast." It has serious faults, both of construction and characterisation. Yet it both holds and stirs the reader by its manifest sincerity and earnestness. Lancelot Smith is a good deal of a prig, and it is a little difficult to believe in Tregarva. Here Kingsley is idealising, and here he is at his worst and weakest. But the moment Kingsley comes to deal with scenes and things he knows, with the hunting-field, with the trout-stream, with the life of squires, farmers, game-keepers, and poachers, he writes with infinite vivacity and charm. If his Lancelot Smith is not convincing, Crawy (the poacher) and Harry Verney (the keeper) are vital figures. He has rendered them to the life,—the misplaced ingenuities, the shifty courage, the thwarted manhood of the poacher, born disinherited, and crushed out of shape by ages of social tyranny; the faithfulness and honest pride of the keeper, whose last words, as he lies shot, are, " There ain't such a head of hares on any manor of the county, and them's the last words of Harry Verney!" In this, as in all his books, Kingsley is strongest when he is at close quarters with the common people. His art goes upon lame feet until his sympathies are kindled by contact with the poor and disinherited. His picture of the village feast, with the dull bestiality, its dim-eyed sodden boors, touched with no warmth of true merriment, with their muddy romance, their spiritless pleasures, their brooding sense of injury, is vivid and startling and indelibly true. It is the thrilling note of humanitarianism that dominates this and all the most impressive scenes in the book.

"Alton Locke" is a novel conceived in the same vein, but with a greatly widened range of power. His faculty of characterisation has ripened; it is altogether more accurate and skilful. The book contains one figure wholly admirable—old Mackaye, of whom Carlyle said, "my invaluable countryman in this book is nearly perfect. . . . His very dialect is as if a native had done it; the whole existence of the rugged old hero is a wonderfully splendid and coherent piece of Scotch bravura." The questions discussed in this volume go to the very root of the social problem. He has looked on London with the same penetrating and sympathetic eye which had already discovered the miseries and maladies of the rural population. He writes now in a sustained frenzy of passion and indignation, exposing the evils of his time with a ruthless realism which is profoundly impressive. "Alton Locke" is his best book, because it is the book most representative of the man. It shows us Kingsley at his noblest, and it is besides a memorial of a movement very remarkable in itself, and still of unexhausted potency in its influence on society.

The book is not only his best book, but so much remains unaltered in social conditions that it may still be regarded as a book with a message. Nevertheless, it must be allowed that Kingsley contributes nothing very positive to the solution of the problem he presents with so much vigour. He exhibits the common weakness of prophets—of Carlyle, for example—that he finds the denunciation of evil much easier than the discovery of a remedy. Prophets rarely have the gift of constructive statesmanship, and Kingsley is no exception to the rule. Another thing worth notice is that Kingsley's radicalism is a kind of aristocratic radicalism. His sympathies are with the people, but he is scarcely a democrat. He is a Socialist, but with such curious reserves that it is doubtful if the flannel-collared Socialist of to-day would have owned him. He had a good deal more sympathy with a well-ordered feudalism than with genuine Chartism. His temper was mainly the Tory-democrat temper; his hope of national salvation lay in the squires rather than the people.

In " Alton Locke " his bitterest satire is directed, not against the classes, but the demagogic leaders of the masses. One or two things he saw clearly and truly; and the chief was that the rift between the classes was spreading. He had very vague ideas of how it was to be healed. In his later prefaces to " Two Years Ago " he seems to imagine that the Crimean War, which every statesman of note to-day does not hesitate to denounce as a stupendous blunder, was to be the means of a new reconciliation of society. Such a declaration makes us suspect that Kingsley never really grasped the social problem with any approach to accuracy. His sympathies were true enough, but his was not the order of mind that patiently investigates facts and discovers remedies. One could wish that it had been otherwise, though such wishes are futile. But Kingsley did one thing with splendid efficiency: he pictured the conditions of the problem with such intense vividness and sympathy that he did much—perhaps more than any other man of his time—to rouse the mass of men to its consideration. Other writers may suggest the remedies; it is, after all, no small service to get the facts stated in such a way that they lay hold of the popular imagination, and melt the frost of callousness which has kept the sympathies of a nation stagnant.

The moral earnestness of Kingsley was his most distinctive quality, but that alone would scarcely have made him a popular novelist. Fortunately for his fame he possessed also an eye of extraordinary quickness for natural beauty, a thoroughly masculine temperament capable of appreciating the joys of mere living, and a very noble sense of chivalry. Nothing that he saw of sadness and disorder in the world around him could prevent him from praising God for life. He has the art of writing about gloomy things without writing gloomily. He never loses sight of blue sky and the secure stars. His joy in life is absolute, and almost boisterous. Hence there is a wholesome, gladdening, uplifting power in all his writings. He is never so charming as when he touches with a vivid brush the things of Nature—never so animated as when he paints the pleasures of a strenuous life—never so inspiring as when he speaks of woman and sings like a troubadour the praise of chivalry.

Kingsley's passion for Nature was a kind of intoxication. It is not the calm, sustained Nature-worship of Wordsworth; it is a feverish ecstasy, yet it is equally virile and authentic. Fine scenery inebriates him. The best passages in his novels are those in which he describes with the eye of a naturalist and the zest of a boy some aspect of sea or land, forest or open heath, which has impressed him. In his " Prose Idylls " —a book which never enjoyed the popularity it deserved—there are some exquisite pieces of Nature-rendering, which once read are not easily forgotten. The same faculty is found in his poetry; indeed, it is difficult to imagine a poet who is not a lover of Nature. But it will be noticed that Kingsley's passion for Nature is not merely not Wordsworth's, but it is totally unlike it. It is the feeling, not of the mystic, but of the Indian hunter—a frank sense of being akin to the earth, of delight in her magnificence, of keen-edged sensations produced by contact with her. There was a certain animal vigour in all Kingsley's sensations. He speaks of himself as tempted to a hunter's life on the prairies; and it is easy to see that it is the ocean-like vastness and freedom of the prairie which has fascinated his imagination. He did not easily accommodate himself to the trammels of civilisation. He felt in himself a need for boundlessness—a thirst for the desolate and barbaric places of the earth. And in its way this was a message worth delivering. It is probable that it has been a powerful factor in the expansion of England. Many a youth, reading Kingsley's fascinating descriptions of wild Nature, has been fired with a desire for emigration. If nothing else has happened, he has felt that cities are a poor substitute for Nature, and has sought some better acquaintance with the green country lying at his door. And, in an age like ours, it is obviously a great thing to make men feel that Nature has claims upon them, and that no man can be said to fulfil his own best instincts who knows only the sooty pavements of the city.

It was natural enough that a man who felt these things as keenly as Kingsley did should have had something to say upon field sports. And by another natural transition we see how easy it was for him to reach his conception of the "Muscular Christian." It matters very little to us that Kingsley protested against this term, and considered it an opprobrious nickname invented by his enemies; most of us will see nothing in it to excite indignation, and, as nicknames go, it is both just and felicitous. For what does it amount to? Simply this, that Kingsley saw around him numerous specimens of a flabby, nerveless, flaccid Christianity which he utterly despised. Such people virtually, though not by professed creed, held the body in contempt. They were all intent on saving the soul— "their dirty little souls," as Kingsley scornfully said. They had no interest in any sort of games—games were a sinful waste of time. They were infected by the old Puritan prejudice against sport of all kinds. As for vivid delight in Nature, they did not know what it meant; and if they did, would have characterised it as a sinful worship of the creature instead of the Creator. Was that the sort of religion that England wanted? Kingsley asked. Was that the sort of religion which made nations great? Was it any merit, or any proof of superior spirituality in a youth, that his muscles were flabby, that he did not know how to use his fists on occasion, that he spent his time in meditation on his own soul and its future prospects, when a world full of innocent means of enjoyment lay round about him?

Kingsley answered in his impassioned way that such a youth was a fool and a prig. He professed himself the " chaplain of Esau," the wild man and the hunter: Jacob, who cheated his way to a fortune, had plenty of apologists. He elevated into new dignity the athlete, the man of fine animal vigour and physical courage. And he endeavoured to show that a man could be both an athlete and a Christian—that he might be brave, heroic, hardened into physical endurance, soldierly, skilled in sport, but none the less a Christian, who feared God, reverenced duty, and lived chastely.

Religion was with him the cultivation and sanctification of the whole man. The most deadly of all heresies was contempt of the body, and development of the soul at the price of the body. The soul developed by such a process, he would have said, was not worth anybody's saving. We may not need to be told these things to-day, when athleticism has triumphed all along the line; perhaps the time has come when it is necessary to insist on the other side of the truth, and tell men that sanitation is not salvation, and that the life is more than meat, the soul more than the body. But in Kingsley's day the message was needed, and he drove it home with a cogency and fervour worthy of an apostle. After all, Kingsley's " Muscular Christian " is a very admirable conception, and one of which neither he nor we have any reason to be ashamed.

If " Alton Locke " was Kingsley's best book, as being most representative of the spirit of the man, " Westward Ho! " is his greatest book, as being the most representative of his powers as a novelist. It has many of the characteristics of a great book—a large canvas, a stirring theme, a noble story told with immense spirit and vivacity, and full of passages that come near to epic dignity. Here he works at the full measure of his power, with complete zest and freedom. Amyas Leigh is an authentic piece of manhood. We can believe in him, which is not always the case with Kingsley's heroes. We can believe in his adventures, and we follow them with breathless interest. And we believe also in the general picture of the times which Kingsley draws. The case may not be altogether as Kingsley states it. His pretension to historic accuracy has been constantly attacked; but he is as accurate as Scott, who regarded history as a treasure for the plunderer, who naturally takes what he wants, and rejects what is useless to him. Granted the principle, we are only concerned with the result; for no sensible reader expects sound history in fiction, though he may unwittingly swallow a great deal of fiction in history. Kingsley achieves this great result; he re-creates in his own vivid fashion the England of Elizabeth. He interprets to us the spirit and fashion, the romance and adventure, the faith and courage, the heroism, chivalry, and rising patriotism of those great and spacious times. " Westward Ho ! " is a book which has so much of greatness that, had Kingsley died at thirty-five, says Mr. Leslie Stephen, " we should have speculated upon the great things which we had lost." It is upon this book that his reputation chiefly rests, and by it his rank as a novelist must be determined.

If Kingsley fails of the highest rank among modern novelists, the reason lies in his versatility. He attempted too many things to do them all equally well, or even to do one with entire perfection. It is not given to the greatest man to unite in himself the functions of the parish clergyman, the social reformer, the controversialist, the historian, the preacher, the poet, and the novelist, without some sacrifice of one power in the service of another, and that general diminution of efficiency which is the result of power applied to too wide an area. What is gained in superficies is lost at the centre. Kingsley, in his energetic passion to lead a full life, did not perceive this truth. Possibly we are the gainers by his ignorance. We could ill spare his poetry for the sake of his novels, and many of us would be inclined to say that such gems of lyrical expression as " Oh, that we two were maying," " The Three Fishers," and " Loraine Lorree," with their poignant, penetrating pathos, strike a rarer note of genius than anything in his more ambitious prose. Still less could we spare the noble example of a life not only lived at highest pressure, but consistently lived for great things. Kingsley, in being less than a great novelist, is also more—he is a teacher of singular force, who through many forms of activity communicated many impulses to his race, all of which make for loftier ideals of life, for enlarged humanitarian sympathies, and for that spirit of heroism and duty without which nations miss the hour of their visitation and perish from the earth.

XV *

GEORGE MEREDITH

*George Meredith, born in Hampshire, February 12th, 1828.
Published "Poems," 1851; "The Shaving of Shagpat," 1855;
"The Ordeal of Richard Feverel," 1859; "Evan Harrington,"
1861; "Modern Love, and Poems of the English Roadside,"
1862; "Sandra Balloni," 1864; "Rhoda Fleming," 1865; "Vittoria," 1866; "Adventures of Harry Richmond," 1871; "Beauchamp's Career," 1875; "The Egoist," 1879; "The Tragic
Comedians," 1881; "Diana of the Crossways," 1885; "One of
Our Conquerors," 1890; "The Amazing Marriage," 1896. Still
living.*

THOSE who have met George Meredith in recent years will retain a vivid memory of an extraordinarily vivacious old man, eloquent, humorous, rich in various knowledge, whose intellect age has scarcely dimmed with even a passing shadow, and whose natural force of mind is scarce abated. Virility is the outstanding quality of Meredith's old age. Virility is also the outstanding quality of all his work. The zest of life possesses him. He writes constantly as one for whom human life is a boundless good. Not even the long neglect of his contemporaries has been able to save the native sweetness of his temper, or reduce its buoyancy. Yet few great writers have been received with greater coldness by

* The basis of this chapter is found in the writer's article on George Meredith published in "Quest and Vision," 1892.

the public. His first book of poems appeared at the same time as Tennyson's "In Memoriam." More than thirty years were to elapse before the general verdict gave him a place with the immortals.

This delay of recognition is due in great part to the wilfulness and novelty of Meredith's style. It is a style brilliant almost beyond example in his contemporaries; but it is at times wilfully obscure in an almost equal degree. To those who love splendour, subtlety, and felicity of diction, combined with the most penetrating and suggestive thought, the writing of George Meredith is an unboundaried paradise. Roam where you will, a profusion of things dear to the delicate and discerning palate are found. Or, to change the figure, never was there so coruscating a style. The page perpetually breaks in star-sparkles; it flashes with all sorts of pyrotechnic displays, it is volcanic with eruptive radiance. Sometimes it is almost mischievously coruscating, as though a boy exploded crackers under you for the mere pleasure of seeing you jump. But one never knows how soon or suddenly the fire may go out, and you may find yourself plunged into the darkest by-ways of obscurity. Mr. Meredith has described Carlyle's style, and in doing so has partially described his own:

A style resembling either early architecture or utter dilapidation, so loose and rough it seemed; a wind-in-the-orchard style, that tumbled down here and there an appreciable fruit with uncouth bluster; sentences without commencements running to abrupt endings and smoke, like waves against a sea-wall, learned dictionaries giving a hand to street-slang, and accents falling on them haphazard, like slant rays from driving clouds; all the pages in a breeze, the whole book producing a sort of electrical agitation in the mind and joints.

Neither of Carlyle nor Meredith is this description wholly true; but, as Carlyle might have said, "it is significant of much" in both. To complain of too great brilliance is, no doubt, a novel complaint, yet in Meredith's case it is a very real one. Conceive a concert wherein all the music is *allegro,* or a gallery entirely full of Turner's most gorgeous sunsets, and you have a not inapt illustration of the effect produced by a continuous reading of George Meredith. The most brilliant thing suffers by a want of contrast. The last slow and solemn movement in a great sonata is all the more striking by contrast with that which has preceded it; the finest Turner is yet finer if we see it after having seen some study of soft and tender greys. We miss the point of rest almost altogether in Meredith's work. He is so infinitely vivacious, versatile, and witty, so fertile in jest and epigram, so agile in the leaps and glances of his thought, so wayward and surprising, so conspicuously acute and clever, that less nimble minds pant breathless behind him, and even the nimblest have a difficulty in keeping pace with him. "She ran ahead of his thoughts like nimble fire," he says in one place of Mrs. Caroline Grandison. It is a just description of his own treatment of his readers; and sometimes the fire we have followed with panting eagerness suddenly dances a will-o'-the-wisp fantasy of mirth and leaves us knee-deep in the bog. When once we become used to his method, no writer can afford so much intellectual exhilaration; but it is little wonder, when we consider it, that the regular novel-reader is bewildered by so uncommon a guide and prefers some one much duller and safer. Intellectual gymnastics, however brilliant, are not what that patient and somewhat dull creature, " the general reader," looks for in a novel.

It is altogether too late to enter upon the question so often raised in connection with Meredith's work—whether science ought to find a place in novels; the question is rather how large a space ought science to occupy. If this is a scientific age, and if the novel holds the mirror up to the age, science must needs be adequately reflected in it. Moreover, as one of Meredith's critics has truly said, the way of advance in English fiction lies through George Eliot and George Meredith—that is, through the only two novelists of our time who have come to their task with a complete scientific equipment. Is their work the better or worse for this equipment ? It may be answered that it is both. After all, the novel is not a psychological, and still less a physiological, treatise; and there are moments in the writing of both George Eliot and George Meredith when it becomes this and nothing more. The more a novelist knows the better will he write; but when he pauses in his story to display his knowledge he becomes a pedant and ceases to be a novelist. The worst fault of Browning also lies in this direction; there are times when his poetry runs into pedantry, and the reader of the " Paradise Lost " will note the same tendency in Milton. But it is possible, and it is common, to exaggerate these blemishes, and people who do not care to be at any trouble in their reading triumphantly push these blemishes forward as an excuse for their intellectual indolence. To such people poetry and fiction are simply ingenious relaxations for the idle moments of life, of which they have too many, and they naturally demand the old commonplaces of pursu-

ing love and ultimate marriage-bells as the beginning
and end of fiction, and resent a style of fiction which is
charged with the gravest matter and is meant to make
men think. Toward such readers George Meredith,
and not less George Eliot and Browning, take up an
attitude of irreconcilable defiance. They do so because they regard their art as a serious business. They
are of Milton's temper, and approach their task with
a solemn invocation that what is dark in them may
be illumined, what is weak strengthened, that they may
rise to the height of their great argument. A sacred
fire burns in them: for they are prophets, not hire-
lings; voices, not echoes; artists, not artificers. Milton,
George Eliot, and Browning have already triumphed,
and compelled the world to listen: will not George
Meredith also triumph in due season?

Nevertheless, nothing could be more unjust than to
say that George Meredith cannot tell a story or that
his style is consistently obscure. The bulk of his stories
are admirably conceived and executed, and for the
most part the style is marvellous in its suppleness, its
unflagging force and grace, its subtlety of flavour and
suggestion, its flashes of inspiration, its intense con-
cision, its actual splendour and poetry of phrase, its
searching directness and nervous strength. He is a
prose Browning, and his phrases are often as haunting
as Browning's. He is the comrade of George Eliot,
but is George Eliot's master both in force of intellect
and poetic magnificence of diction.

Why, then, we ask again, has it taken thirty years
for Meredith to be known, and even now not widely
known? The real reason lies in the fact that he has
not the universal note of the popular writers.

Dickens, in his best work, and in spite of much that was tawdry, had that note; and George Eliot, also, in spite of much that was stiff and scholastic, at least in her earlier volumes. " David Copperfield " has a charm for the least and most cultured, and so has " Adam Bede." The shopman and the student alike read them, and each feels the charm, though it may be through widely differing channels. But great as are " The Ordeal of Richard Feverel " and " The Egoist," they are not conceived on that broadly human scale which is bound to draw all eyes, to move all hearts. They have height rather than breadth, a quality that is Miltonic rather than Shakespearean. They appeal irresistibly to the cultured, but scarcely at all to the crowd. Style, whether too brilliant or too obscure; science, whether too obtrusively or too frequently thrust to the front, would not be sufficient barriers to dismay the mass of readers if the story itself struck the universal note and appealed to the deep heart of humanity.

To recur again to a name which is inseparable from Meredith's, we may say that he and Browning stand in the same category. It is impossible to suppose that either can be widely read. Browning is not a people's poet, nor is Meredith a people's novelist. But in spite of this Browning, in his teaching and his influence, stands at the back of all the most influential teachers of our day, and is daily being reinterpreted by a thousand lips to ten thousands of persons who are ignorant of his poetry. In the same way Meredith is a fruitful force, working not directly but indirectly on the mass of readers, not in his own person so much as in a far wider degree through the persons of others who have received the impact of his teaching. It is perhaps not as we could wish it, and not as he could wish it. But if it be for the present a thing inevitable there is this compensation, that as the race progresses he will become more and more visible in the general life, and may be read together with Browning by new generations, when those who had their reward in this life are utterly forgotten.

The two great weapons in which Meredith excels are satire and humour. The satire is never less than excellent, for in the mere literary finish of his biting epigrams he is unsurpassed by any writer of English, either past or present. The fault of the satire is that it is not kindly, and it can be cruel. It is as keen as a surgeon's knife, and as cold. It lays bare all the hidden disease of the human soul, and cuts relentlessly, almost savagely, through the intervening filaments. Not in all literature is there to be found so terrible an exposition of selfishness as in the character of Sir Willoughby Pattern, the Egoist. If it were possible to light up a human body from the inside, so that it should become transparent to us, like a glass bee-hive, in which we see every movement of busy wing or tentacle, so that in like manner we might discern every little beating nerve of man, every throb and palpitation of remotest vein and artery, it would be an apt figure of how Meredith treats the soul of man. He conceals nothing—he concedes nothing; he simply flashes his terrible searchlight into the secret places of the heart, and things explain themselves. Coiling one inside the other, restless with vehement and loathsome vitality, we see the mass of serpentine motives, the mean and wicked impulses, which lurk in the bottom of the human ego. Pleasant?—no, it is not pleasant; but

how true it is! How wholesome it is for us to be
driven sometimes into this searching analysis of ourselves! We pause a hundred times in the reading of
the " Egoist " and shudder, for we have found out
something about ourselves which we did not suspect,
or of which we were fearfully and faintly conscious,
as of a skeleton in the cupboard, known to us, but
judiciously and gratefully ignored. Meredith refuses
to be our accomplice in any such deception. He forces
us to face the ghastly secret of the human cupboard.
" Sacred reality," he tells us, is the goddess he wor-
ships; and he argues that it cannot be wise or right for
any of us to go about in ignorance of what we really
are. His satire is the child of relentless truth; it is
indeed truth itself, naked, severe, uncompromising.

No more striking example of this rigorous satirical
analysis is to be found than in Meredith's exposure of
what Sir Willoughby's desire for purity in woman
really means. He demands of his betrothed that she
should be cloistral. " Women of mixed essences,
shading off the divine to the considerably lower, were
outside his vision of women." He demands " purity
infinite, spotless bloom." The commonplace observer
will at once say, Of how admirable and clean a nature
must be this man who can be content with nothing
less than " purity infinite " in woman. Not at all, says
Meredith—entirely the reverse. It is nothing but a
" voracious æsthetic gluttony." " It has its foundation in the sensual," and this vast and dainty exacting
appetite is lineally " the great-grandson of the Hoof."
Why does he frantically demand this immaculate, this
more than human bloom? It is the exaction of a
gluttonous, sensual appetite. It is more than that; for

him there must needs be fashioned "a perfect speci-
men designed for the elect of men." There the secret
is out; the demand is but another tentacle of that ink-
spitting cuttlefish Egoism, which works uneasily in the
mud of the human heart, and stretches itself on all
sides in insatiable craving. "And," adds Meredith,
"the capaciously strong in soul among women will
ultimately detect an infinite grossness in the demand
for purity infinite, spotless bloom." What you have
supposed the demand of austerity is the passionate
shriek of voluptuousness, and the strong-souled among
women will find you out.

Meredith's satire allied to analysis is sometimes cruel,
but when it is allied to humour it is delightful. It is
then the smack of the sea-salt that gives edge to the
sunny breeze. He can be droll, quaint, genial; he
can jest and gambol like a boy or shout with Homeric
laughter. He who has not read "Evan Harrington"
has before him several hours of unmitigated laughter.
For broad humour—in one or two instances a trifle
too broad for good taste—it would be hard to surpass
that memorable cricket supper at the Green Dragon,
Fallowfield, and the eccentric behaviour of John Raikes
thereat. The hat of John Raikes alone is provocative
of infinite mirth. "I mourn my hat. He is old—I
mourn him yet living. The presence of crape on him
signifies he shall ne'er have a gloss again. The fact
is my hat is a burden in the staring crowd. A hat like
this should counsel solitude." In another spirit, but
as genially humorous, is the famous description of Mrs.
Caroline Grandison, in "Richard Feverel." "She was
a colourless lady, of an unequivocal character, living
upon drugs, and governing her husband and the world

from her sofa. Woolly Negroes blessed her name, and whiskered John Thomases deplored her weight." She had rapidly produced eight daughters, and felt the solemnity of woman's mission. A son was denied her. Her husband, the quite unobjectionable gentleman, lost heart after the arrival of the eighth, and surrendered his mind to more frivolous pursuits. After that disappointing eighth she also lost heart and "relapsed upon religion and little dogs." But to give samples of Meredith's humour were an endless task. It runs through a hundred variations, from the keenest to the broadest; it smacks of Jingle and of Falstaff; it is sometimes plain farce, at others finished comedy; it is acute, genial, caustic; it is now hilarious with boyish buoyancy and good spirits, now the product of masculine good sense and piercing insight, now a shaft of laughter playing round a fountain of tears; and, widely as it differs, running through the gamut from the verbal quip to the profoundly human delineation, from merely comic to half-tragic laughter, it is a pervasive element, with which all his books are lavishly endowed. As a mere humorist Meredith is as superior to those ephemeral writers who pass as such to-day as is Shakespeare to Douglas Jerrold.

To Meredith, as to Thackeray, and with equal ignorance and lack of insight, the term "cynic" has been generally applied. If the cynic is he who sneers at good, then no man has less deserved the reproach. But when such terms are used no one stops to consider what they imply, and to call a man a cynic is the only refuge of Philistine mediocrity, which above all things dreads satire, and is afraid of being laughed at for not understanding what breeds laughter in others. We may admit that there is sometimes a disagreeable flavour in some of Meredith's scenes and phrases. One knows not how to define it, except to say that in such cases his robust masculinity touches in a fugitive fashion the verge of grossness. But of cynicism, of the spirit which mocks and derides, he has no trace; on the contrary, one is struck by the broad humanity of his writings, their essential buoyancy and good humour. And this is the more remarkable when we recollect that he has been condemned by the public to thirty years of almost total neglect, during which period he has had the mortification of seeing a score of writers with not a tithe of his genius press to the front and become the acknowledged representatives of English fiction. The " Ordeal " of George Meredith will make one of the most surprising chapters of that history of literature which our sons will write one day. For him, as for Browning, has been ordained a quarter of a century of deaf ears and mocking mouths; and how much does it say for the genuine greatness of each that they were able to keep a tranquil soul, an unembittered mind, and emerge from the cloud of neglect as the great optimists of their generation!

If we will take the trouble to analyse this so-called cynicism, we shall see at once that its component elements are really moral intensity and love of " sacred reality." To tell the plain truth is often to say a bitter thing, and for a good many people anything bitter is called cynical. And the supreme moral value of George Meredith's writing is its absolute witness to truth. He glosses over nothing. He sees clearly " the reddened sources " from which even the noblest passions spring. He is profoundly convinced that we can gain nothing in the long-run by ignoring any element of truth about ourselves. To leave the body out of consideration in our epitome of man is as fatal a blunder as to ignore the soul. To collect only the finest qualities of a man or woman into a sort of odorous nosegay and call that human nature is to commit an outrage on justice. The earth grows weeds as well as flowers, and so does human nature. Let us have, then, the whole truth, and nothing but the truth; it will do us less harm to know everything than to know only what it will please us best to know. That is the great lesson of his greatest book, " Richard Feverel "; and never was a lesson taught with more impressive power. " The system," as he derisively calls it, that marvellous system which is to produce a perfect youth by picking and choosing among the elements of things, by building walls here to close up dangerous paradises, and opening gateways there into sterile moral Saharas, by twisting this proclivity into grotesqueness, like a bruised vine upon a pole, and diverting the natural course of that taste or passion till it makes for itself feculent puddles instead of flowing purely in its natural bed—this system, carefully pieced together, mechanical, rigid, meant to mutilate life at every point, and produce perfection by mutilation, in the end works nothing but havoc, ruin, and death to all whom it concerns. And the secret of its failure lies in the fact that it is not based upon the truth of things. " Great is truth, and must prevail," is the constant chant of George Meredith; and not less passionately than Carlyle does he perpetually affirm that truth is always wholesome, and a half-truth is the worst of lies.

The moral intensity of Meredith often becomes almost prophetic in its passion. "You cannot cheat nature," he insists over and over again. Nowhere in fiction is there a more tremendous sermon on the inevitable consequences of sin than in that chapter of "Richard Feverel" called "The Wild Oats Plea." Every youth should read it; it is a prophet's scroll to be thrust into his hand as he steps over the threshold of boyhood into the fulness of manhood. Sir Austin Feverel calls upon two ancient intimates, Lord Heddon and Darley Absworthy, "useful men though gouty, who had sown in their time a fine crop of wild oats, and advocated the advantage of doing so, seeing that they did not fancy themselves the worse for it." He found one with an imbecile son and the other with consumptive daughters. "So much," he wrote in his note-book, "for the wild oats theory!"

Darley was proud of his daughters' white-and-pink skins. Beautiful complexions, he called them. The eldest was in the market, immensely admired. There was something poetic about her.

She intimated that she was robust, but toward the close of their conversation her hand would now and then travel to her side, and she breathed painfully an instant, saying, "Isn't it odd? Dora, Adela, and myself, we all feel the same queer sensation—about the heart; I think it is—after talking much."

Sir Austin nodded and blinked sadly, exclaiming to his soul, "Wild oats! wild oats!"

Lord Heddon vehemently preached wild oats also. He was of opinion that a lad is all the better for a "little racketing when he's green." He had always found the best fellows were wildish once, etc.

"How's your son?" asked Sir Austin.

" Oh, Lipscombe's always the same," replied the gouty advocate of wild oats. " He's quiet—that's one good thing; but there's no getting the country to take him, so I must give up hopes of that."

Lord Lipscombe entering the room just then, Sir Austin surveyed him, and was not astonished at the refusal of the country to take him.

" Wild oats! wild oats!" again thinks the baronet, as he contemplates the headless, degenerate, weedy issue and result.

He was content to remark that he thought the third generation of wild oats would be a pretty thin crop.

The " Ordeal of Richard Feverel " is a great book because it is a profoundly wise book. The wise books of the world, the books which embalm the deepest lessons of experience and thus attain to a sort of sacred value, are few, and thus become of necessity the classics of literature. This is such a book, and it is not only wise but witty, and is throughout executed in Meredith's most brilliant manner. There are sayings in it which cannot be forgotten; they are as memorable as the sayings of Gautama or Confucius, of Marcus Aurelius or Augustine, and might be the fit texts for great sermons.

Take, at random, some half-a-dozen sentences from that half-tragic note-book of Sir Austin's "The Pilgrim's Scrip," a book in which every record has the diamond's worth and lustre, and let us hope, the diamond's unchanging endurance too.

How profoundly religious are these aphorisms:

Expediency is man's wisdom. Doing right is God's.
Until he has had some deep sorrow he will not find the divine want of prayer.

Who rises from prayer a better man, his prayer is answered.
For this reason so many fall from God who have attained to Him, that they cling to Him with their weakness, not with their strength.

And how keenly do these cut:

Nature is not all dust. Through Nature only can we ascend. St. Simeon saw the Hog in Nature, and took Nature for the Hog.

It is the tendency of very fast people to grow organically downward.

O women, who like and will have for hero a rake! how soon are you not to learn that you have taken bankrupts to your bosoms, and that the putrescent gold that attracted you is the slime of the Lake of Sin!

Or, to conclude with three that touch a sunnier height:

The compensation for injustice is that in the darkest ordeal we gather the worthiest round us.

There is for the mind but one grasp of happiness—from that uttermost pinnacle of wisdom, whence we see that this world is well designed.

And this most perfect of lovers' petitions:

Give me purity to be worthy the good in her, and grant her patience to reach the good in me.

And these are but the chance gleanings of a book which it has taken all these years to lift into even moderate eminence, and which beyond its wisdom and its humour has every quality of art and genius which can make a novel great. The one consolation in the remembrance is that in this long ordeal of injustice George Meredith has not failed to gather the worthiest round him.

To catalogue qualities, and speak of pathos, humour, and imagination, and make quotations is an easy task, but one feels that after all it amounts to little. The real greatness of George Meredith lies in something deeper and more inclusive; it is that he is a great poet who has chosen chiefly to work in prose. His poetic force is behind all he writes; it is the animating soul of all. It is perpetually thrusting aside the heavy garments of prose and flashing out upon us in thoughts and phrases which startle and fascinate us as only poetry can. How exquisite is that whole picture of Richard reading the diary of the dead Clare, with its secrecies of unconfessed affections, its pathetic humbleness, its meek reproach!

He could not read for tears. It was midnight. The hour seemed to belong to her. The awful stillness and the darkness were Clare's. Clare Doria Forey! He knew the music of that name. *It sounded faint and mellow now behind the hills of death.*

Is not this poetry too?—

He pronounced love a little modestly, as it were a blush in his voice.

When Sandra's song is finished, the stillness settles back again " like one folding up a precious jewel." And where are there any passages in the whole realm of fiction so full of lyric rapture, so intoxicating in their charm of perfect beauty, as those which describe the first waking of love in Richard Feverel? George Meredith's greatest moments are in the interpretation of young love and nature, and here he does both.

The little skylark went up above her, all song, to the smooth southern cloud lying along the blue; from a dewy copse standing dark over her nodding hat the blackbird flitted, calling to her with thrice mellow note; the kingfisher flashed emerald out of the green osiers; a bow-winged heron travelled aloft, seeking solitude; a boat slipped toward her containing a dreamy youth.

.　　.　　.　　.　　.

Stiller and stiller grew nature, as at the meeting of two electric clouds.

.　　.　　.　　.　　.

To-morrow this place will have a memory—the river and the meadow, and the white falling weir. His heart will build a temple here, and the skylark will be its high-priest and the old blackbird its glossy-gowned chorister, and there will be a sacred repast of dewberries. . . .

Golden lie the meadows, golden run the streams, red-gold is on the pine-stems. The sun is coming down to earth, and walks the fields and the waters.

The sun is coming down to earth, and the fields and the waters shout to him golden shouts. He comes, and his heralds run before him and touch the leaves of oaks and planes and beeches lucid green, and the pine-stems redder gold, leaving brightest footsteps upon thickly weeded banks, where the fox-glove's last upper-bells incline, and bramble-shoots wander amid moist, rich herbage.

.　　.　　.　　.　　.

For this is the home of enchantment. Here, secluded from vexed shores, the prince and princess of the island meet; here, like darkling nightingales, they sit, and into eyes and ears and hands pour endless ever-fresh treasures of their souls.

.　　.　　.　　.　　.

Out in the world there, on the skirts of the woodland, a sheepboy pipes to meditative eve on a penny whistle. Love's musical instrument is as old, and as poor; it has but two stops, and yet you see the cunning musician does thus much with it.

.   .   .   .   .

The tide of colour has ebbed from the upper sky. In the west the sea of sunken fire draws back, and the stars leap forth and tremble and retire before the advancing moon, who slips the silver train of cloud from her shoulders, and with her foot upon the pine-tops surveys heaven.

Young as when she looked upon the lovers in Paradise, the fair immortal journeys onward. Fronting her it is not night, but veiled day. Full half the sky is flushed. Not darkness; not day; but the nuptials of the two.

A soft beam travels to the fern-covert under the pine-wood where they sit, and for answer he has her eyes—turned to him an instant, timidly fluttering over the depths of his, and then downcast; for through her eyes her soul is naked to him.

"Lucy! my bride! my life!"

The night-jar spins his dark monotony on the branch of the pine. The soft beam travels round them and listens to their hearts. Their lips are locked.

Pipe no more, Love, for a time! Pipe as you will, you cannot express their first kiss—nothing of its sweetness, and of the sacredness of it nothing. St. Cecilia up aloft, before the silver organ-pipes of paradise, pressing fingers upon all the notes of which Love is but one, from her you may hear it.

The women-characters of George Meredith are worthy of an essay to themselves. They are intensely living, and intensely human. It was one of Lord Byron's fads to pretend disgust at seeing women eat. It has been well said of George Meredith's women that they eat and are not ashamed. Woman is to him no sentimental abstraction, no impossible deity; it delights him to show us that she is flesh and blood, and none the worse for it; that in intellectual power she is mate of man, and in moral power his superior, because she lives closer to the heart of nature; that, in fact, the angel is as false a description as the animal, and that in any case the correcter our estimate of her the higher will be her honour. He will have nothing to do with the doctrine that woman is but "undeveloped man," and he roundly denounces it as a lie. The masculine and feminine are for ever different in scope, sphere, and essence; yet men " who have the woman in them without being womanised are the pick of men. And the choicest women are those who yield not a feather of their womanliness for some amount of manlike strength—man's brain, woman's heart." She needs no spurious daintiness to recommend her. Let her come to us in native naturalness, and she will save us; for "women have us back to the conditions of primitive man, or they shoot us higher than the topmost star." Again and again does George Meredith insist, as Mr. Le Gallienne admirably puts it, that " a man's relations to woman, how he regards her, how he acts toward her, are the most significant things about him." And for the man who misapprehends or misuses her there is tragic vengeance; " for women are not the end but the means of life, and they punish us for so perverting their uses. They punish society."

The chief thing, from the moral point of view, which fills the mind after a thorough perusal of George Meredith's works is their robust hopefulness. He has gone down to the sources of life; he has uncovered its worst secrets; he has surprised the unsuspected and dragged into light the ignored elements of conduct; he has been utterly true in his fealty to " sacred reality," but he has retained, in and through all, his geniality, his faith in God and man, his hope for the world. He has told us that the only chance of happiness is the belief that this world is well de-signed, and this is his own belief; and he adds through the lips of his Diana of the Crossways, "*Who can really think and not think hopefully?*" Like so many of his aphorisms, this is one that goes to the root of things and expresses a philosophy. It would seem to teach that pessimism is the disease of shallow minds, a surface complaint which attacks mainly the less forceful and efficient natures of the race; the wider and deeper natures have too strong a vitality to be its victims. Go deep enough, he says, and you will find that the source of hope and vital joy are not dried up. You will find no chaos, but a most Divine Cosmos, to know which is to rejoice in life. Despair is a disease; the sane and sound nature must needs be hopeful. A little thought, like a little knowledge, is a dangerous thing, and may breed pessimism. A little more thought takes one out of the storm-belt into the far-reaching sunlight. "*I think it al'ays the plan in a dielemmer,*" says the wise Mrs. Berry, "*to pray God and walk for-ward.*" Nor can any better plan be invented for the guidance of bewildered souls. There is, of course, a thoughtless optimism, as there is a thoughtless pessim-ism—the optimism of those who recognise no problems or dilemmas in life, and whose gaiety is the mere frisking ebullience of the happy animal. But the glory of George Meredith's optimism is that, having seen the worst, he believes in the best. Having touched the lowest depth, he still has eyes to discover the starry height, and has ears to hear the music of the spheres. In this resolute and intelligent optimism he and Robert Browning once more find themselves akin; nor can the spirit of Meredith's work be better expressed than by putting into his lips the well-known verse of Browning:

I have gone the whole round of creation: I saw and I spoke;
I, a work of God's hand for that purpose, received in my brain
And pronounced on the rest of His handwork—returned Him
    again
His creation's approval or censure: I spoke as I saw,
I report as a man may on God's work—*all's love, yet all's law.*

With so much of real and rare genius, with a temperament essentially poetic, with a style full of felicity and surprise, with a mastery of means rarely surpassed by any great artist, it would seem that George Meredith has all the qualities which secure and win fame. And yet a doubt remains which is not easily dismissed. The doubt lies in the direction already indicated—viz., Meredith's failure to interest the broad average of mankind. Is he, after all, a vogue? Does he belong to the esoteric class of writers who appeal only to the initiated? Will he ultimately find his rank with such a writer as Landor, who possessed undoubted genius, and was in the strictest sense a great writer, yet failed of popular fame, and must always fail, because he had neither the instinct nor the will to address himself to the popular taste? Such questions can scarcely be answered by Meredith's contemporaries; but even the most reverential of his contemporaries may be excused some uneasiness in their contemplation. For, as one returns to the study of Meredith after an interval of years, the critical mind is increasingly conscious of an element of brilliant artificiality in his work. He has never discovered the truth that the last art of profundity is simplicity. One suspects also a certain element of contempt for humanity in Meredith's temper—the contempt of the superior person, who despises the vulgar average, and counts their praise or blame as of little consequence. This is Landor's great fault, and it has circumscribed his fame. In the writer of fiction it is a fatal fault. For in the writer of fiction something more is needed than the most brilliant intellectual gifts; he needs above all that kind of sympathy which enters into and interprets common life—the broad human touch which we find in all the truly great novelists, from Defoe to Dickens, which is the real secret of their enduring influence. Nevertheless, the outstanding fact is clear, that Meredith's contribution to the imaginative literature of his age is of a quality so high, and an achievement so rare and distinguished, that, if it does not put him in the first rank of novelists, it gives him a position which is unique and conspicuous. He is the most intellectual of English novelists. With such a fame he may rest content. If he does not take rank with Scott and Thackeray, he does appeal, as no other English novelist does, to the ear of a discriminating culture. Like Landor, he will " dine late; but the dining-room will be well lighted, the guests few and select."

XVI

THOMAS HARDY

Thomas Hardy, born at Upper Rockhampton, Dorset, June 2nd, 1840. Published "Desperate Remedies," 1871; "Under the Greenwood Tree," 1872; "A Pair of Blue Eyes," 1872-3; "Far from the Madding Crowd," 1874; "The Hand of Ethelberta," 1876; "The Return of the Native"; "Two on a Tower," 1882; "The Mayor of Casterbridge," 1884-5; "The Woodlanders," 1886-7; "Tess of the D'Urbervilles," 1891; "Jude the Obscure," 1895. Still living.

TO Thomas Hardy must be conceded the first place among the later novelists, although it is probable that his claim, for a considerable time to come, will not be admitted without dispute. Those who look first to the purely intellectual qualities of a novelist will easily justify the primacy of Meredith, who as a brilliant philosophic thinker, working in the medium of romance, has no rival. Compared with the subtly coloured page of Meredith, Hardy's page is plain and grey; destitute alike of those surprises and felicities which make Meredith's writing so exciting to the cultured reader. But if Hardy's style has little splendour, it has a certain grave Lucretian lucidity which is very impressive. He ranks with Crabbe among the sternest painters of man's social life. His chief aim is truth; and hence whatever superficial graces he may lack, he never fails in the grace of a severe sincerity. The parallel with Crabbe may be pushed further. He has much of Crabbe's relative narrowness of vision, with a corresponding intensity, except that in Crabbe's case this narrowness is unavoidable, but with Hardy intentional and deliberate. Crabbe lives in a narrow world from necessity, Hardy from choice. It is his boast that in this narrow world, among people of the humblest social type, he finds the great elements of the human drama, and the development upon a tragic scale of all those motives which would have contented the dramatic genius of Sophocles and Aeschylus.

Two outstanding facts may be briefly noted. The first is that Hardy's perfect knowledge of rural life is his by inheritance and training. He was born in the heart of the woodland, at Upper Bockhampton, near Dorchester, a place so tiny that it is scarcely known to the ordnance maps. A recent writer, in describing it, says, " In country parlance it is an outstep spot, difficult of access even to those who know the neighbourhood. The walk thither from the market-town, in spring or summer, is delightful to those who love the green pageantry of Nature. Just a narrow track across a meadow is taken, and the doors of the modern world swing to their closing, and an entrance is gained into a region where life is hushed by the sway and tremble of leaves, mirrored in a stream that seldom breaks the garment of stillness by a liquid rush or fall. . . . Upper Bockhampton is but the germ of a village, and continues to this day, in point of dimensions, in a state of unambitious infancy, bespeaking the first primitive needs of human nature without any visible hint of sophisticated desires. The cottage home is there seen in its typical simplicity—the living-room stone-flagged,

the ceiling cross-beamed, the chimney spacious, with a
fire of wood on the hearth enclosed by uncemented
bricks." In this primitive abode Hardy was born, and
there, but the other day, his mother died. It is a rare
thing in literary biography to find a man of genius
so deliberately rooted to the soil of his birth that the
larger world has no attractions for him. Even the
greatest novelists have felt change of scene necessary
as a stimulus to their art, and it is the habit of most
modern novelists to seek new backgrounds for their
work, in order to retain public interest. It rarely
happens that backgrounds so sought are impressive, or
even true. They may have a certain superficial accur-•
acy—the accuracy of the guide-book, as George Eliot's
Florence has in "Romola"—but they fail to convey
the spirit of the scene. Art expresses best what is
normal to the artist. Scenery has to be felt, and
slowly absorbed, before it can be truly described. The
secret of Hardy's unique power in rendering rural
scenes, is that they are essential to himself. They are
a part of his own blood and fibre. They belong to his
heritage as peasant and woodlander, and are expressive
of his temperament.

A second notable feature of his art is a certain spirit
of continuity in his design. Perhaps it was from
Balzac he derived his idea of a series of books which
should represent with more or less fulness the human
comedy, but he interprets the idea after his own
fashion. He creates for himself a district called Wessex—re-naming the actual towns, rivers, and hills in
a nomenclature which is meant to be no more than a
thin disguise of the real nomenclature. Thus Casterbridge is Dorchester, Budmouth Regis is Weymouth,

Warbourne is Wimbourne, King's Bere is Bere Regis, Sherton Abbas is Sherbourne, Shaston is Shaftesbury, Wintoncester is Winchester, and so forth. Within this area every road is known to him, every legend, every antiquarian reminiscence, together with hundreds of family histories and traditional episodes. The names he uses for his characters are usually local names, peculiar to the soil. The result of this painstaking fidelity is an extraordinary air of verisimilitude in his stories. They are not so much stories, in the conventional use of the term, as histories interpreted by the imagination. It is true that he does not, like Balzac, introduce the characters of former novels into succeeding stories, expecting us to recollect them, and recognise them as actors in one common and continuous drama, but he attains the same effect of continuity even more subtly by retaining the same scenery. It is a bold experiment, which might easily produce the same sense of sameness, but Hardy conducts it with such supreme skill, that familiarity becomes a new bond of attraction. We begin to be interested in these scenes for their own sake, and we realise the truth of his contention that there is in their apparent peace ample material for Sophoclean drama, all the passions that torture or deprave humanity lying like volcanic fire beneath the apparent secular repose. Greatness of design must always be reckoned as one of the most original features of Hardy's art. He may or may not have succeeded—this is a question for the critic—but he stands alone among English novelists in the coherent definiteness of his scheme.

Here, then, to begin with, is what we may call the large note in literary art. Hardy sets himself to a task which is meant not only to be an adequate expression of his own genius, but a broad synthesis of human life. He has certain definite convictions to express, and in order to express them he invents a wide framework, and he adopts a logical scheme. Just as Balzac takes a group of people and develops them; just as Zola follows the same immense ideal; so Hardy annexes for his purpose a district of England of which he has special knowledge, and peoples it with the creatures of his art. Although he does not write his novels as a deliberate series, yet they are all closely connected in spirit and design. The people he depicts are in reality members of one family. They represent primitive, and almost primeval types. They epitomise the struggles and passions of the race. They propound in their histories the eternal riddle of the universe. Thus, the first and clearest impression conveyed by Hardy's novels is of fundamental brainwork in their conception. Every slightest detail is thought out with exactness; he obeys no chance impulses, and never wanders from the path which he has set himself. It may be said of many novels which are distinctly works of genius that, while they represent a certain phase of the author's thought, they do not represent any fundamental truth, nor do they even represent the real secret of the author's idiosyncrasy. But this cannot be said of Hardy. He has no dealings with the casual. He is always at work upon his scheme. And this extraordinary definiteness of aim, this spirit of severe dedication to his task, produces an epic force, which constitutes the " larger note " in literary art.

The names of Balzac and Zola naturally suggest themselves in relation to continuity of design, but we must not be misled by the parallel. In the main qualities of his art, Hardy has little in common with them. Hardy's art is marked by strong original features which are peculiar to himself. Some of these we may now consider.

Putting them in the order of their significance, we may range these qualities thus: Nature-worship, austerity, logic, melancholy, humour.

The Nature-worship of Hardy controls and colours all his writing. Towards religion, in the conventional sense, his temper is hostile; he is a pagan, whose faiths and sentiments are rooted in a world so ancient that the religious thoughts of the last two thousand years fail to find any point of contact with it. He regards the entire problem of Christianity much as an antique Roman of Virgil's countryside might have regarded it. Such religious sentiment as he has attaches itself to things immemorially sacred—the march of seasons, the loom of silent powers weaving the web of life, the worship of fecundity, the spirit of creativeness, the sense of the eternal in time. Wordsworth has no deeper passion for the silent hills than he for the woodlands, valleys, and wide heaths of Wessex. Hence his men and women are not so many persons set against a background of Nature, but they are its vital growths and manifestations. Nature interprets them, and they interpret Nature. The scenery of the woodland is essential to the understanding of such characters as Giles Winterbourne and Marty South. Divorced from the scenery they are weak and meaningless; moving in it, they are so much a part of it that they express its primeval grandeur. There is an actual sympathy between them and the woodland. The tree-roots know the touch of Winterbourne's skilled hand; they will grow for him, as they would not for another. Egdon Heath is much more than the background of that great story " The Return of the Native "; it is a brooding and a shaping presence, touching the life of each actor in the drama in turn. In this art of producing entire unity between the man and the scene in which he moves Hardy is supreme. Hetty Sorrel and Adam Bede might have lived in any pleasant rural hamlet; but Winterbourne and Marty South belong to one scene only, and are inconceivable apart from it. Even the virtuous and sturdy persons Wordsworth celebrates might exist apart from the actual hillsides where he found them; but Hardy's peasants are as much products of a particular soil as the glades in which they live. Nature herself breathes and speaks through them; and so much is this the case, that as we follow their fates it is with the sense that Nature has a constant hand in the business, she is the predominant partner, and they are as much the products of her inscrutable will as the leaves upon the tree, or the crops upon the field.

To depict scenery is not in itself a novel art; but to render the spirit of scenery is rare, and it is still more rare to render it through human personifications in whom its peculiar qualities are concentrated. What is it that rivets the gaze on the apparently paltry fortunes of Mrs. Yeobright, Clym, Eustacia Vye, and Wildeve in " The Return of the Native "? It is the sense of something elemental acting in them, and acting and re-acting through them. They are the handiwork of powers older than the oldest civilisation; they move to the silent rhythm of forces ancient as the stars.

Thus they become elemental through perfect unison with the eternal elements of things. And for the spectator of the drama, Egdon Heath is the symbol of the elemental. The human artist is unseen; " haggard Egdon " is the spell-worker. The eye never loses the vision of Egdon presented in the first pages of the book. We see its barrenness and beauty; we feel its awe, its separate and peculiar solitude, its immense antiquity, older than all empire, and *older than the sea itself;* and there is subtly conveyed to us the sense that the drama of the Yeobrights and Eustacia Vye is of an equal antiquity and grandeur. It never occurs to us that they are quite ordinary people; Egdon Heath sublimes them. If we think of it, this is one of the most extraordinary miracles of art. And this power of creating and maintaining perfect unison between the physical world and human character is a power found in varying degrees in all Hardy's novels. It is in reality a method of interpreting Nature much more subtle than the most eloquent description of Ruskin's, or even those exquisite passages of depiction that linger longest with us in the pages of Wordsworth and other great poets. It reveals a closer intimacy of passion, in which the personality of the artist is wholly subdued or extinguished; he standing aside that Nature may be all in all.

It is a secondary matter, but nevertheless a great matter, in Hardy's art, that his actual pictures of Nature have a rare exquisiteness of fidelity. It would be difficult to name any other English writer who has shown so true and fine a colour sense. Notice, for example, the part that colour plays in this description of Egdon Heath:

A Saturday afternoon in November was approaching the time of twilight, and the vast tract of enclosed wild known as Egdon Heath embrowned itself moment by moment. Overhead the hollow stretch of whitish cloud shutting out the sky was as a tent which had the whole heath for its floor. The heavens being spread with this pallid screen and the earth with the darkest vegetation, their meeting line at the horizon was clearly marked. . . . The face of the heath by its mere complexion added half an hour to evening; it could in like manner retard the dawn, sadden noon, anticipate the frowning of storms scarcely generated, and intensify the opacity of a moonless midnight to a cause of shaking and dread.

In a totally different tone of colour, but equally exact, is the description of dawn in the opening chapters of " The Hand of Ethelberta."

A huge inflamed sun was breasting the horizon of a wide sheet of sea, which, to her surprise and delight, the mansion overlooked. The brilliant disc fired all the waves that lay between it and the shore at the bottom of the grounds, where the water tossed the ruddy light from one undulation to another in glares as large and clear as mirrors, incessantly altering them, destroying them, and creating them again; while further off they multiplied, thickened, and ran into one another like struggling armies, till they met the fiery source of them all.

In the " Woodlanders " is a yet more daring transcript of aerial sublimities:

Between the broken clouds they could see far into the recesses of heaven, the eye journeying on under a species of golden arcades, and past fiery obstruction, fancied cairns, loganstones, stalactites, and stalagmites of topaz. Deeper than this their gaze passed these flakes of incandescence, till it plunged into a bottomless medium of soft green fire.

And with this power of reporting large effects in scenery of sea and sky and broad heath, there is also joined the most observant eye for minute and humble details in ordinary landscape.

They went noiselessly over mats of starry moss, rustled through interspersed tracts of leaves, skirted trunks with spreading roots whose mossed rinds made them like hands wearing green gloves; elbowed old elms and ashes with great forks in which stood pools of water that overflowed on rainy days, and ran down their stumps in green cascades. On older trees still than these huge lobes of fungi grew like lungs. Here, as everywhere, the unfulfilled intention, which makes life what it is, was as obvious as it could be among the depraved crowds of a city slum. The leaf was deformed, the curve was crippled, the taper was interrupted; the lichen ate the vigour of the stalk, and the ivy slowly strangled to death the promising sapling.

These are but casual examples of a singularly fertile art. There is no book of Hardy's that does not abound in Nature-pictures, some delicately etched, some composed of broad masses of colour, but all carefully observed by a consummate artist. But their chief quality, as we have seen, is not in the beauty or daring of the detached picture, but in its relation to human destinies. Nature and man are constantly engaged in expressing the same thought. We are often reminded, in reading Hardy, of Millet's picture of " The Angelus," in which the bowed peasants and the scenery of bare fields and setting sun in which they are placed are so intimately interwoven that the pathos of the picture is as much in one as in the other; it is a whole so harmonious that every detail has equal significance. Hardy himself has insisted, in a striking passage of the " Woodlanders," that the true charm of the country is less in contour than in memory. The dweller in woods

must know all about those invisible ones of the days gone by, whose feet have traversed the fields that look so grey from his windows; recall whose creaking ploughs have turned these sods from time to time; whose hands planted the trees that form a crest on the opposite hill, whose horses and hounds have torn through that underwood; what birds affect that particular brake; what bygone domestic dramas of love, jealousy, revenge, or disappointment have been enacted in the cottages, the mansions, the street, or on the green.

In other words, Nature is only seen aright through man, and man is interpreted through Nature.

Next to the spirit of Nature-worship in Hardy, we may rank the spirit of austerity. One of the commonest mistakes about Hardy is that he is the deliberate exponent of the coarser passions, with the implication of licentiousness in thought and temper. The mistake arises from a total misunderstanding of Hardy's attitude toward life. His attitude is really that of the moralist and satirist, of the pagan rather than the Christian type. He sees no reason why the plain facts of life should not be plainly reported, and he reports them with uncompromising sincerity. The worst that can be charged against him is defect of delicacy, a certain bluntness of feeling which betrays him into errors of taste. It offends us to find woman spoken of as the female animal. There is, in " Jude the Obscure," one incident in the first meeting of Jude and Arabella which is unpardonable in its coarseness. But is it not a fair question whether this defect of delicacy is not the result of environment rather than of temperament? Country folk, who are brought into daily close contact with animal life, have usually a very blunt way of describing gross facts which the more reticent social spirit of towns conceals. The fact exists; it is well known to everybody; what is gained by treating it as non-existent? Reuben, the tranter, in "Under the Greenwood Tree," says,

> "Well, now, that coarseness that's so upsetting to Ann's feelings is to my mind a recommendation; for it do always prove a story to be true."

The real country-dweller is apt to assume that all that is true comes within the scope of discussion, and hence he is unaware of coarseness, which to a more fastidious mind is a cause of blushes. But who would assume that the townsman is more virtuous than the farmer, because he employs euphemisms where the farmer would use blunt speech? The reverse is often the case; the townsman's prudishness becoming a form of vice, and the countryman's bluntness being significant of a certain masculine sanity of nature.

Hardy, by birth, habit, associates and long residence, belongs to the country. He uses a country frankness in describing the facts of life, a kind of pagan freedom. But the real student of country life knows perfectly well that in spite of these frank habits of speech the character of the countryman has much more austerity than that of the townsman. He is knit together by firm unyielding fibre; his moral judgments are apt to be harsh; if he be a pagan, he has also a certain pagan hardness as the substratum of his character. And Hardy entirely conforms to this type. His faults of taste are the faults of an over-masculine temperament. His bluntness is the bluntness of strength. At the root of his character is the countryman's austerity, the hard-fibred masculine temperament, unrefined by the use and habit of towns, and incapable of euphemism. Nature is coarse, and he who lives close to Nature insensibly acquires, together with the strength he draws from her primal bosom, something of her unembarrassed contemplation of things which artificial civilisations are in a hurry to conceal or forget.

These things belong, however, in the main, to the domain of morals; and to be exact, to morals in their relation to social sentiment. The austerity of Hardy is an intellectual rather than a moral quality. His mind is one of the Lucretian order, grave, sad, sombre, and dominated by an overwhelming sense of law. His austerity is the Lucretian austerity of a peculiarly solemn genius, brooding over life rather than immersed in it, detached, separate, and viewing men and women with a kind of scornful commiseration. He and joy stand very far apart, in spite of his many moments of delightful humour. He is overweighted with the burden of the world. His lips smile, but in their curve lurks perpetual irony. His eyes have the prophet's severity; he is as one who looks through the dim veil of life to those pitiless forces which control and create it. Let the reader thoroughly acquainted with the writings of Hardy call to mind the groups of people in his books; the bowed peasants, toiling beneath grey skies, the relentless developments of fate that overtake them, the hard silent heroisms they display, their acquiescence in calamity as a thing inevitable, their rigid tearless endurance of the blows of circumstance, and he will begin to realise how much the spirit of austerity governs Hardy in all his creations. There is the clang of a pitiless mechanism in all, as there is in the great poem of Lucretius. He is without suavity, he stands apart upon an icy peak, watching with sombre eyes the insignificant struggles of a lower world, at once intent, ironically sympathetic, but, like Nature, implacable. There is no other novelist who stands so aloof from life; there is none with the same hardness of mental grain, none who more than distantly resembles him in the quality of intellectual austerity.

One fruit of this austerity is the air of dignity which is patent in all Hardy's writings. His mind is of such gravity that it cannot condescend to trivial issues; it moves constantly among the large and deep things of life. It has been truly said by Mr. Lionel Johnson that the " dignity of his work comes from his occupation with dignified natures "; for although the men and women he depicts belong to the simplest social order, they are all stamped with Nature's own dignity. They, like their creator, know nothing of the lighter emotions. Their love, their hatred, their pride are terrible forces, working out insatiable tragedies. They possess the dignity of all large and simple natures. Their emotions are strong and deep; they have in them something akin to the resistless flow of tides, the steady culmination of seasons, the sweep of stars upon a predetermined curve of space. Gabriel Oak and Michael Henchard are excellent examples of this quality. Each is no more than a plain labourer, but in the stoical endurance of the one, and the tremendous passions of the other, we are transported into the atmosphere of Greek tragedy. They belong to the old pagan world;

they have a fortitude, a force, a sombre dignity, which we instinctively feel is characteristic of a world far older than the Christian era. Shakespeare might have found a place for them in his dramas; no other mind since Shakespeare's has been capable of conceiving them.

From the intellectual austerity of Hardy is derived that powerful logic which governs all his creative work. It is the logic of events, infinitely lucid, infinitely pitiless, never swerving by a hair's breadth from its appointed sequences. There is a mathematical quality in Hardy's art; not in vain was his early life devoted to architectural studies. He builds his story as he would build a house; the strain of every part is calculated, every stone has its place, every crumb of mortar bears its part. The common fault of inexperienced novelists, as of inexperienced architects, is imperfect calculation. Those who have had to examine a number of architectural plans will know how often it happens that in what seems an admirable design glaring deficiencies exist; a staircase is left out, no provision is made for the lighting of a passage, or the roof is pitched so low that the upper rooms are uninhabitable. A judicial verdict on such designs would be that the aesthetic sense has been gratified at the expense of the mathematical; and the same verdict would apply to many novels in which the art of apportioning cause to effect is conspicuously absent. But in Hardy's novels the broad sweep of design is always based upon an almost meticulous accuracy of detail. He forgets nothing. From the moment when the story is sufficiently advanced for us to grasp the nature of its problem, we can forecast the issue. We know that neither sentiment nor pity will turn him aside from the path dictated by a hard rationality. The stars in vain fight in their courses, and the sun is in vain commanded to stand still; things being as they are, the results will be as they must be. And, to indulge once more in architectural metaphor, each part is of equal value in the equilibrium of the whole. Slight incidents, which we barely notice at the time, reappear later as controlling forces of destiny. Seeds of action, dropped carelessly, startle us with sudden explosions of life. The colour of a thread of hair introduces us to the gallows. A hot glance of passion ruins a life. The story, when it begins to move, moves with an increasing momentum to an ineluctable goal. The logic of events tramples its way over human hearts to its axiomatic close, knowing no respite, and is proof against the excited prayer or appeal of all protesting sentiment.

No quality in Hardy's work is so marked as this, and none is so impressive. Many writers have great gifts of imagination, but little gift of invention; in Hardy the gifts are in equipoise. It would be equally true to say that he produces his effects by largeness of design, and by minute finish of particulars. When he described " Under the Greenwood Tree " as a piece of painting in the Dutch manner, he rightly laid stress on his habit of minute perfection. It is the manner of Gerald Dow and Van Huysum, each of whom excels in the elaboration of detail. The picture is built up by multitudes of slight touches, by the use of the finest brush; infinite care being taken to produce the dewdrop on a cabbage-leaf, the bloom upon a peach, the brilliant sheen upon a copper pot or an insect's wing.

But Hardy did less than justice to himself in insisting on this elaboration of detail as the chief feature of his art. There is something more, a breadth of design, a magnificence of detail, as though to the delicacy of Gerald Dow's art there were added the poetic grandeur of Rembrandt. The various tavern scenes, and the Mayor's dinner, and the dancing in the booth, in the " The Mayor of Casterbridge," are entirely in the spirit of Dow's or Ostade's art; but it is a totally different spirit which meets us in the wild heath where Henchard seeks a shelter for his mortal agony. It is the brush of Rembrandt that is at work here. Yet the final grandeur is the logical climax of converging trivialities. In each separate incident there is an element which proves necessary in the completion of the whole. When we close one of Hardy's greatest books the deepest impression is always of something fated and inevitable in the sequence of event, and this impression rests equally upon his skill in episode and his power of climax, his genius in invention and his genius for imagination, the coherence of his logic, and his power of penetrating vision. He is, in effect, a man of science, turned dramatist, a mathematician dealing with dramatic and poetic material.

From a mind so constituted we might have expected a variety of moral qualities, such as calmness, temperance, sanity; how comes it, then, that the logic of Hardy constantly expresses itself in a passionate melancholy? The most probable answer is that he is too narrowly logical to see life in its full perspective. He reasons on too slender premises. Determined to set down precisely what he sees in life and no more, he is incapable of looking beyond life. The future has no existence for him. His view of life is microscopic rather than astronomic. His eye is fixed upon a brilliantly lit lens, beneath which the contortions of the pitiably futile creature known as man are faithfully exhibited; it does not occur to him that the same creature has authentic relations with infinity. It is difficult to recall any leading figure in Hardy's books who sees life in large perspective, who feels that romance of the infinite which manifests itself in genuine religious emotion. Not one looks beyond the earth, not one is consoled by any thought of future opportunities and vindications. And hence, in spite of the great note of tragedy which is heard ever and again, Hardy makes us feel that life is a little thing, appointed to derision and disaster, the contortions of a " mollusc on a leaf," the flight of a gnat in a sunbeam. Some sense of the gravity and splendour of human life is necessary to that self-reverence which is the true source of all cheerful or hopeful views of life. But Hardy sees no element of gravity or splendour in human life; it is sordid, cruel, mean, and therefore he cannot regard it with cheerfulness. He is, to use his own phrase, " unreconciled to life," and his disbelief in life—in its vital good, its moral base, its hidden goal, its possibilities of sublimity or indefinite evolution—produces in him a constant temper of scornful anger deepening into bitterest melancholy.

It is by no means the worst thing that can happen to a man that he should be " unreconciled to life," for there is a species of divine discontent from which all progress springs. But Hardy's lack of reconciliation to life is purely negative. He does not resent her discord only to seek some possible rhythm, he does not realise her gloom only to be " stung with hunger for full light." He does not so much as suggest a solution of the human problem. He is resolved to live without one, as a Stoic to whom nothing greatly matters, and yet the very bitterness of his reflections makes us feel how much it matters. He is too angry not to care; the very violence of his aversion to life is significant of acute feeling. Who will show us any good? is his constant cry. Most people would see some good in a home full of children, but even that spectacle excites Hardy's anger.

If the heads of the Durbeyfield household chose to sail into difficulty, disaster, starvation, disease, degradation, death, thither were these half-dozen little captives under hatches compelled to sail with them—six helpless little creatures, who had never been asked if they wished for life on any terms, much less if they wished it on such hard conditions as were involved in being of the shiftless house of Durbeyfield. Some people would like to know whence the poet whose philosophy is in these days deemed as profound and trustworthy as his verse is pure and breezy, gets his authority for speaking of " Nature's holy plan."

The Durbeyfield children are plainly doomed to destruction by what he takes pains to inform us is " an unsympathetic First Cause." It is in the same spirit that the last sentence of the great tragedy of " Tess " is written:

Justice was done, and the President of the Immortals [an Æschylean phrase] had ended his sport with Tess.

Many similar passages might be quoted, all coloured with the same melancholy. No doubt it is in part a heritage of temperament. Possibly also it may be traced in some degree to the influence of solitude on a sensitive mind, for melancholy is a quite common feature of rural life. But in the main its source is that peculiarly narrow logic of the scientific mind without faith, which sees life microscopically rather than astronomically. The thread of life upon the lens *is* insignificant enough till we see it as part of the universal life; the drop of water is contemptible till we see it lifted into clouds, and woven into rainbows. But the ultimate of life is what Hardy never sees. The highest vision he has is of an "Unfulfilled Intention," from which nothing can be hoped, and which is therefore but an elaborate mockery on the part of the President of the Immortals.

Apart from reasons clearly discernible in the nature of his teaching, one can only guess at causes of melancholy which are part of the author's own personality; but it seems probable that the solitude of country life, to which reference has been made, may rank with the major causes. Writers on country life have much to say about its joys, but they rarely penetrate the secret of its melancholy. Nor is it easy to analyse it. It owes something to the solemnity of the earth itself, something to the sense of relentless forces always at work behind the veil of things, yet more to the habit of self-introspection, the turning over and over in the mind of a few thoughts, the harping on the same string. The man who leads a broad, busy, adventurous life is rarely given to pessimism. In moving freely about the world, he gets a sense of the variety of the forces at work. He does not trouble himself to frame a theory of life, because he finds so much to contradict all theories, the good and the bad alike. Nor does he dwell overmuch on the grim and awful aspects of life. His thought flows nimbly; his interest in new objects is constantly excited; there is no time for the blood to stagnate into the black poisonous clot which corrupts the heart. But with the man of reflective mind, living in solitude, the process is reversed. The thought is continually turned in upon itself, and gradually becomes morbid. Things come to be seen out of proportion, and the real perspective of life is lost. One suspects that the morbid strain in Hardy's genius is the product of causes such as these. By living the life of a solitary he has learned to write with extraordinary mastery of that corner of the world which he knows; but it is at the sacrifice of much that might have made him a happier man, and possibly a more efficient artist. Shakespeare owed much more to London than to Stratford; possibly Hardy would have depicted life with a broader synthesis had he known the city as well as he knows the hamlet and the woodland.

And yet, mixed with all Hardy's melancholy, there is one of the finest gifts of humour ever possessed by an English novelist. If in anything Hardy does betray authentic kinship with Shakespeare, it is in this gift of humour. His peasants often seem to have stepped direct out of Shakespearean comedy. Joseph Poorgrass is as great a humorous creation as Bottom or Justice Shallow. He belongs, indeed, to the same England, the archaic racy England of Shakespearean comedy, fruitful in types of character, over which the steam-roller of advanced civilisation has not passed.

Hardy's peasants have the delightful, unconscious

grotesqueness of pure comedy. They have the whims and oddities of children who have not attained that stage of enlightenment when self-consciousness produces self-distrust and reticence. They are full of quaint conceits, and their very language has a sort of stilted solemnity which is irresistibly comic, just as the talk of children is often comic by the employment of words chosen for their sound rather than their sense. They are unconsciously and delightfully profane. " Poor Charlotte," says Coggan; " I wonder if she had the good fortune to get into heaven when a' died. But a' was never much in luck's way, and perhaps a' went downwards after all, poor soul." It is one of the reproaches of Farmer Everdene's kitchen that not a single damn was allowed: " No, not a poor bare one, even at the most cheerful moment when all was blindest, though the good old word of sin thrown in here and there at such times is a great relief to a merry soul." Concerning which, the maltster replies in grave reprehension, as one who states a moral fact, " Nater requires her swearing at regular times, or she's not herself; and unholy exclamations is a necessity of life." Joseph Poorgrass' apology for drunkenness is worthy of Pecksniff—he only suffers " from a multiplying eye." " A multiplying eye is a very bad thing," says Mark Clark. " It always comes on when I have been in a public-house a little time," says Joseph Poorgrass meekly. " Yes, I see two of every sort, as if I were some holy man, living in the times of King Noah and entering into the ark . . . y-y-y-yes," he added, becoming much afflicted by the picture of himself as a person thrown away, and shedding tears, " I feel too good for England; I ought to have lived in Genesis by rights, like the other men of sacrifice, and then I shouldn't have b-b-been called a d-d-drunkard in such a way." If Dr. Barrow's famous definition of humour, that " it lurketh under an odd similitude, in a plausible reconciling of contradictions, or in acute nonsense," be correct, there are few more triumphant illustrations of humour than the speeches of Joseph Poorgrass.

It is characteristic of all these Wessex peasants that they are much concerned with religion. They are frequently engaged in the attempt to unravel the mysteries of life, and they are never more humorous than when so employed, because their reasoning has that delightful element of topsy-turvy logic which is so charming in childhood. Perhaps this is the secret of their charm; they are children, the ignorant, quaint children of Arcadia. They advance their views on the ways of Deity with all the irreverent frankness of children. They state with the utmost gravity, the most absurd propositions. Thus Mark Clark seriously argues that the power of taking a sufficient quantity of drink is " a talent of the Lord mercifully bestowed upon us, and we ought not to neglect it." Coggan's loyalty to the Established Church is based upon the comfortable assurance that " a man can belong to the Church and bide in his cheerful old inn, and never trouble or worry his mind about doctrines at all. But to be a meetinger, you must go to chapel in all winds and weathers, and make yerself as frantic as a skit. Not but what chapel-members be clever chaps enough in their way. They can lift up beautiful prayers out of their own heads, all about their families and ship-wrecks in the newspapers."

" They can, they can," says Mark Clark, with corroborative feeling, " but we Churchmen, you see, must have it all printed aforehand, or, dang it all, we should no more know what to say to a great gaffer like the Lord than babes unborn." The language of all these worthies is full of Scripture allusions, almost always wrongly used. When Joseph Poorgrass explains to Cain Ball the nature of an oath, he informs him that " 'Tis a horrible testament mind ye, which you say and seal with your bloodstone, and the prophet Matthew tells us that on whomsoever it shall fall, it will grind him to powder." Even Tess, in spite of her Board School education, has visions of centurions still to be seen in the crowded places of the earth. The devil is euphemistically described as " the dark man," or " the horrid man in the smoking house." Odd quotations from Church collects mingle with snatches of monkish lore, and still more ancient pagan superstitions. And, underlying all this quaint jumble of ideas, there is a kind of wisdom; touches of shrewd observation, and the plain man's philosophy based on hard experience. With little knowledge, few pleasures, and the narrowest outlook upon life, Hardy's peasants nevertheless speak as wise men, not as fools.

Hardy has done nothing so well as this rendering of peasant humour. He understands the Wessex peasant thoroughly, and has rendered him completely. It is noticeable that his gift of humour confines itself almost entirely to the Wessex peasant; there is not a trace of humour among the higher social types he depicts. There is no laughter on the lips of Clym Yeobright, or Grace Melbury, or Angel Clare; they are all more or less conscious of the complexity of life. It would seem that education is destructive of humour; in the degree that knowledge widens, the capacity for quaint conceit is lost. Hardy had the good fortune to know the countryside before education had drilled its inhabitants into uniformity. He has caught the last fugitive gleams of a humour that will visit it no more. When we speak of his peasants as Shakespearean, we use an intrinsically right phase, for the peasants of Hardy's romances do literally belong to a world that has altered scarcely at all since Shakespeare's day. They use the same racy words which were familiar when Elizabeth was queen, they express themselves with the same frankness, innocence, and archaic simplicity. And something of the spirit of that Merrie England of Elizabeth yet lingers in them, a spirit of pagan joyousness that flies before the advance of railroads, school-boards, and a popular press.

Of Hardy as a stylist something has already been said. He has not the delicate and discriminating ear of the supreme artist. Such an artist would never have described Wordsworth's poetry as "breezy," or have used such a phrase as "mounting a humid steed." In most of Hardy's writing there is also a certain laboured stiffness. He has no natural eloquence of language; one can imagine him almost as surprised as his reader when a really fine phrase flashes from his pen. He is apt to be pedantic, especially in his constant references to art. These are so frequent that without a tolerably competent knowledge of Dutch and Italian pictures many of his allusions will be meaningless to his readers; and in purely rural drama it is irritating, in any case, to be distracted by such allusions.

The same criticism applies to his frequent introduction of scientific references. A capital instance of this intrusion of science to the detriment of a story occurs in " A Pair of Blue Eyes." The finest scene in the entire book is the adventure of Knight and Elfrida on the cliff, when Knight's life is in peril; but it is much injured in effect by the geological reflections of Knight. The passage in which these reflections are expressed is in itself nobly written.

Time closed up like a fan before him. He saw himself at one extremity of the years, face to face with the beginning and all the intermediate centuries simultaneously. Fierce men, clothed in the hides of beasts, and carrying, for defence and attack, huge clubs and pointed spears, rose from the rock, like phantoms before the doomed Macbeth. . . . Behind them stood an earlier band. No man was there. Huge elephantine forms, the mastodon, the hippopotamus, the tapir, antelopes of monstrous size, the megatherium, and the myledon—all, for the moment, in juxtaposition. Farther back, and overlapped by these, were perched huge-billed birds and swinish creatures as large as horses. Still more shadowy were the sinister crocodilean outlines—alligators, and other uncouth shapes, culminating in the colossal lizard, the iguanodon. . . . These images passed before Knight's inner eye in less than half a minute, and he was again considering the actual present. Was he to die? He dared not move an inch.

One would like to be sure that all these images did pass before Knight's mental eye in half a minute, but it seems improbable. A man fighting for his life on a crumbling cliff-face has other things to think of than geology. But even if a man of Knight's scientific mind might be conceived as indulging in these reflections, two pages of writing were not necessary for their record. The story pauses for a lecture on geology, and, fine as the lecture is, yet it leaves an unpleasant sense of pedantry. This habit of pedantry is Hardy's worst fault. But in the main his style is eminently lucid. If he lacks the finest kind of literary discrimination, he is nevertheless the master of a singularly compact and nervous style; a trifle too laboured it may be, not gracious nor eloquent, but grave, masculine, and usually impressive in its sincerity.

Opinion will be divided on the relative values of Hardy's books; but it may be confidently claimed that few authors who have written so much have written so little that is not memorable. "The Pursuit of the Well-Beloved" is his only entire failure, and there are parts of "Jude the Obscure" which suggest the decadence of genius. "The Trumpet-Major," "The Hand of Ethelberta," and "Desperate Remedies" are also books that fall below the first rank. But we have left at least five books which deserve to rank with the highest products of English fiction, viz., "The Return of the Native," "The Woodlanders," "The Mayor of Casterbridge," "Far from the Madding Crowd," and "Tess of the D'Urbervilles"; and not far behind these come "Under the Greenwood Tree," with its inimitable country charm, and "A Pair of Blue Eyes," with its pathetic note of tragedy. In these five greater books assuredly a rare genius is enshrined. They bear that severest test of fiction, the possibility of constant re-perusal, and they bear it triumphantly. We can as little imagine these books forgotten in any subsequent generation as the greater works of Jane Austen, Scott, Dickens, or Thackeray. It would indeed be difficult to name any books in which the art of fiction has been carried to a higher point of perfection; they are great alike in design and execution, and display the fullest resources of a creative art. Upon these books the fame of Hardy will rest, as upon an impregnable foundation. Men may adopt new philosophies, and attain to a wider synthesis of life, which may do something to discredit Hardy's teaching; but as long as the mind of man is capable of being moved by the note of pure tragedy, as long as pastoral drama has a charm and humour a fascination, as long as the mental eye rests with delight on strong and simple types of character, as long as enough sincerity remains in the reader to prefer the plain realism of life to its sentimental counterfeits, so long will the work of Thomas Hardy live. And unless the future bring with it some irretrievable decay of taste, some general decadence of literary instinct, in which the gods of gold shall be overthrown to make room for the gods of clay, this means that Hardy's fame will be a prolonged and imperishable fame.

XVII

ROBERT LOUIS STEVENSON

Robert Louis Balfour Stevenson, born in Edinburgh, November 13th, 1850. Published "An Inland Voyage," 1878; "Travels with a Donkey in the Cevennes," 1879; "Prince Otto," 1885; "The Strange Case of Dr. Jekyll and Mr. Hyde," 1886; "Kidnapped," 1886; "The Master of Ballantræ," 1889; "The Wrecker," 1892; "Catriona," 1893; "The Ebb-Tide," 1894; "Weir of Hermiston," 1896. Died in Samoa, December 3rd, 1894.

AMONG the writers of later fiction Robert Louis Stevenson occupies a place apart, not only by the nature of his work, but by virtue of a fascinating and unique personality. It was his supreme fortune to be treated as a classic before his death, a fate that has happened to few, and to scarcely any one whose period of toil was so brief as his. Yet, as a novelist, it can hardly be allowed that he ranks with the greatest. His most popular stories, " Treasure Island," " Kidnapped," and " Catriona," are written with immense vivacity, but no one would think of putting them in the same category with the greatest works of Cervantes or Balzac, of Thackeray or Scott. He himself would have been the first to repudiate such a claim. He is entirely frank in confessing that he does not wield an easy pen. He never thinks of the immense fecundity of invention, and the careless, masterly ease of Scott without despair. He says, in speaking of Scott, " I cannot compete with that—what makes me sick is to think of Scott turning out ' Guy Mannering' in three weeks. What a pull of work! Heavens, what thews and sinews! And here am I, my head spinning with having re-written seven not very difficult pages, and not very good when done." In a darker mood he writes, " I think ' David Balfour' a nice little book, and very artistic, and just the thing to occupy the leisure of a busy man; but for the flower of a man's life it seems to me inadequate. Small is the age; it is a small age, and I am of it." What, then, is the secret of the unique fascination which Stevenson exercises over his contemporaries? It lies in personality, charm, and style. It is perfectly true that he cannot write with the supreme ease of Scott, whose work was a pastime rather than a labour; but he has the rarer art which Scott had not, of infusing into all his work an element of something intimate and spiritual, which all who are sympathetic to him must feel, and find delightful.

There are many writers capable of producing admirable and even memorable books, who, nevertheless, fail to quicken in us any slightest ripple of interest concerning themselves. There are other writers whose most careless page is steeped in so keen a personal element that our admiration for their work is from the first curiously intermingled with affection for themselves. It is to the latter class that Stevenson belongs. He has the secret of charm. He admits us to the intimacies of his soul. He explains with the alluring frankness of a child his motives, recapitulates his errors, registers his fluctuations of health, of feeling, of opinion, discloses his methods of thought or labour, and altogether interests us in the problem of himself quite as much as in the story he tells or the plot he weaves. He is a bland and genial egotist, but without a trace of vanity; it is the egotism of a child. We read his books with the curious sense of a haunting presence, as of some light-footed Ariel; or, in more solemn moments, of a spiritual form hovering near us. There is a body terrestrial and a body celestial; the celestial body floats very near us in the limpid atmosphere of Stevenson's best work. It is given to few authors to produce this effect. We feel it in the work of Montaigne, of Ruskin, of Charles Lamb, and it is an effect which only genius can produce. Perhaps we can best measure by such a test the long-debated differentiation of talent and genius; the man of talent interests us in his work, the man of genius makes his work the medium through which we are interested in himself.

Stevenson has another element of genius which is equally rare; the gift of an inimitable style. Perhaps one should hardly speak of it as a gift, since he himself has taken pains to inform us by what infinite labour it was attained. He has stated that "elbow grease" is the secret of his success. From earliest boyhood he admits the tendency to write, but with him it was never a casual indulgence, nor was the achievement of his style a fortunate discovery. In those old Edinburgh student days which he has so perfectly depicted, he was to the academic eye a mere idler, attending as few classes as possible, and wholly without thirst for academic honour. When he presented himself for a certificate in the engineering class, Professor Fleming Jenkin, whose life he was afterwards to write, said, "It is quite useless for you to come, Mr. Stevenson. There may be doubtful cases; there is no doubt about yours. You have simply not attended my class." He indulges in a sly thrust at the model student when he says, " Most boys pay so dear for their medals that they never afterwards have a shot in their locker, and begin the world bankrupt." It would be interesting to know what the model student thought of him. Certainly in those days few persons, perhaps none, augured distinction for this long, lean, dreamy-eyed youth, whose chief joy was in silent rambles on the Pentlands, and whose inhuman carelessness of academic reputation was only equalled by his barbarian pleasure in free winds and solitude. But he had a university of his own, and was graduating after his own fashion. This university was provided by " a nameless trickle that springs in the green bosom of Allermuir, and is fed from Holkerside with a peren-nial teacupful, and threads the moss under Shearer's Knowe, and makes one pool there overhung by a rock, where I loved to sit and make bad verses." It was there he ceaselessly experimented in the art of word-weaving. He began to see that words were something more than the mere counters of speech; they had roots, and bloom, colour and fragrance; they were histories and biographies; they embalmed the thoughts of dead generations, and had associations which linked them with an immeasurable past; they had also the secret of music in them, and were capable of endless modulation and harmony under the touch of a deft hand, and by the regulation of a quick ear. It is a lesson which every great stylist has to learn, but few have ever gone about it with such systematic patience. In one pocket the boy carried the book he was reading, in the other the book which contained his experiments in writing; and in no class-room of the University of Edinburgh was there more indefatigable labour going on than beside this "nameless trickle" of the Pentlands, in this green university of the hills.

This sense of the richness of words is one of the most striking qualities in all Stevenson's writings. Of all the constant and delightful surprises of his pages, cadence is the chief: the unexpected harmony which is obtained by the use of some sonorous and resonant word. We may open his books at random, and be sure that this music will greet us. Here, for example, are half-a-dozen phrases, taken at hazard as the book happens to fall open:

The high *canorous* note of the north-easter on days when the very houses seem to stiffen with cold.

The song of hurrying rivers.

The green-gold air of the east at evening.

At every town the cocks were *tossing* their notes into the golden air.

The sad immunities of death.

The great conflagrant sun, tumultuary, roaring aloud, inimical to life.

The fountains of the Trade were empty. Where it had run but yesterday, and for weeks before, a roaring blue river, *charioting* clouds, silence now reigned, and the whole height of the atmosphere stood balanced.

Consider the mere sound of these phrases, the satisfying depth of harmony that fills the ear on their rotund utterance. In his essay on "The English Admirals," Stevenson says characteristically that Cloudesley Shovel is a mouthful of quaint and sounding syllables; and in all that he has written he has the liveliest ear for the charm of all quaint and sounding syllables. But it must be noted that Stevenson never chooses a word for its mere sound, but for its truth and fitness. His boyish experiments taught him, above all things, the art of observation; they were not the bookish pastimes of a precocious boy in a library, but of a youth sitting on a green hillside, and beneath a sky full of travelling clouds, who found in language the medium of interpretation that the painter finds in line and colour. It is scarcely possible to describe the high piping note of the north-easter by a better word than " canorous," or the joyous morning note of the cock by a truer phrase than " tossed into the golden air." It is not until we attempt to alter these phrases, to transpose or amend them, that we discover how perfect they are. And we perceive at the same time by what labour they have been forged, by what close attention to the niceties of sound, to the truth of nature, to the demands of art. Of no writer of our day is the saying truer that his is the art which conceals art, the ease and flexibility which are the disguises of eternal labour.

But it is obvious that the work of a novelist cannot be judged by any verbal felicities of expression, however rare. The main work of a novelist is to depict human life, and to disclose the secrecies of human character. Stevenson himself was perfectly aware of this. He claimed to be a psychologist or nothing. Can we find in his work the creative instinct, the power of vivid and true characterisation which gives vitality to the puppets of his pen? Few writers have less cause to shrink from such a test. We may place to his credit such vital figures as John Silver, the sea-cook in " Treasure Island." Alan Breck in " Kid-

napped," Captain Nares in "The Wrecker." In
Silver and Captain Nares there is an almost brutal
vivacity of life. We see them in their habit as they
lived, we recognise them in every turn of expression,
idiomatic of their own minds. Nor is this quite all.
The portrait painter can produce the external traits
of character, and even suggest the internal essence,
but it needs the psychologist to analyse the soul.
Stevenson judged himself aright when he claimed
to be a psychologist, or nothing. There is a
subtlety of insight in his presentation of character
which is rare even in the greatest novelist. It goes
to the very roots of motive, it touches the secret coils
of conduct, it exhibits men not as they appear to the
world, but as they appear to themselves and their
Maker.

We have a palmary example of this power in Robert
Herrick, in the "Ebb-Tide." Herrick belongs to a
class which arouses all the psychologist's instinct in
Stevenson. Here is a man who has failed in life not
through vice, but weakness. A fatal incompetence,
and an incapacity of fixed aim and deliberate effort,
have brought him at last to be the comrade of Huish,
the cockney cad, and Davis, the broken-down drunken
sea captain on the beach of Papeete. The three men,
made comrades by misfortune, sail away upon a stolen
ship. Self-contempt eats the soul of Robert Herrick
throughout that tragic voyage, but he submits to his
environment. He sees his duty, but cannot do it.
The ship comes at last to a solitary island, and there
Herrick's fate touches its grim climax. Attwater, the
owner of the island, reads his character when he asks
him what the "puppy is doing between two wolves."

In the bitterness of his shame Herrick sees no escape but suicide, and then follows an analysis of the thoughts and emotions of the despairing man, which it would be difficult to parallel in modern literature. Herrick slips silently at midnight into the water of the lagoon, resolved on death.

A very bright planet shone before him, and drew a trenchant wake along the water. He took that for his line and followed it. That was the last earthly thing that he should look upon; that radiant speck, which he had soon magnified into a City of Laputa, along whose terraces there walked men and women of awful and benignant features, who viewed him with distant commiseration.

From these flights of fancy he was aroused by the growing coldness of the water. Why should he delay? Here, where he was now, let him seek the ineffable refuge, let him lie down with all races and generations of men in the house of sleep. It was easy to say, easy to do. To stop swimming; there was no mystery in that, if he could do it. Could he? And he could not. He knew it instantly. He was instantly aware of an opposition in his members, unanimous and invincible, clinging to life with a single and fixed resolve, finger by finger, sinew by sinew; something that was at once he and not he— at once within and without him; the shutting of some miniature valve within the brain, which a single manly thought would suffice to open—and the grasp of an external fate ineluctable as gravity. To any man there may come at times a consciousness that there blows, through all the articulations of his body, the wind of a spirit not wholly his; that his mind rebels; that another girds him and carries him whither he would not. It came now to Herrick with the authority of a revelation. There was no escape possible. The open door was closed in his recreant face. He must go back into the world and amongst men without illusion. He must stagger on to the end with the pack of his responsibility and disgrace, until a cold, a blow, a merciful chance ball, or the more merciful hangman, should dismiss him from his infamy. There were men who could commit suicide; there were men who could not; and he was one who could not.

His smile was tragic. He could have spat upon himself.

Such is the picture of Herrick, Oxford graduate, beach-comber, comrade of thieves, without faith, without resolution, whose final confession is—" I am broken crockery; I am a burst drum; the whole of my life is gone to water; I have nothing left that I believe in, except my living horror of myself,"—and it is something more than a character that is presented to us by the subtle art of Stevenson: it is the exhibition of a soul in torture.

Another characteristic of Stevenson's art is the poetic sense of nature which it everywhere displays. This is, perhaps, its most delightful quality. It appears in his first book, when he describes his outdoor life as donkey-driver in the Cevennes; it appears in his last, where he paints with a full brush the rugged scenery of Scotland, whose fascination survived through all his years of exile. Like the French doctor of one of his stories, he was a connoisseur in sunrises. Could he have chosen, he would have lived always in the fields, where, as he says, " God keeps an open house." One of his most charming pictures is of his outdoor sleep among the woods—the blue darkness lying along the glade when he slumbered, his sleep soothed by the " indescribable quiet talk of the runnel over the stones," and the dawn waking him to the moment. And in spite of all the maladies that laid him by the heels, Stevenson remained all his life a hater of houses, a lover of open spaces, a gypsy at heart, who submitted with intense reluctance to the smug comfort of a life beneath roofs.

Sunrise has often been painted, but rarely with more truth and charm than in this description which occurs in Stevenson's " Prince Otto."

The Princess Seraphina, suddenly deprived of her throne by a miniature revolution, flees into the forest, and spends, for the first time in her life, a night under the naked heavens. Suddenly she becomes aware of a glow of transfiguration in the woods, and with joy catching at her voice, cries, " O, it is the dawn ! "

Soon she had struggled to a certain hill-top, and saw far before her the silent unfolding of the day. Out of the east it welled and whitened; the darkness trembled into light; and the stars were extinguished like the street lamps of a human city. The whiteness brightened into silver; the silver warmed into gold: the gold kindled into pure and living fire; and the face of the East was barred with elemental scarlet. The day drew its first long breath, steady and chill: and for leagues around the woods sighed and shivered. And then at one bound the sun leaped up: and her startled eyes received day's first arrow, and quailed under the buffet. The day was come plain and garish: and up the steep and solitary eastern heavens the sun, victorious over his competitors, continued slowly and royally to mount.

Take again, as a companion picture, the tropic daybreak as the *Farralone,* the stolen ship in " The Ebb Tide," begins to open up the unknown island. It is four in the morning when the sound of breakers is first heard.

The sound was continuous, like the passing of a train: no rise or fall could be distinguished: minute by minute the ocean heaved with an equal potency against the invisible isle; and as time passed, and Herrick waited in vain for any vicissitude in the volume of that roaring, a sense of the eternal weighed upon his mind. To the expert eye the isle itself was to be inferred from a certain string of blots along the starry heaven. There was little or no morning bank. A brightening came in the east: then a wash of some ineffable, faint, nameless hue between crimson and silver, and then coals of fire. These glimmered awhile on the sea-line, and seemed to brighten and darken, and spread out, and still the night and the stars remained undisturbed; it was as though a spark should catch and glow and creep along the foot of some heavy and almost incombustible wall-hanging, and the room itself is scarce menaced. Yet a little after, and the whole east glowed with gold and scarlet, and the hollow of heaven was filled with daylight.

And then, to take one more example, executed on a larger scale, what description of a sea-storm can be at once truer and more impressive than the description of the gale the *Norah Creina* meets on the way to Midway Island in " The Wrecker "?

By dinner I had fled the deck, and sat in the bench corner, giddy, dumb, and stupefied with terror. The frightened leaps of the poor *Norah Creina,* spanking like a stag for bare existence, bruised me between the table and the berths. Overhead the wild huntsman of the storm passed continuously in one blare of mingled noises; screaming wind, straining timber, lashing rope's end, pounding block, and bursting sea contributed; and I could have thought there was at times another, a more piercing, a more human note that dominated all, like the wailing of an angel; I could have thought I knew the angel's name, and that his wings were black. It seemed incredible that any creature of man's art could long endure the barbarous mishandling of the seas, kicked as the schooner was from mountain side to mountain side, beaten, and blown upon, and wrenched in every joint and sinew, like a child upon the rack. . . . God bless every man that swung a mallet on that tiny and strong hull! It was not for wages only that he laboured, but to save men's lives.

It is in passages like these that Stevenson moves and holds the hearts of his readers. Nature still remains, in spite of cities, the open Bible, toward which God's creatures turn with undying interest and curiosity, and no writer is truly great who cannot read afresh, and teach us to read, the beauty of that Bible. Stevenson has done this. He has spoken to the poet that exists in every man. He has hung the common room of life with inimitable tapestries woven on the looms of God. He has brought to tired men in cities a new vision of the wonder of the earth. Great statesmen and great soldiers whose names are famous have done less to help mankind with all their toils, for of all boons that men can bring to man none is greater than to give vision to his eyes, and make him feel the grandeur of that elemental life of which he is a part.

This sense of the elementary grandeur in human life is a marked feature in all Stevenson's works. It is this which constantly imparts dignity to episodes of action which in themselves are mean. There is an energy of touch altogether Homeric in his best stories, a delight in human daring, and a sense of a large music running through human life, full of incomparable rhythm and noblest diapason. An instance of this is found in the picture he draws of Carthew, the broken gentleman, who recovers his hold on life by earning his hard wage as a navvy, working night and day through the Australian rains to keep the trains running on a washed-out line. Carthew recognises " the answering glory of battle " in such a task. The mountain shakes and nods seaward; the rare trains come creeping and signalling; the navvies clutch at trees and shrubs and watch in choking silence; and Carthew, sick with sleeplessness and coffee, with hands softened and cut to ribbons by the wet, watches too with mingled fear and exultation. In this " continual instancy of toil," hitherto lacking in his misdirected life, he had found " the true cure of vital scepticism." The curt words of praise from the engineer's grim lips " fall on the ears of the discarded son like music." Toil and venture re-create in him the spirit of a man. And it is in commenting on this scene that Stevenson reveals his own spirit. He declares that no man can know much of human life whose own career is " sedentary, uneventful, and ingloriously safe." Let such men paint pictures or write stories if they will, but let them forbear judgment on man and his destiny, " for it is a thing with which they are unacquainted. Their own life is an excrescence of the moment. . . . The elemental life of man, spent under sun and rain, and in rude physical effort, lies upon one side, scarce changed since the beginning."

It is this mode of thought which makes Stevenson's stories in the right sense heroic. It is common to speak of the chief figure in a novel as the hero of the story; but in few instances is he truly heroic. Stevenson's heroes are heroic. They are one and all engaged in dramas of action. They suffer hunger, nakedness, thirst, peril, and in all quit themselves like men. Alan Breck, fleeing through the heather, holds us fascinated by his gaiety, his impudence, his resourcefulness. The Master of Ballantræ, black-hearted villain as he is, charms us by his contempt of fate. Even Huish, the cockney cad in " The Ebb-Tide," the most entirely contemptible of creatures, has the grace of courage. Stevenson knew well that whatever appetite may fail in man, his appetite for heroism remains insatiable. "Ingloriously safe" as his own life may be, he thrills to the note of peril and adventure. And hence, when Stevenson rehabilitated the old pirate and adventure story, he was doing a real service to his age, by attracting men to that spectacle of rude Homeric struggle, the taste for which no civilisation has the power to extirpate, or even to subdue.

But Stevenson was a moralist too, and a moralist even when he wrote of pirates. Mr. Henley remarked this characteristic in his famous sonnet upon Stevenson, a sonnet which is as vivid a piece of impressionism as can be found in English poetry.

> In his face,
> Lean, large-boned, curved of beak, and touched with race
> Bold-lipped, rich-tinted, mutable, as the sea,
> There gleams a brilliant and romantic grace.
> A spirit intense and rare, with trace on trace
> Of passion, impudence, and energy.
> Valiant in velvet, light in ragged luck,
> Most vain, most generous, sternly critical.
>
> .   .   .   .   .
>
> A deal of Ariel, just a streak of Puck,
> Much Antony, of Hamlet most of all,
> And something of the Shorter Catechist.

The description sounds paradoxical, but it is perfectly accurate. Beneath much that is wayward and bohemian in Stevenson's temperament there runs the hard strata of the Shorter Catechist, as beneath the soft loam there may often be found the wedge of rock which turns the sharpest weapon. It was the heritage of his Scotch birth and training. The Scot can rarely escape the pressure of those profound and serious

thoughts which constitute religion, and Stevenson carried religion in his very bones and marrow. He makes
no effort to conceal the fact. He speaks of his own
religious experiences with the fervour of a St. Augustine or a Wesley. He tells us that his own life came
about "like a well-handled ship," because there stood
at the helm "the unknown steersman whom we call
God." Amid the grimy horrors of his most powerful,
but least pleasant book, "The Ebb-Tide," he breaks
forth into praise of the grace of God; there is nothing
in the world "but God's grace. We walk upon it; we
breathe it; and we live and die by it; it makes the
nails and axles of the universe." That which gives his
great scenes their most impressive element is not
merely their force of imagination or of truth; it is this
subtle element of religion which colours them. The
difference between a great scene of Scott and a great
scene of Stevenson is that while the first impresses us,
the second awes us. Words, phrases, sudden flashes
of spiritual insight, linger in the mind and solemnise
it. We feel that there is something we have not quite
fathomed in the passage, and we return to it again and
again to find it still unfathomable. Wonder and astonishment sit throned among his thoughts, the wonder of the awe-struck child at Divine mysteries, the
enduring astonishment of the man who moves about
in worlds not realised. It is this intense religious
vision which gives Stevenson a place apart among his
contemporaries; in his own phrase, it holds him with
a force "ineluctable as gravity."

The working of this temper is seen in two directions;
in the spiritual background which he gives to all his
stories, and in his vivid sense of the reality of Evil.

There is a striking and almost grotesque illustration of the first in " The Ebb-Tide."

Attwater, the athlete and mystic, and Captain Davis, Huish, and Herrick, the detected rogues from the stolen ship *Farralone,* are seated on the verandah of Attwater's house after dinner. Attwater, with deliberate cruelty, has probed the consciences of the three unhappy men. Suddenly he strikes a silver bell at his side, and asks them to observe its effect.

The note rose clear and strong; it rang out clear and far into the night, and over the deserted island; it died into the distance, until there lingered in the porches of the ear a vibration that was sound no longer. " Empty houses, empty sea, solitary beaches," said Attwater. " And yet God bears the bell. And yet we sit on this verandah, on a lighted stage with all heaven for spectators." The captain sat mesmerised. At length, " bursting with a sigh from the spell that bound him," he stammers out, " So you mean to tell me now that you sit here evenings, and ring up—well, ring up the angels—by yourself?" " As a matter of historic fact, one does not," replied Attwater. " Why ring a bell when there flows out from oneself and everything about one a far more momentous silence? The least beat of my heart, and the least thought in my mind echoing into Eternity, forever, and forever, and forever?"

Think of that scene, and try to imagine it. The three men are there to plan the murder of Attwater, and he knows it. It is a sordid, grisly episode of greed and crime you watch. Suddenly, as though the veil were rent, the horror of Eternity rushes into view. At the sound of the bell the silent hosts of judging angels are assembled, and the Last Assize begins. Metaphorically speaking, that bell of alarm rings through all the stories of Stevenson. He writes as one who sees behind all earthly shows, the vision Marvell pictures in his poetry:

> Time's winged chariot hurrying by
> Deserts of vast Eternity.

And there can be little doubt that the extraordinary power with which Stevenson rivets the attention even in his slightest stories is due in great part to this element of spiritual vision, rare in all writers—rarest of all in novelists.

Another story in which the same silver bell resounds is " Markheim," but in this the moral truth is plainer. Markheim is another of the men Stevenson was so skilled in depicting, the man who fails in life through weakness. His weakness at last brings him to an act of crime. Late on Christmas Eve he visits a curiosity dealer of his acquaintance, and deliberately murders him for gain. Here again is an episode as grisly and sordid as could be imagined. But in the same instant that the earthly crime is consummated the spiritual drama commences. Markheim suddenly trembles with a dreadful sense that he is not alone. He is " haunted and begirt by presences." The twenty-four stairs he climbs to the upper chamber, where he means to rifle the dead man's goods, are " four-and-twenty agonies." There comes " a flash of ice, a flash of fire, a bursting gush of blood," and Markheim stands " transfixed and thrilling," for at last he knows there *is* a following step. It is his own Soul that confronts him. The unhappy man begins to plead his case with every casuistry known to guilt. Circumstance, and not he, is responsible for his crime. He was born and has lived in a land of giants who have dragged him by the wrists, the giants of circumstance. He is no worse than others whose crimes are undetected. He hates evil, even while he does it, and that should count to him for righteousness. In any case, this was meant to be his last crime. To-morrow he will begin the world anew, with a resolution that cannot fail of high results. And then his Soul put one tremendous question to him:

" For six-and-thirty years you have been in this world. I will propose one simple question, and as you answer I shall read to you your moral horoscope. You have grown in many things more lax. . . . But granting that, are you, in any one particular, however trifling, more difficult to please with your own conduct, or do you go in all things with a looser rein?" And Markheim's answer is, " No, in none; I have gone down in all."

And at that point the drama ends. The features of the ghostly visitor " undergo a wonderful and lovely change." Markheim has confessed his guilt, and calls for the police to take him. But the Soul smiles, knowing that in that penitent confession the better nature is at last triumphant in the man, and over the darkened stage, as in Goethe's great drama, the angelic voices cry, " Not ' lost,' but ' saved ! ' "

It will be seen at once that this story is in effect an allegory—for fable and allegory Stevenson always had a strong liking—and his power of allegory at last found expression in what must always be regarded as a masterpiece, " Dr. Jekyll and Mr. Hyde."

The seed-thought of this appalling fable is familiar enough: it is the ancient Pauline description of the war in our members, so that the thing we would we do not, and the thing we would not, that we do. Dr. Jekyll is the wise physician, prudent, wealthy, respected, famous. Mr. Hyde is the worse self that dwells in his members. By an accidental discovery Dr. Jekyll finds out how to separate these two personalities. He can at will cease to be Dr. Jekyll, and become Mr. Hyde. When he wearies of the virtues of Dr. Jekyll he can adopt the vices of Mr. Hyde. He is secure of secrecy —for who would dream of connecting the deformed monster, who steals out of Jekyll's house, bent on midnight lust and murder, with the wise physician, known far and wide for the goodness of his life, and the breadth of his charities? The good and evil are each real, and each intolerant of the other. The man is literally torn between the good and evil natures; in his right mind given to serious and religious thoughts; in the guise of Mr. Hyde greedy of abominable vices, repenting and sinning in turn; to the last desirous of good, but impotent of achieving it, and all the time conscious that the ape-like thing within him grows stronger for each fresh liberation and indulgence. It is on this fact that the whole tremendous moral of the story lies. "This was the shocking thing," writes Stevenson, "that the slime of the pit seemed to utter cries and voices; that the amorphous dust gesticulated and sinned; that what was dead and had no shape should usurp the offices of life. And this again: that that insurgent horror was knit to him closer than a wife, closer than an eye; lay caged in his flesh, where he heard it mutter, and felt it struggle to be born; and at every hour of weakness, and in the confidence of slumber, prevailed against him and deposed him out of life."

The appalling moment comes when Mr. Hyde can

no more be transformed back to Dr. Jekyll. There is no longer a Dr. Jekyll left, only a Mr. Hyde, waiting for the hangman, and yet it is the soul of Jekyll that cries frantically from the lips of Hyde.

Such is the story, and although horror pursues us as we read it, no one can read it without a stirred conscience; no one can lay it down without some sincere resolve to set a closer guard upon his virtues, and put a stricter curb upon his follies.

In these three illustrations from his stories we have some indication of Stevenson's place as a moralist. Here is the Shorter Catechist indeed; a Calvin of the imagination, a Knox speaking in fables. Let it, however, be remembered that he had a hopefulness in human nature not found in Calvin, and a charity not found in Knox. Men need to hear the stern voice of the indignant moralist—no age needs it more than ours—but they have an even greater need to hear the voice that bids them hope. That voice of hope is never wanting in Stevenson. He rarely fails to recognise some positive good in the worst nature that may be turned into account. Bellairs, in " The Wrecker," one of his ugliest villains, has the virtue of self-sacrifice; and while he pictures all the baseness of Davis, he reminds us, too, " of the endearing blend of his faults and virtues, the sudden shining forth of a tenderness that lay too deep for tears," in this base man's affection for his children. He makes no scruple to talk of the grace of God even in relation to his worst rogues. He counsels the worst against unfruitful remorse, which he calls " an unclean passion." His vision of evil is penetratingly clear; his vision of the power of man to achieve good is not less clear; and so into the lips of erring mortals he puts that noble prayer, which expresses so much of his own valiant and hopeful spirit, " Help us with the grace of courage, that we be none of us cast down when we sit lamenting amid the ruins of our happiness or our integrity; touch us with the fire from the altar that we may be up and doing to rebuild our city."

No estimate of Stevenson can be complete that does not take full account of his poems, his essays, and his familiar letters. His poems resemble Emerson's, in a certain pregnant felicity of phrase and a relative inability to master the technical means of expression. Yet he was by nature a poet, lavishly endowed with the two great qualities of the poet—imagination and sympathy. It is by virtue of these qualities that he has written quite the best, because the truest, essay that has ever been written upon Robert Burns. Carlyle has not surpassed him in sincerity, and at some points he has altogether surpassed Carlyle in the friendly yet searching insight with which he has interpreted the darker secrets and the worst motives of Burns' tragic life. His sketch of Villon is equally memorable in its subtlety of insight, and is, besides, a most picturesque and vivid reconstruction of lost history. But the essays which will take the highest rank are naturally those which are most expressive of the author's own personality. In his power of minute self-revelation he resembles Montaigne. It matters little of what he writes; he never fails to project some lovable, or at least fascinating, image of himself across the page. The spirit of candour with which he expresses himself is the spirit in which he regards mankind. There is a fine catholicity about him which makes him able to apprehend the most diverse natures, and to sweep into the orbit of their lives at unexpected angles. Beggars, gypsies, sailors, shepherds, rude chestnut-gatherers of the Cevennes, and abnormal creatures like Villon—he finds something in each which corresponds to something in himself, and he shares with them what he has finely called "man's enduring astonishment at his own position." His own position was sufficiently astonishing. If ever man had just cause to write gravely, and even bitterly, on matters pertaining to human destiny, it was this man; yet his spirit is throughout touched not only with a stoic courage, but with inimitable gaiety. His "supreme and splendid characteristic" is, as Mr. Chesterton has so finely phrased it, "a certain airy wisdom, a certain light and cool rationality, which is very rare and very difficult indeed to those who are greatly thwarted or tormented in life." It is levity indeed—it is Mr. Chesterton's word—but it is a reasoned levity, "the flower of a hundred grave philosophies."

Yet though we accept the term, we can only accept it as a mental characteristic. The "airy wisdom," the "light and cool rationality," play over profound moral depths. He uses many bye-paths, but they always conduct him to the great issues of life. In his lightest mood his eye is busy with the things that lie beneath the surface. Thus the foul air of an emigrant car suggests this notable flash of criticism:

I think we are human only in virtue of our open windows. Without fresh air you only require a bad heart and a remarkable command of the Queen's English to become such another as Dean Swift; a kind of leering, human goat, leaping and wagging your scut on mountains of offense.

In the same way the spectacle of the Chinese emigrants opens up illimitable thoughts:

For my own part [he says] I could not look but with wonder and respect on the Chinese. Their forefathers watched the stars before mine had begun to keep pigs. Gunpowder and printing, which the other day we imitated, and a school of manners which we never had the delicacy so much as to desire to imitate, were theirs in a long-past antiquity. They walk the earth with us, but it seems they must be of different clay. They hear the clock sound the same hour, but surely of a different epoch. They travel by steam conveyance, yet with such a baggage of old Asiatic thoughts and superstitions as might check the locomotive in its course. Whatever is thought within the circuit of the Great Wall; what the wry-eyed, spectacled schoolmaster teaches in the hamlets round Pekin; religions so old that our language looks a halfling boy along-side; philosophy so wise that our best philosophers find things therein to wonder at; all this travelled alongside of me for thousands of miles over plain and mountain.

It is not the facile and joyous essayist who speaks in this passage, but the serious-hearted observer of life. In one of his earliest books, the " Travels with a Don-key in the Cevennes," full as it is of the light-hearted and mercurial spirits of youth, the same trait is pres-ent. The delightful humour of the early chapters conducts us to the country of the Camisards and the monastery of Our Lady of the Snows; or perhaps I should say that the humour accompanies rather than conducts us, for the special charm of the book is its varying mood, and that in no mood whatever is the humour out of sight. It is the surest of all bonds between writer and reader, and we are equally con-scious of it, whether we goad the unhappy Modestine up the mountains, or discuss theology with the monks of the Trappist retreat. It seems a perfectly natural thing with Stevenson to be one moment laughing over the imbecilities of an unhappy ass, and the next gravely discussing the martyrdom of the Camisards, and thrilling in heart to the noble speeches of the accused leader, Séguier:

"Your name?" they asked.

"Pierre Séguier."

"Your domicile?"

"Lately in the desert, and soon in heaven."

"Have you no remorse for your crimes?"

"I have committed none. My soul is like a garden full of shelter and of fountains."

In the familiar letters the same characteristics are even more clearly displayed. It is very possible that the day may come when of all that he has written the letters will be most cherished as his real testament to the human race. The eye that has grown careless over his essays or his stories will kindle afresh over these more intimate confessions, which display a courage, a vivacity, and a joy in life which would be remarkable in a strong man, but are almost unique in a man whose whole life was spent in the shadow of death. The mind lingers long over such a confession as this: "Sick or well, I have had a splendid life of it, grudge nothing, regret very little, and—take it all over—would hardly exchange with any man of my time, unless perhaps it were Gordon, or our friend Chalmers" —Chalmers being the great missionary and heroic martyr of New Guinea. The strenuous life never had a more convinced advocate, nor a more conspicuous example than this man, who amid constant disappointment and difficulty could write with boyish cheerfulness, " Still, it's good fun." He deliberately set himself to achieve what he has called " the great task of happiness." He will sing no " Miserere "; that particular piece of music, he tells us, he takes to be the composition of an atheist. He believes " in the ultimate decency of things ": " Ay, and if I awoke in hell, should still believe in it." He wonders when he listens to the loud song of the crickets at the close of the day round his ruined hut on the Silverado mountain, " why these creatures are so happy, and what was wrong with man, that he also did not wind up his day with an hour or two of shouting." The lesson he has to teach is the saving virtue of manliness; and from these familiar letters the most gallant of human souls greets us, speaking in high soldierly accents to the timid, in cheerful irony to the recreant, in warm encouragement to the struggler, in human-hearted sympathy to all. The spirit of his whole life is expressed in the prayer he wrote for the beginning of the day's toil: " Give us to go blithely about our business. Help us to play the man; help us to perform the petty round of irritating concerns and duties with laughter and kind faces "; and in the evening prayer, written but twenty-four hours before his death, " Call us up with morning faces, and with morning hearts, eager to be happy, if happiness shall be our portion; and if the day be marked for sorrow, strong to endure it."

Stevenson died as he lived; to the last full of zest in life, happy, buoyant, laborious. He who had lived all his days in expectation of death, when it came experienced no premonitory shadow—" God's finger touched him, and he slept." His death brought a grief to thousands of homes the wide world over, to thousands of men and women to whom he was much more than a writer—a counsellor, an inspiring presence, a dear and beloved friend. When he once praised his native cook for his skill, saying, " Great is thy wisdom," the man replied, " Great is thy love." And it might be said of Stevenson himself, that great as was the admiration men felt for his wisdom, the love he inspired was yet greater. He had in a rare degree " the genius to be loved," which is after all the noblest form of genius. He earned the highest reward of genius, which is to live in the affectionate memory of men. His work for the world is very far from done because his bodily presence is withdrawn from it; he remains, and unless all the signs be false, must long remain, as a spirit in men's thoughts, strengthening the feeble, uplifting the timid, and animating the strong to a wise and heroic use of life. The verses written on his tomb in far Samoa express excellently that strenuous zest of life which animated him to the last:

> Under the wide and starry sky
>   Dig the grave and let me die.
> Glad did I live, and gladly die,
>   And I laid me down with a will.
>
> This be the verse you grave for me,
>   Here he lies where he longed to be,
> Home is the sailor, Home from the sea,
>   And the hunter home from the hill.

But there is another element they do not express, the continued life of memory, the restless ardour of the soul, felt long after the body is dissolved in dust, the influence which the great writer exercises over the mind of succeeding generations, which is his most enduring triumph. That part of the epitaph others must write for him; and it cannot be better written than in the famous and familiar lines of Matthew Arnold, which commemorate all those prophetic souls to whom it is given to speak to the universal soul of their race:

> Ye, like angels, appear,
> Radiant with ardour divine,
> Beacons of hope ye appear!
> Languor is not in your heart,
> Weariness not on your brow,
> Ye alight in our van! at your voice
> Panic, despair, flee away;
> Ye move through the ranks, recall
> The stragglers, refresh the outworn,
> Praise, reinspire the brave.
> Order, courage return;
> Eyes rekindling, and prayers,
> Follow your steps as ye go,
> Ye fill up the gaps in our files,
> Strengthen the wavering line,
> Stablish, continue our march,
> On, to the bound of the waste,
> On, to the City of God.

XVIII

RELIGION IN FICTION

George Macdonald; J. H. Shorthouse; Mrs. Humphrey Ward; Olive Schreiner; Mark Rutherford.

FICTION, being both a transcript and a criticism of life, nothing that pertains to life is alien to it. The novelist, guided by his own temperament, deals with that aspect of life which is most familiar or interesting to himself, and naturally from time to time there arises a novelist of distinctive religious genius. So far as English fiction is concerned there is much in the national temperament and history to explain the existence of what may be called the religious novel. It can escape no student of history that all the great causes which have most powerfully moved the English mind have been in essence religious causes. The greatest series of battles ever fought on English soil were struggles between antagonistic religious creeds. The Puritan stood primarily for certain spiritual truths; it was an accident of his time that these truths involved the cause of political liberty. His antagonist also claimed the consecration of a creed which, beginning with certain ecclesiastical convictions, was found to involve the entire theory of monarchy. Twice in her history England has got rid of a king, but the original cause of offence in each instance was as much religious as political. With such antecedents it is nothing more than might be expected that English fiction should reflect in an unusual degree the religious temper of the race.

One of the results of long training in liberty of thought is that the average Englishman holds himself competent to discuss any subject under the sun, however intricate and philosophic, and to pass an opinion on it which he deems worthy of respect. Naturally the novelist shares this estimate, which is common to the nation. He is quite indifferent to the charge that he has had no special training for the discussion of theological problems. His opinions are as good as other people's, and he claims the right to state them. Hence in a nation much given to religious thinking, delighting in debate for its own sake, in the main profoundly sincere in its desire for truth, and easily impassioned by spiritual ideas, it is inevitable that religion should be constantly expressed in fiction.

But here it becomes necessary to distinguish, with some care for exact definition, what may be properly described as a religious novel. Clearly it is not the novel into which religion enters as one among many composite qualities, or the novel in which a sense of religion is more or less accidental, because most really good novels answer to this description. Thackeray, as we have seen, has many passages touched with the purest spirit of piety; Dickens, with a much slenderer sense of religion, nevertheless attempts its exposition; Kingsley writes always with distinct religious aim. There are passages in both Charlotte Brontë and George Eliot which might have been written by some passionate poet of religious ideas, some St. Catherine or St. Theresa—notably the noble close of " Villette," the preface to " Middlemarch," the sermon of Dinah Morris on the village green, and the spiritual experiences of Maggie Tulliver. Even Daniel Defoe has rare moments when he makes us conscious of the things that lie " on the other side of Time," and in Stevenson this consciousness is always dominant. Yet in the strict sense of the term not one of these writers has produced a religious novel. They have touched the religious chord because it is one of the common chords of humanity. The effort of their art was to sweep the full compass of life, and they could not, as mere artists, ignore the religious chord.

The religious novel proper is that which centres itself expressly, definitely, and by distinct limitation on the exposition of religious ideas or the statement of theological problems. It may take into its scheme a wide or a narrow area of human action, but it will take no more than is necessary to its special purpose. It may create types of character as vital as any that may be found in more secular forms of fiction, but that is a question of the power of the artist, not of the intention of his art. In other words, the religious novel is a novel in which the faculty of creative imagination is definitely devoted, and in some instances subordinated, to the exposition of religious ideas.

Such a definition may serve in the work of discrimination, but it is indicatory rather than judicial. Where, for instance, are we to rank such books as Mrs. Beecher-Stowe's " Uncle Tom's Cabin " and Hawthorne's " Scarlet Letter "? Both are great books, so great that no history of fiction can ignore them. It is probable that no novel ever written has had such an immense popularity or has exerted so

great an influence on human affairs as " Uncle Tom's
Cabin." In its power of simple pathos, in its passionate humanitarianism, in its instinctive art, it is unique.
It has the rare kind of greatness which belongs to a
large and simple design faithfully executed. If it
has ceased to be read, it is because the cause it pleaded
is won—the highest possible tribute to its influence.
Hawthorne's novel has the same merit of complete
simplicity of design, but united with a profound moral
insight, and governed by a fine and rare artistic sense.
It has the purity and the " severity of perfect light."
Its theme is sin and conscience, and in this sense it
is a religious novel, as " Uncle Tom's Cabin " is a religious novel by virtue of the religious spirit which
conceived and informs it. Yet in the strict sense
neither quite answers the definition of a novel completely devoted to the exposition of religious ideas.
Neither could have existed apart from the religious
sense, but neither binds itself to the sole exposition of
religious ideas. For, in the main, Mrs. Stowe is
humanitarian rather than religious; and if we distinguish between the spirit of Hawthorne's art, and
the material on which it works, we recognise in him
the spirit of the Greek dramatist dealing with the large
issues of fate, and only touched incidentally by modern
theological conceptions.

Putting aside, then, the vast array of novels which
appeal to religious sentiment—some of them fairly
meritorious, most of them poor in theme and faulty
in construction—there are not more than three or
four names which stand for high achievement in this
realm of literature. Foremost is the name of George
Macdonald, a writer of real genius, whose influence

in contemporary religious thought has been much greater than the present generation is aware of. The pivot of his entire theological system is the Fatherhood of God, with its logical corollaries of human perfectibility and universal restoration. In his own way he has uttered in fiction the message which Maurice uttered in theology, and Tennyson and Browning in poetry. He nowhere minimises sin, but he everywhere teaches that evil cannot last for ever. Eternal sin enduring in the presence of eternal holiness is to him unthinkable. Somewhere, sometime, love will be supreme; and of all the souls which God has made, not one will be lost, or

> Cast as rubbish to the void
> When He hath made the pile complete.

He once said characteristically that when Protestantism revised the Eschatology of Rome it eliminated the wrong thing; it should have retained Purgatory and left out Hell. With the religious value of these conclusions the critic of fiction has nothing to do; all that he has to do is to observe the method of their expression, and how far they have or have not served the purposes of imaginative art. It may be at once replied that in George Macdonald's writings these conceptions have, at all events, not hindered the freedom of his art. They are so much a part of himself, that it is as natural for him to write of dour Scots Calvinists trying to shed their ancestral creed, as it is for Kipling to write of soldiers and machinery. That the controversialist sometimes deposes the artist no one will deny; so also the artist in Kipling is sometimes subservient to the ship's engineer. The great thing, however, is that the writer should be sincere, and then his art will be sincere. Macdonald has this entire sincerity, and it has been the secret of his wide-spread influence.

The general spirit of Macdonald's teaching may be best studied in such books as " David Elginbrod " and " Robert Falconer." Here, for example, are certain passages in " Robert Falconer " which deeply penetrate the memory, and do so because they move the heart:

One thing is clear to me, that no indulgence of passion destroys the spiritual nature so much as respectable selfishness.

    .   .   .   .   .

"They are in God's hands," he says of fallen women; "He hasn't done with them yet. Shall it take less time to make a woman than to make a world? Is not the woman the greater? She may have her ages of chaos, her centuries of crawling slime, yet rise a woman at last."

    .   .   .   .   .

"Did you ever observe that there is not one word about the vices of the poor in the Bible, from beginning to end?"
"But they have their vices?"
"Undubitably. I am only stating a fact. The Bible is full enough of the vices of the rich. I make no comment."

Of a poor, gin-sodden woman with a smiling child in her arms, he says:

A child, fresh from God, finds its heaven where no one else would. The devil could drive woman out of Paradise; but the devil himself cannot drive Paradise out of a woman.

And where is there a more tenderly exquisite picture of the contrition of a soiled soul than this? Falconer is reading the story of Magdalene to a company of sinners:

Some one sobbed again. It was a small, slender girl with a face disfigured with small-pox, and save for the tearful look it wore, poor and expressionless. Falconer said something gentle to her.

"Will He ever come again?" she sobbed.

"Who?" said Falconer.

"Him—Jesus Christ. I've heard tell, I think, that He was to come again some day."

"Why do you ask?"

"Because," she said, with a fresh burst of tears, which rendered the words that followed unintelligible. But she recovered herself in a few minutes, and, as if finishing her sentence, put her hand up to her poor, thin, colourless hair, and said, "My hair ain't long enough to wipe His feet."

A much less influential writer, but a more delicate artist, is Mr. Shorthouse, the author of "John Inglesant." "John Inglesant" is a book about which opinion is much divided. Its worst fault is lack of spontaneity. It betrays the implacable drudgery by which it was produced. It resembles a much worked-on picture, touched and retouched into laborious perfection; and there is no kind of picture less acceptable to the true critic of art, who rightly prefers the rough vigour of a sketch in which genius is unembarrassed and careless of detail. But the large brush of the unconscious artist does not belong to Mr. Shorthouse; he works with the finest of brushes, slowly and with elaboration, until the perfection of the part becomes a kind of imperfection. It is this over-elaborateness which makes the book appear tedious to many readers. It is packed too tight with thought; its impact is not direct enough; it is too dialectic; which is the common vice of the religious novel. Yet it has many passages of extraordinary brilliance. The battle of beliefs, and the much greater battle between flesh and spirit, have rarely been described with such masterly analysis. And because it is in parts so restrained as to be almost frigid, when the true passionate fire of vehement emotion begins to burn it burns with surprising intensity. There is a kind of eloquence in Mr. Shorthouse's best writing only comparable with those almost lyric outbursts which we find in Charlotte Brontë's writings— the last pages of " Villette," for example, the description of Rachel's acting, or the description of Eve in " Shirley."

Who can read unmoved the passage which pictures the vision of Christ which comes to Malvolti, the murderer of Inglesant's brother?

He came down the steps—and He came to me. He was not at all like the pictures of the saints, for He was pale and worn and thin, as though the fight were not yet half over—ah, no!— but through this pale and worn look shone infinite power, and undying love, and unquenchable resolve. The crowd fell back on every side, but when He came to me He stopped. "Ah!" he cried, " is it thou? What doest thou here? Knowest thou not that thou art Mine? Thrice Mine—Mine centuries ago, when I hung upon the Cross of Calvary for such as thee— Mine years ago, when thou camest a little child to the font— Mine once again, when forfeit by every law, thou wast given over to Me by one who is a servant and a friend of Mine. Surely I will repay." As He spake a trembling ran through the crowd, as if stirred by the breath of His voice. Nature seemed to rally and to grow beneath Him, and heaven to bend down to touch the earth. A healing sense of help and comfort, like the gentle dew, visited the weary heart. A great cry and shout rose from the crowd, and He passed on; but amid ten thousand times ten thousand I should know Him, and amid the tumult of a universe I should hear the faintest whispering of His voice.

Equally powerful, but in another way, is the memorable picture of the night in the forest with Lauretta, with its fierce temptation. Inglesant realises that a trap has been set for his soul. In the moonlight every leaf of the forest shone with unnatural distinctness; the silence was terrible; it seemed as though Nature herself waited breathlessly to see his ruin.

The sylvan arcades seemed like a painful scene-piece upon a Satanic stage, supernaturally alight to further deeds of sin, and silent and unpeopled, lest the wrong should be interrupted or checked. To Inglesant's excited fancy evil beings thronged its shadowy paths, present to the spiritual sense, though concealed of set purpose from the feeble human sight. . . . The hour was admirably chosen, the place perfectly adapted in every way, as if the result, not of happy chance, but deeply concerted plan. Why then did he hesitate? . . . He had prepared the way for the tempter, and this night even he had disregarded the warning voice and drifted recklessly onward. We walk of our own free will, heated and inflamed by wine, down the flowery path which we have ourselves decorated with garlands, and we murmur because we reach the fatal goal.

The deadly glamour of moonlight faded suddenly; a calm, pale, solemn light settled over the forest . . . a fresh and cooling breeze sprang up and passed through the rustling wood, breathing pureness and life. The day-spring was at hand in the eastern sky.

The rustling breeze was like a whisper from heaven that reminded him of his better self. It would seem hell overdid it; the very stillness for miles around, the almost concerted plan, sent flashing through his brain the remembrance of another house, equally guarded for a like purpose, into which years ago he had forced his way to render help in such a case as this. The long-past life of those days rushed into his mind—the sacramental Sundays, the repeated vows, the light of heaven in the soul, the kneeling forms in Little Gidding Chapel, the face of Mary Collet, the loveliness that blessed the earth where she walked, her death-bed, and her dying words.

He came back into the room. Lauretta lay upon a couch, with rich drapery and cushions, her face buried in her hands. . . . As he entered she raised her face from her hands, and looked at him with a strange, apprehensive, expectant gaze. He remained for a moment silent, his face very pale; then he said, slowly and uncertainly, like a man speaking in a dream:

"The fatal miasma is rising from the plain, Lauretta. This place is safe for neither of us; we had better go on."

The dramatic impressiveness of the scene is evident, but its spiritual force is yet more obvious. And this is the greatest quality of the writer—a certain delicate and subtle power of spiritual apprehension, which has given to his one noticeable book a very high place in literature, and a still higher in the category of religious novels.

Of a wholly different spirit is Mrs. Humphrey Ward. It has been somewhat the fashion of late to decry her, but few will deny that at times she is both a delicate and powerful artist. Considered merely as a novel, " Marcella " is her best book, and the chapters which describe the life and fate of Hurd the poacher are admirable examples of pathos and realism. In these chapters she competes with Kingsley, and excels him. But as a religious novelist her chief claim is based on " Robert Elsmere." Few books have ever attained so great a vogue. " Robert Elsmere " was the subject of innumerable reviews; it was preached about and denounced in hundreds of pulpits; all the forces of the Church were rallied to oppose its conclusions, and for a considerable time little else was talked of among thoughtful people. And yet, what was the dangerous thesis which it expounded? Nothing more than this—the conclusions of the Higher Criticism on the Book of Daniel. Two figures absorb the attention—an atheistic squire, and a peculiarly sensitive and not very robust-minded young clergyman, who appears to think that the entire cause of Christianity depends upon the date at which the Book of Daniel was written. It is an amazing situation. The Higher Critics have travelled a long way since " Robert Elsmere " was written, and so far as we can judge have done very little harm to Christianity. The last shot is fired, and still the citadel remains uninjured; much heavier batteries than those which demolished the faith of Elsmere have been called into action, and yet the popular faith in Christianity shows no diminution.

A later generation is thankful to the critics for labours which have made the Bible more interesting by making it more intelligible; and the common-sense verdict has been reached, that it is of small consequence whether there was one Isaiah or two, as long as the marvellous poetry of the book moves the heart and uplifts the soul; or for what purpose, or when, the Book of Daniel was written, as long as it does undoubtedly expound moral ideas without which nations cannot thrive. Had these conclusions been general when " Robert Elsmere " was written, the book would have attracted no notice.

A much more powerful writer, greater alike as artist, thinker, and poet, is Olive Schreiner.

When her famous " Story of an African Farm " appeared under the *nom de plume* of Ralph Iron, it attracted little attention. The title was not inviting, nor did it give a suggestion of the true range of the book. It is one of the ironies of criticism that the same eyes which saw all manner of deadly elements subversive of Christian faith in " Robert Elsmere " should have been so slow to perceive the much more perilous stuff contained in this book. For here we have an indictment directed, not against certain details in Christian evidence, but against the scheme of the universe itself. The thoughts that move in Olive Schreiner's mind are of a kind that make " a goblin of the sun." Life is for her one long irony ; she might have said with Heine, " The irony of God lies heavy on me." Heine himself never harangued the Almighty with words winged with a bitterer passion of revolt. Scorn of life, of its mingled littleness and cruelty ; scorn of the human mind, of its imbecility and irrational make-believe ; scorn of love, as a passion base and futile ; scorn of all accepted creeds, of all social systems, and above all, and bitterer than all, self-scorn, which mocks the heart capable of adoring ideals it has no strength to follow, of capitulating to creeds it has not power to believe, of hungering for food which it knows is not bread,—this agony of scorn is the chief note in this extraordinary book. She walks among broken lives ; she treads everywhere on broken hearts.

The boy Waldo breaks his heart over a God who gives him no sign. Em breaks her heart over a lover who is false to her. Lyndall herself dies in lonely agony, the victim of some horrible blunder for which no explanation is offered. Why seek to explain what has no explanation? Why interrogate God or Nature? Each is alike dumb, each is but a name. Why set your heart on lofty things? The higher your ideal, the more certain are you to be tortured. Life plays a hundred brutal tricks upon the helpless puppet Man; but life reserves its utmost ingenuity of malice for the best. The more delicate your powers, the more fine and sensitive your nature, the more ruthlessly will life pursue you with malevolence. Waldo's little machine, on which he has expended all his hopes, suddenly trampled under-foot in sheer lust of cruelty, is a parable of life itself; even so, brute force is always happiest when it is trampling on the weak. The only people who can get through life with tolerable equanimity are the thick-skinned people. Tant' Sannie, the Boer woman, does not suffer because she is insensitive. It is only low organisms such as hers that are fitted for such a world as this; manifestly the world is no place for people with brains and ideals and sensitive emotions, who are always striving to lift themselves out of the primal mire where man was first fashioned. So the bitter indictment runs, with an ever-deepening note of agony. Revolt throbs in every page. The phrases are dipped in heart's blood and living flame. No more significant book has ever been addressed to Christian readers; very few books in the last half-century of fiction display anything like the same intense and subtle genius.

Yet the book is not all bitterness; if it were, it would scarcely have attracted its thousands of readers, the great majority of whom have no acquaintance with the theological problems discussed by its author. The secret of its power is that it is a broadly human book, a human document of first-rate importance. It records a spiritual experience, it is one of the great

confessions of literature, and there is no kind of book
so certain of fame as the book which is genuinely confessional.   Here is a young girl, brought up in the immense loneliness of the African veldt; imperfectly
educated, yet touched with the unrest of modern knowledge; full of beautiful idealism, yet forced into contact with a kind of life which is coarse and constricted;
seeking in vain amid a sordid environment for some
soul capable of correspondence with her own; stretch-
ing out her hands to life in a passion of baffled desire;
forced by the loneliness of her position to think her
own thoughts, to follow her own intuitions, to guess
wildly at truth, without the least opportunity to correct her thoughts by the standard of general experience; and in seeking to express the voices of her own
soul, she becomes the spokesman of multitudes of
lonely and unguided lives. For the true problem Olive
Schreiner presents to the world is not a problem of the
intellect, but the problem of the heart.   How paltry
are the questions discussed by Mrs. Ward compared
with the questions discussed by this untutored girl!
And how shallow is the disquiet created in the mind
of Elsmere compared with the fierce agony of soul
which this book reveals! Here, indeed, " the wounded
is the wounding heart." A few people here and there
may be troubled over the authorship of the Book of
Daniel, but here is a much deeper and more catholic
kind of trouble—trouble over the mystery of life, the
anguish of fruitless prayers and ruined hopes, the
abominable pain endured by men and women capable
of lofty things, but helpless in the grip of circumstance; rage against the injustice of life, the eye to
see a path the feet will never tread, the will to do the

great things fate forbids. It is the tragedy of the caged life that beats against the bars, and sinks at last exhausted by its fruitless struggle. And it is a common tragedy· old as humanity itself, and hence the fascination of the book. All who have struggled in vain, all who have had high dreams which have melted in the light of common day, all who have sought the unattainable, all who have stood amid the broken idols of ideals and creeds, find in Olive Schreiner an interpreter, and her confession is the confession of their own baffled wills.

The book also pleads a cause—the cause of woman. It is essentially a woman's protest on behalf of women, intensely felt, and spoken with infinite energy and eloquence. " Pathos, wit, humour, epigram, dialectic; tenderness and scorn; sarcasm, irony, and banter; things original and things indisputable; touches of poetry and pleading, followed instantly by the bitterest invective,—all are here, and all are expressed with masterly ease and vigour." " We bear the world, and we make it," she says of woman.

The souls of little children are marvellously delicate and tender things, and keep for ever the shadow that first falls on them, and that is a mother's, or at best a woman's. There never was a great man who had not a great mother—it is hardly an exaggeration. The first six years of our life make us; all that is added later is veneer; and yet some say, if a woman can cook a dinner, or dress herself well, she has culture enough.

Of all the injustices wrought in the earth, no injustice is so great as that which is constantly visited on woman. The responsibilities of the race are confided

to her, yet she herself is scarcely treated as a responsible creature. A dimple in the cheek, or a finely
turned wrist, will serve her better in the struggle of
life than brains and intellect.

The less a woman has in her head, the lighter she is for
climbing.

It is delightful to be a woman, but every man thanks the
Lord devoutly that he isn't one.

The same note of bitterness is found in the writings
of Mark Rutherford, whose "Autobiography" has
become a classic for readers of discernment, and
whose remarkable stories, "The Revolution in Tan-
ner's Lane" and "Catherine Furze," have won for
themselves an abiding place in modern fiction.

The characteristic note of these books is a certain
sad lucidity of vision. They are the confessions of an
over-sensitive mind, for which the riddle of existence
has proved too hard. They depict the struggles of a
human soul in search of truth and faith; the wish to
believe, at war with the conditions of belief; the
martyrdom of a fine nature, too scrupulously honest
to purchase peace by those conventional casuistries
which rule commonplace minds; the tragedy of a
superior nature, forced by the hand of fate into association with natures either mean or narrow, or dull
and unillumined, which are capable of no response,
and indeed of no vital contact with his own. Mark
Rutherford, with all his capacity for both delicate
thought and passionate emotion, is thrust into the
narrowest of worlds. It is useless to declare his real
thoughts, for no one would understand them. He is
supposed to have been trained for the ministry, in a

college where not a single problem of faith or religion has ever been stated honestly. His instructor was an elderly gentleman, with a pompous degree of Doctor of Divinity—"a gentleman with lightish hair, with a most mellifluous voice, and a most pastoral manner, reading his prim little tracts to us, directed against the shallow infidel. About a dozen of these tracts settled the infidel, and the whole mass of unbelief, from the time of Celsus downwards."

He becomes the minister of a stagnant church in a stagnant little town, where the only person who can afford him the least degree of intellectual comradeship as an atheistic printer. He drifts from this to a yet more stagnant Unitarian chapel; finds that the longer he preaches the less he has to communicate; plunges at last into the vortex of London life, enduring all the indignities of the poor and unconsidered; attaining at last just enough faith in altruistic ideals to attempt a little social work for the outcasts of Drury Lane. This is the brief story of the "Autobiography"; but it is told with such extraordinary intensity, it abounds in such vivid sketches of character, it is so pregnant with emotion, so exquisitely phrased, so rich in subtle analysis of the most secret passions of the heart, at once so frank, subtle, and sympathetic, that it possesses an incomparable charm, and ranks with the highest works of imaginative genius.

"No theory of the world is possible" is the last word of Rutherford's message. With perfect frankness he admits that he has erred in attempting to grapple questions too big for him, and he counsels men against the folly of too exorbitant curiosity. His only positive counsel is the old counsel of stoicism.

There is no condition of life from which a man may not extract some grains of happiness, if he does not retain his fortitude and the readiness to find joy in simple pleasures. Men constantly make the mistake of asking too much of life. They expect ideal affections, and scorn the plain bread of human love. The woman whom Rutherford despised for her intellectual limitations becomes in the end his honoured wife. Some natures, and especially natures of unusual depth and sweetness, never reveal their riches except in the hour of trial. If any justification can be found for what seem the senseless sufferings of human life, it is that these sufferings do liberate the best elements of fine characters. One of the most tender passages in the " Autobiography " describes the process by which a young girl, whom he loved little because he thought her dull and stupid, becomes a perfect nurse to his sick wife:

Faculties unsuspected grew almost to full height in a single day. . . . I remember once going to her cot in the night as she lay asleep, and almost breaking my heart over her with remorse and thankfulness,—remorse, that I, with blundering stupidity, had judged her so superficially; and thankfulness that it had pleased God to present to me so much of His own divinest grace. . . . My love to Marie was love to God Himself as He is—an unrestrained adoration of Him, adoration transfigured into love, because the revelation had clothed itself with a child's form. . . . I had seen the Kingdom of God through a little child.

He who can thus misread his fellow-creature may well ask himself whether he has not also misread God. If no theory of the world is possible, there may nevertheless exist enough of hint and suggestion to encourage hope, or at least to make a wise man diffident in denial.

The proper attitude, the attitude enjoined by the severest exercise of the reason is, " I do not know "; and in this there is an element of hope, now rising and now falling, but always sufficient to prevent that blank despair which we must feel if we consider it as settled that when we lie down under the grass there is an absolute end.

It may be doubted if any writer has ever rendered mental agony with such power as Mark Rutherford. Doubt is for him not a philosophic balancing of probabilities; it is a cruel force which rends his heart in twain. And his doubt goes very much beyond the questioning of this or that assumption of orthodox faith; it arraigns the whole scheme of things. He is unable to discern any sign that the " soul of the universe is just." He uniformly represents the comfortable rewards of life as falling to the unworthy, or at least to persons of featureless character. He pictures person after person, lavishly equipped with fine faculties of thought or affection, either denied the opportunity of their development, or put into a position which makes *these* very faculties a means of torture. He himself is a case in point. There should have been some place in society which he might have occupied with content and honour, but he never found it. He has an immense capacity for friendship, he would gladly have died for a friend; but he finds repeatedly that the ardour is all upon his side, that he calls thrice upon a friend for once that his friend calls on him, that he has stooped even to the point of shame and humiliation to give a love which no one values. He is made to feel that he is a superfluous person, nearly useless to the world. The agony of loneliness is sometimes too great for endurance. Yet something remains to him; for the Gospel of Christ reinterpreted by the conditions of his own life comes back to him with new emphasis and consolation. Christ also was lonely. His Gospel is particularly designed to be the gospel of the lonely and the despised. It has nothing to say to the prosperous whom the world suffices.

The story of Jesus is the story of the poor and the forgotten. He is not the Saviour of the rich and the prosperous, for they want no Saviour . . . but every one who has walked in sadness because his destiny has not fitted his aspiration; every one who, having no opportunity to lift himself out of his narrow town or village circle of acquaintances, has thirsted for something beyond what they can give him; everybody who, with nothing but a dim daily round of mechanical routine before him, would welcome death if it were martyrdom for a cause; every humblest creature, in the obscurity of great cities or remote hamlets, who silently does his or her daily duty without recognition,—all these turn to Jesus and find themselves in Him. . . . There is no Saviour for us like the hero who has passed triumphantly through the distress which troubles us. Salvation is the spectacle of a victory of another over foes like our own.

It may be objected that reflections of this kind are better suited to the essay than to the novel, and it must be admitted that in the strict sense of the term the " Autobiography " is doubtful fiction. Much of it is but thinly disguised personal confession; perhaps, if the truth were known, there is not a single invented incident in the entire book. Yet the hand of the creative artist is visible in every line. Whether the people he pictures are idealised types or portraits of known persons—and perhaps they are something of each—it is certain that they are rendered with extraordinary vividness.

No extract, and no series of extracts, can do justice to the writings of Mark Rutherford. They have qualities which give them a place apart in later literature. He speaks as one who has greatly suffered, and hence he speaks as no other can to the suffering heart. He is the interpreter of inarticulate natures. The actual message which he has to deliver may be brief, but it is vital because it has been tested and sanctified by experience. He writes also with a curious pregnancy of phrase. His style is austere and simple, shorn of all redundancy, of all deliberate eloquence or laboured novelty, yet it is the most suggestive of styles. It is a triumph of severity and compression. Those who read his books once find themselves returning to them again and again; they hold the mind with an incomparable charm; they quicken thought, they reveal the deep things of life, and, in spite of their quiet rejection of orthodox faith, they have a strange power of creating that larger faith which is based, not on dogma, but on the universal instincts of humanity. Other writers of religious fiction represent certain phases of thought and feeling peculiar to their time; Mark Rutherford deals with the great secular thoughts of humanity. Sincere and accomplished as a writer like Mrs. Humphrey Ward may be in the examination of religious problems, yet her message seems shallow and almost insincere in comparison with the message of Mark Rutherford. For here is authentic suffering—here is spiritual tragedy which goes to the very roots of life; and hence the influence which Mark Rutherford exercises over minds that are sympathetic with him is unique. It is perhaps more perilous to forecast the future of books than of nations; but it would not be surprising if the writings of Mark Rutherford, or at least his " Autobiography," should take rank with the famous classics and the imperishable treasures of English literature.

XIX

AMERICAN NOVELISTS

Nathaniel Hawthorne, 1804-1864.   Edgar Allan Poe, 1809-1849.

THE history of American fiction is brief, as is natural in the case of a people whose own history is brief.   In the early days of a great people there is little room for the development of those arts which minister to the æsthetic and the imaginative faculties.   The tasks of practical and constructive civilisation must needs be the first employment of a pioneer nation.   The conquest of the wilderness, the building and ordering of cities, the gradual driving of the wedge of light into the darkness of the aboriginal waste, the development of the land and its resources, the pushing on of the railroad, the provision for the elementary needs of life, all the vast epic of labor, all the absorbing romance of commerce—these are the first chapters in the history of any new civilisation.   Not until wealth is accumulated and leisure is achieved can literature flourish.   And the last form of literature to arise is fiction.   A kind of life which in itself is fiercely romantic feels no need of the romance of the pen.   It is only when a nation begins to recall and recollect its past that there is room for the author whose work is in essence a criticism of life.

Nevertheless, America has produced at least two writers who deserve to rank with the great masters and makers of fiction. The first of these is Nathaniel Hawthorne. Hawthorne's life was lived at a period when the throes of initial civilisation were over in that portion of America in which his lot was cast. The civilisation of New England had been accomplished. It was possible to draw breath and to gain a coign of vantage from which sober perspective was attained. The story of the past was full of suggestion to a philosophic mind. It abounded in splendid episodes of valour and heroism; it was dominated by austere ideals of duty; it was the story of the making of manhood, under the plastic stress of difficulties and vicissitudes scarcely paralleled in the history of any people. Here was the material to hand for a great artist, a great philosopher, and Hawthorne was both. He had a mind of singular depth, which brooded much over the secrets of personality. The men who founded New England were themselves fascinated by the problems of philosophy and they transmitted the tendency. Nothing in the heroic details of their lives seemed to them so important as the history of their spiritual emotions, their relation to the unseen world and the problem of their eternal destiny. They retained through generations the characteristics of the Puritan movement which begot them. Stern and hard, and unimaginative as they appeared, yet each thrilled to the romance of the infinite. They were conscious of vibrations of light from far-off worlds. They moved in the constant awe of a divine tribunal, dimly seen, but acutely realised in every fibre of their consciousness.

Hawthorne inherited this temperament to the full. But he added to it something that was rare in the New England temperament, something indeed that was historically hostile to it, the gift of the artist, who is so far detached from life that he can analyse, review, and judge it. He could understand the past and yet be sceptical of its conclusions. He sympathised, but he also criticised. This painful quality of scepticism is vital to the artist; not till doubt dissolves the hardness of tradition is any real criticism of life possible. But the more necessary is the interpretive sympathy, which comprehends modes of life and thought which the conscience no longer regards as authoritative. Hawthorne possessed all these characteristics, and it is in virtue of them that he became the greatest writer of fiction whom America has produced.

Reference has already been made to Hawthorne's greatest work "The Scarlet Letter." It is this book upon which his fame as a writer of fiction must rest. For to be ranked with the makers of fiction something more is needed than high artistic efficiency: the maker of fiction is he whose work is both perfect and original. Hawthorne triumphs completely under this last. There is much in his other books that any writer might have been proud to produce. He has written nothing that does not bear the marks of long, and often profound meditation. The reader of his "Note Book" will not need to be informed how sedulously Hawthorne tabulated ideas, suggestions of thought, traits of character, passing flashes of intuition into human motive and conduct. His style also is distinctive, though often laboured. He is at all times a master of felicitous phrase. But chief among all his qualities and characteristics is a certain awful sombreness of imagination. His mind brooded perpetually over the more tragic and austere aspects of human life. Of vivacity, that happy nimbleness and levity of thought, which is so characteristic of the modern American, he reveals no trace. He belonged to an older world. His eye scans not the surface but the depth and issue of things. In his milder moods he can observe life with a kind of faint geniality, but such moods are infrequent. His real concern is always with the soul. His whole temper is introspective. Hence his sketches of manners, while truly observed and finished with that exquisite art which never failed him, always impress us as laboured. He does the thing well, but it is not the thing that he was born to do. How different is the movement of his genius when he approaches the intricacies and subtleties of the soul. Here his full power is revealed. He fascinates us because he is fascinated himself. He becomes a wizard, a magician before whose touch the inmost doors of personality fly open. The sombre brooding mind, the mind of the philosophic thinker, deeply tinged with the serious thinkings of a long race of men and women, to whom the affairs of the soul were the only real concerns of life, here finds its most adequate and therefore its most characteristic expression.

In the " Scarlet Letter " we have Hawthorne's peculiar genius in its ripest manifestation. Perhaps the most remarkable characteristic of the story is the artistic restraint which characterises it. Here is a story which in weak hands might easily have become melodramatic, and in careless hands offensive to the moral sense. The fineness of Hawthorne's artistic gift saves him from the first error and the Puritan austerity of his temperament from the second. In his hands the story has all the sombre dignity of Greek drama. Two sinful creatures confront us, but while their sin is never veiled, it never alienates our sympathy. We understand them too well to despise them. The dangerous proverb that to know all is to forgive all, finds some degree of justification as we contemplate the nature and the stages of their misdoing. No apology for their sin is hinted at or offered: on the contrary it bears upon it from the first its predestined condemnation. If we contrast the similar episode of Arthur Donnethorne and Hetty Sorrel we are at once aware of the enormous gulf that yawns between a spiritual and a scientific estimate of human life. For George Eliot, in spite of a temperament essentially moral and even religious, sees but dimly in the realm of the spiritual. On the contrary, Hawthorne's genius is essentially spiritual. George Eliot is content to paint outward consequence; Hawthorne is concerned with the much more awful tragedy of inward defilement. George Eliot sees a moral problem; Hawthorne a spiritual. The thing that George Eliot bids us see is weakness; a weak man who is the prey of evil passion, and a weak girl who is the victim of idle vanity. Let them be reprobated, but let them also be pitied: it is so that Nature in her inscrutable irony has fashioned them by heredity and environment. But simply because Hawthorne is the child of an austere Puritanism, he treats the whole problem from a very different standpoint. Mistress Prynne is not a weak woman. She is cast in a mould of antique breadth and dignity. She is radically a pure woman, not liable to the seductions of petty vanity or the gusts of thoughtless passion. And, again, while the minister is weak of will, yet he also has all the spiritual instincts in their fullest force. This is a putting of the tragedy of passion remarkable alike in its breadth and daring. The difference in the method of Hawthorne's statement of the most ancient of all problems and George Eliot's is this: that whereas George Eliot, in common with most novelists, choose weak natures to illustrate a common frailty, Hawthorne chooses strong and dignified natures, and in doing this he raises the austere theme to the height of pure and great drama.

It is this feature of the book that fixes it so indelibly upon the mind and makes it so alarming. We can read of Hetty Sorrel's bitter folly without a pang of self fear. " It is not so with us and cannot be," we say. We can contemplate as David did the far-off sin with feelings in which pity and scorn and anger are in turn predominant, but our withers are unwrung. But Hawthorne comes to us with the terrible allocution " Thou art the man." In showing us the corruption of the good and the frailty of the strong he makes us tremble for ourselves. Terror seizes upon us as we read—a terror that shakes the spirit. For Hawthorne is more than a novelist depicting an event, he is a prophet who seizes on the reins of the soul. The summed up spiritualities of a long Puritan ancestry speak in him, and they speak to the deepest soul of man.

" The Scarlet Letter " has for its dominant motive expiation—that motive which is the source of so much that is great and moving in Greek tragedy. Yet with that firmness of touch, that undeviating perception of inexorable fate which characterises all great tragedy, there is mingled another element rare in any tragedy, which may be best described as spiritual subtlety. We are made to feel that the " Scarlet Letter " is not so much embroidered on the dress of Hester Prynne as scorched upon her heart. In like manner, although no emblem of shame burns upon the heart of the minister, we know that his shame consumes him, and the suffering thus endured by slow degrees becomes noble because it is purgatorial. In moral stature these two guilty persons tower far above their accusers and their judges. They at least know the meaning of love, which is a knowledge never attained by the narrow, vindictive natures that surround them. The bitter cruelty of the wronged husband is a worse sin than that committed against him by the minister whom he hates. In making this clear, Hawthorne breaks with the Hebraic ideal which is the root of Puritanism, and expresses the most characteristic truth of Christianity. For of all the sayings of our Lord none are so startling, and indeed so revolutionary as these two : that she who loves much is forgiven much and that he who hates his brother, even upon what seems a just cause, is in danger of hell-fire. Such axioms are so far above all common conceptions of morality that even moral thinkers find it safer to forget them. He alone is fitted so much as to contemplate them who surveys life from a great height of purity. For to purity alone is given the insight which understands guilt. Hawthorne has that understanding—the understanding which is insight. Thus, in treating a theme often enough treated by novelists and dramatists, Hawthorne has displayed a spiritual delicacy altogether unrivalled, and without diminishing the element of drama has carried the whole theme into the difficult realm of spiritual allegory.

Judged from whatever standpoint we may choose to accept, " The Scarlet Letter " is a masterpiece. In style, in method, in spiritual force, it is a great book and it remains not only the noblest achievement of American literature, but ranks with the masterpieces of universal literature. In many of the qualities common among great novelists Hawthorne was deficient. He is often more of an essayist than a novelist. His mind is not fecund, not rapid; the careless ease of the great improvisor is unknown to him. He struggles for expression; his ideas come to birth by severe throes. He is too exigent a critic of himself to abandon his mind to the force of his ideas. That full, wide, effortless sweep of power found in Scott, and Balzac, and the Brontës, is not his; excellent as are all his books, yet they often fail to please or fascinate: the mind wearies of an excellence that is technical. But in " The Scarlet Letter " his entire power works freely, without let or hindrance. His genius soars at last untrammelled, like a pure flame long repressed. No happier fate can happen to an artist than to find his genius and his task so exquisitely adjusted that the result is perfect. It may happen but once in a long career, yet the true artist knows that on this one occasion his whole career stands justified; it was for this hour that he was born and by its record he must live. To Hawthorne in the course of a long literary career there came this one perfect moment, this consummate hour. " The Scarlet Letter " is the book that he was born to write, for no other could have written it; and it is the permanent memorial of a rare and delicate genius.

The second great name in American fiction is Edgar Allan Poe. He shares with Hawthorne but one quality, a taste for the occult. In every other respect he is totally dissimilar. He knew little of the element of restraint either in his art or in his life. His life was woefully misdirected. In his art he cannot be acquitted of the charge of charlatanism. He was vain, violent, and without conscience. His poetry, genuine as it is, is full of tricks and mannerisms, and he is not above exposing the trickiness of his method when it pleases him to do so. But with all his faults and limitations he was a man of supreme literary ability and a great artist. The power that he possessed was limited, but it was genuine and of rare quality. He was incapable of producing the deliberate and sustained novel: but in the art which produces the short story he was a master. His genius is fugitive, brilliant, brief in its expression, but nevertheless it is genius of a kind unique, separate, and astonishing.

Few men have united in the same degree analytical acumen with imaginative force. From the first faculty sprang a series of stories which deal with the mysteries of crime, of which the " Murder in the Rue Morgue " is the outstanding example. Later generations which have marvelled over the method of Sherlock Holmes will find that Poe used precisely the same method in his stories which deal with crime and the wiles of criminals. The similarity is so close that it cannot be accidental. We have the same acute observation of trifles, the same deductions based on circumstances in themselves unnoticeable, the same piecing together of evidence, until what seems an insoluble enigma becomes a mathematical demonstration. But Poe is at all times superior to the author of Sherlock Holmes. He deals with deeper motives, his psychological skill is more subtle, and the secret of his puzzle is more carefully concealed. "The Gold Bug" is probably an example of the finest cryptogram in literature. Many writers have used a similar motive, including Stevenson in his "Treasure Island," but none has displayed so complete a mastery of means. There is something almost diabolic in the cleverness of Poe in this kind of a story. The detective story may be but a poor form of art, but it undoubtedly has great fascination for the reader; and, if it is to be truly successful, requires singular gifts of penetration and analysis in the author. Poe's gift of analysis enabled him to lift what is radically a poor form of art into superb excellence. He invested the detective story with the dignity which belongs to the display of real thought, and the depiction of real tragedy. In this respect he must be ranked with the masters of fiction.

But Poe possessed another kind of power even more remarkable, viz., an extraordinary vividness of imagination. That his imagination was disordered and radically diseased few can doubt. He revels in horrors, he loves the monstrous, the deformed, the abnormal: the world as he sees it is the phantasmagoria of a drunkard's appalling dreams. But in spite of much that is grotesque and repulsive, Poe compels our admiration by the extraordinary force of his imagination. By his mere use of words in many instances he produces on the mind a sense of fear, of haunted twilight, of immeasurable melancholy. The " Fall of the

House of Usher " is such an instance. Put into bald prose there is no story and nothing to tell, but Poe uses words as music is used in the interpretation of emotion. He strikes a long chord which reverberates through the soul: produces wailing notes that thrill us with the premonition of disaster: a sombre gloom fills the mind; with nothing real, nothing tangible before us, we shiver as though a spectre touched us; and this reverberant horror grows with every new phrase, till utter eclipse overwhelms us and the blood chills in the veins. How is it done? We can only reply by a kind of magic. It is as though the Mephistopheles, who a moment ago laid bare the realities of this gross life with sneering cleverness, now waves a wizard's wand, grows pale with occult ecstasy, soars in thin flame, slowly withdraws the forbidden curtain of destiny and shows us in wavering awful outlines the hooded forms that haunt the outer darkness of a demon world. Balzac has endeavoured to produce this effect, but with scant success. Stevenson has succeeded in such a story as " Thrawn Janet." But Poe alone is a master of horror, the true wizard who alone knows this entire secret of literary occultism.

No writer in English literature has dealt so entirely with the more fugitive and phantasmal forms of the imagination. In his best tales he inspires a sort of breathless terror. But what is more remarkable is that in the realm of the wildest fantasy the coolness of his logical faculty is undisturbed. He can give the aspect of complete reality to things that in themselves are incredible and impossible. An excellent example of this power is in the story which he calls " A Descent into the Maelstrom."

Manifestly no such adventure could have happened. But Poe, by the calm matter-of-fact way in which he assumes the possibility of the adventure, at once compels attention, and sustains it. In this respect he resembles Defoe, with whom he has no other gift in common. He writes both as a mathematician and a dreamer: and this not alternately, but with a complete fusion of qualities which seem not only far apart, but antagonistic. And in all his writings there is a most careful attention to style. He is a master of phrase, using words with a scholarly attention to the nicety of their significance and a poet's perception of their harmonies. The result is a series of stories which have become classical. They have survived the test of time and are probably more widely known and read to-day than at any period since their production. Their unique excellence is proved by the fact that while they have had many rivals, they are still unrivalled. Both as poet and prose writer Poe still stands in the first rank of imaginative writers, and is one of the few men of creative genius in American literature.

In that literature many other writers will be found of great excellence, but upon the whole Hawthorne and Poe are the only writers whose contributions to fiction have unique value and distinction. No reader of intelligence will forget the graceful work of Washington Irving, and the wonderful popular gift of Harriet Beecher Stowe. The native genius of Mrs. Stowe is quite extraordinary, and had her artistic training been equal to her natural gift, she might have claimed a place among the greatest writers. Among the more recent writers none have produced work of greater excellence than W. D. Howells. A grateful memory will also recall the name of Mark Twain, the unrivalled master of a form of humour essentially of the New World; of Bret Harte, whose earlier stories have real pathos and dramatic instinct; and Oliver Wendell Holmes, whose genial philosophy has been a source of pleasure to multitudes of readers.

During the last decade, American fiction has made great strides. It is significant that the American publisher no longer turns to England to discover authors whose books will captivate the public. American writers are rapidly arising who perceive the romance of their own country and find in the daily life of their own people ample material for the purposes of fiction. Such a writer as the late Frank Norris, whose early death was a national disaster, shows an epic power in dealing with the world of commerce, which had in it the promise of assured greatness; and the path which he took will no doubt be followed by many others. In no country are the materials for a new school of fiction more abundant. Among no people is any new form of genius more warmly welcomed, or generously rewarded. America has not yet produced a novelist comparable in gift and scope of power with Meredith or Hardy; yet it may well happen that the next great master of fiction may arise in America, as more and more the leisure won by industrial success affords opportunity for that life of culture which is the true goal of all civilised endeavour.

XX

CONCLUDING SURVEY

IN the preceding chapters we have traced the growth and development of the English novel in the examples of its greatest masters. Men and women of genius, guided by their own authoritative impulses, have found in prose fiction a means of expression for their religious, philosophic, and social beliefs—for their gaiety, fancy, and humour—for their powers of observation and reflection; and each in turn has contributed some enduring element of personality or art to the novel. The evolutionary principle in this long history is not always apparent. It is only when we measure the distance traversed that we are conscious of its influence. Some "plastic stress," working upon individual genius, has exercised compulsion and restraint, has moulded thought and form. The great writer is the creature of taste as well as its creator. His greatness is reached through a superior sensitiveness to the conditions of his time. Writing to fulfil the necessities of his own thought and emotion, he finds that he has expressed with more or less fulness the characteristics of his age. In the degree that a writer does this, his work is famous, and witnesses to the evolutionary principle.

Some general reflections upon the histories and achievements discussed in the foregoing pages may now be permitted.

First of all, there will doubtless exist on the part of many readers a desire to revise or dispute some of the verdicts arrived at. Imaginative literature differs from every other form of literature in one important feature —viz., that it affords an opportunity for transient distinction, which contains no guarantee of settled fame. It has often been said, and with a considerable measure of truth, that every novelist of real parts has it in him to write one great novel. What this means is, that there is usually some particular province of life known to a novelist with surprising accuracy, and that in writing on such a theme he writes impressively. There are things which he himself has suffered and endured —various poignant emotions of joy or sorrow, conflicts of mind and will, doubts in search of truth, and rebuffs in search of fortune; and even a mediocre writer, writing upon things deeply felt, is often able to produce a book which attracts universal attention among his contemporaries. Every season brings us some novel which achieves distinction. It is read, discussed, admired, and enthusiastic critics predict a new Thackeray or Dickens. Such a book as Du Maurier's "Trilby" is a case in point. The author strikes a vein of observation which is fresh and original—he pictures something he knows; and the result is that his work receives an applause which even a Thackeray or a Dickens would have regarded as unstinted. Later on it becomes clear that the writer has said all he had to say in his first book. He has packed it with his ripest experience of men and things. He has written his own autobiography, and in the nature of things he cannot write it twice. His book is really fine, but it is a *tour de force*. It soon becomes evident that he has not the true creative instinct of the great artist—he has not his fecundity, nor his variety, nor his staying power. A history of fiction, written at the time when his star was paramount, could not ignore him; but in the calm mood of wider retrospect his name is received in silence, not because he has not done well, but because his total achievement is slight.

The history of fiction is full of personal triumphs of this order. It would be possible to mention a score of books by forgotten authors, each of which in its kind may be compared favourably with single works of the great masters. The critics who praised them were not wholly wrong in their judgment; at least, they were not wrong after the fashion of the older critics, who quite honestly put Montgomery's " Satan " in comparison with the poems of Shelley, to the indignant dispraise of the latter. As long as the art of fiction endures there will appear from time to time really admirable and brilliant books which achieve a personal triumph. They well deserve their triumph, because they are the products of intimate experience, motive, and observation.

But in the long run the fame of a novelist must rest upon much broader foundations, if it is to endure. He must be able to deal adequately, not with a phase of life, but with life in many phases. He must draw upon other treasures than those of autobiography. He must have the power of understanding, by imaginative sympathy, lives totally unlike his own, and of creating characters of which his own personal experience gives him no clue. In other words, he must be an artist, seeing the whole of life as much as it is given to man to see it, bringing to his task an instinct no doubt sharpened by experience, but going much beyond experience, into the realms where genius alone can penetrate by the force of its intuitions.

It is by such a test, if we have the skill to apply it, that we can distinguish between what is ephemeral and what enduring, even in contemporary fiction. An author writes a book which is unmistakably a transcript of experience. Some little known part of the world, India, Malay, or even a Scotch glen, is presented to us with vivid force. Types of character, hitherto unknown to us, are drawn with a truth which we feel is vital. We are sure that the writer is telling us what he himself has felt and seen, and we instantly hail him as a great novelist. But the very fact that he does so unmistakably tell us what he himself has felt and seen should put us on our guard. "Well and good," we should say; "he has shown himself a graphic artist—is he also a creative artist?" The thing seen counts for much less than the thing imagined. Any man of highly sensitive powers of observation can describe the things seen; but it needs a much rarer order of mind to describe the things imagined. Kipling has seen his Mulvaney and his Ortheris, but Shakespeare never saw Hamlet, nor Dickens Mrs. Gamp, nor Thackeray Becky Sharp. The former are photographs, the latter portraits. It is not the visual eye, however keen, that can discover Hamlet, or Mrs. Gamp, or Becky Sharp; they are creatures of the imagination, built up, indeed, from much scattered material, but combined by creative art into types of universal life.

When a novelist is accused of something which is improbable or incredible in his story, he usually retorts that he has only described life as he has seen it. The plea appears good, but it is really invalid, because this is the very thing that he should not do. Stevenson's Captain Wicks, in " The Wrecker," puts this point with rare conciseness, when he replies, to Carthew, who pleads that the log-book of *The Flying Scud* is "real life." " So it is; and what better are we for that, if it don't look so?"—thus " sounding unwonted depths of art criticism." It is not enough to describe life as it is—the novelist must make it look like life. The newspaper correspondent describes real life in the slum or on the battlefield, and we are satisfied with his work so long as it is accurate and honest. But we demand of the artist something more—he must not only see life as it is, but he must select and combine from life the elements which are capable of artistic expression. Turner saw landscapes with as true an eye as man ever had, and his thousands of pencil sketches show that he was the most conscientious and delicate of draughtsmen. But Turner's great fame does not rest on draughtsmanship. The landscapes he painted were not the landscapes he saw; they were Nature interpreted through his own wonderful artistic sense. So with the novelist; if he does no more than describe what he has seen he is but a draughtsman; to become an artist he must select and combine the materials won by observation into ideal forms which nevertheless look like life. All art is after all a form of illusion. The statue simulates the living form, the canvas simulates the sunset and the movements of the sea and clouds; the one point with which the onlooker is concerned is that the illusion shall be perfect. The supreme test of the novelist is whether he makes his illusion perfect. These are simple distinctions, but they are absolute in the study of art, whether of the brush or of the pen; and by their application to the work of a novelist we can determine with indisputable justice his real rank in the hierarchies of fiction.

It is because the true novel is a work of art that it is never likely to lose its power over the human mind. It may have its periods of decay, as all arts have; it will also have its resurrections into new forms. The fear has been constantly expressed that fiction is bound to decline through mere staleness or dearth of material. All the love-stories have been told; every possible situation in which lovers find themselves has been exhausted, and all the combinations of plot possible to human ingenuity have long since been appropriated. The modern novelist comes to a field not only reaped, but gleaned. What can he attempt to do which has not been already done, and superbly done, by the great masters of his craft? No doubt it is much more difficult to write a great novel to-day than a century ago, when an immense wealth of unused material awaited the imaginative writer. Yet there is no cause for despair. The old stories become fresh, the trite and worn situations become original, when they are passed through the alembic of creative genius. The great artist makes all things new. Life, after all, contains very few dramatic situations. They consist of events set in motion by the eternal forces of love, jealousy, crime, passion, sorrow, heroism, death. They have been utilised over and over again in every literature of the world. If, in his attempt to depict the constant play of these primal forces upon human char-

acter and destiny, the novelist complains of poverty
of theme, he may be assured that the poverty is not
in the theme, but in himself. Let him bring to his
task the genius of the artist, and although the story
he tells may be as old as Homer or Euripides, it will
nevertheless strike the chord of universal interest. He
may plagiarise freely from his predecessors; no one
will count that plagiarism which transmutes old material into new forms. The palette of the painter
holds no more primary colours to-day than it held in
the day of Titian; the seven notes of music are the
same as when Handel used them; yet both colour and
music are still capable of indeterminable combinations.
The old themes and situations are the primary colours
and the fundamental notes of the novelist; they are
his to combine and to treat as he will. Given a Rembrandt, there is a new art; given a Wagner, there is a
new music; and when the great novelist brings to his
task the true creative instinct, there is the same freshness of conception which makes Rembrandt great in
spite of Titian, and Wagner, in spite of Handel.

In one respect the modern novel shows a great advance on its predecessors—viz., in its technical perfection. Its art may be thin and poor, but its craftsmanship is excellent. The story is usually told with
vivacity and clearness, the plot is skilfully contrived,
the interest is sustained, and the writing often has a
real grace of style. The average of sound literary
craftsmanship is to-day much higher than it ever was.
If we take at random any half-dozen novels of the
present season and compare them with the novels
produced by writers not of the first rank fifty years
ago, we are struck at once by the great advance in

technique. It is scarcely an exaggeration to say that every season there is published one or more novels which would have made a great reputation fifty years go. The average of good craftsmanship in fiction has risen in the ratio of increased literary perception and education among the people. It is much more difficult to reach the front in any profession to-day than fifty years ago, because the number of competent competitors is much larger. In fiction the struggle of existence is keener than in any other form of literature; and the chief fruit of this struggle is, that the competitors have learned the value of competent equipment, they have studied methods, and consequently they are able to produce books which reach a very high level of technical excellence.

But it must not be forgotten that the best technique is a poor substitute for creative genius. The comparison between draughtsmanship and art may once more serve us. There were never so many people in the world who can draw accurately as to-day, and never so few great artists. Any one who examines the works of a thoroughly good art school will be astonished at their general excellence, but he will also feel their want of initiative. We are in much the same position in respect of fiction. We have to say as Reynolds said of a picture which had every quality but genius, " It has not THAT! " It is the large touch, the profound emotion, the creative power, which is lacking. The modern novel tends too much to become the expanded anecdote. The novelist carves cherry-stones—exquisitely, no doubt, but the total result is small. He lights up a corner of existence with flashing brilliance, but he has no eye for the harmonious mass, the large groupings of life. The very insistence on technique narrows him. While he polishes his sentences and contrives the ingenious convolutions of his plot, the broad effects of tone escape him. We may have much to say against a superbly careless writer like Scott, who gave little thought to technique; nevertheless, Scott has THAT—the wide sweep of creative power. Technical excellence is after all only a minor morality in art, and it becomes less a gain than a peril when its value is exaggerated at the expense of creative genius. It then becomes a powerful element in the discouragement of genius, and the triumph of mediocrity.

Much would be gained for the novel of the future by a return to broad fundamental themes. It is true that a great theme can be adequately treated only by a great artist, but he who boldly attacks a great theme at least gives himself the chance of being great. The influence of Flaubert and other writers of his school upon English fiction has not been wholesome, considered only as an influence on art. The search for expression, the passion for meticulous felicity of phrase, the careful, exacting mosaic work of the phrase-maker, tend to barrenness of invention and imagination. Flaubert himself escapes the peril because he was a great man; but his disciples, not being all of them great men, have succumbed to it. It cannot be too strongly insisted that no grace of expression can serve as a substitute for wealth of conception. The greatest novels are uniformly those which deal with broad and simple themes. Laborious phrase-making is neither needed nor present in these novels. They move easily and swiftly; it is their matter which fascinates the mind rather than their form; they attract and hold us, not by virtue of style, though this may be present in abundance, but by the influence they exert upon our sympathies and our emotions. Their subject-matter is of relative indifference. Their scene may be Fagin's kitchen or Gaunt House. The people described may be rascals or heroes. The great point is that, whatever they are, they are swayed by elemental motives, and, wherever they act, the stage is life. The expanded anecdote, the brief episode of passion or of intrigue, cannot compete with these broad and living dramas. They amuse the idle hour of the idle reader, but they reach neither his heart nor his intellect. He who would paint life with fulness, and in doing it achieve the fame that endures when the impertinence of mere notoriety is forgotten, must set himself deliberately to the treatment of the great and trite themes of which mankind never tires, because mankind understands them and delights in them.

The greatest peril of the modern novelist lies in the relative ease with which popularity is won, and the kind of demand made upon his talent by this popularity. No man is so often a victim of what Kipling has called "the damnation of the cheque-book." The moment his work is sought for the temptation to overwrite himself assails him, and in his feverish effort to meet the extravagant demand made upon him it is inevitable that the quality of his work must deteriorate. Another form of the same temptation is the demand of the multitude for the constant repetition of any form of art which has pleased them. Like the painter who must needs go on reproducing variations of a theme which has caught the passing taste, if he is to retain his popularity, so the novelist must stick to the vein in which his first success is won. The public resents versatility either in the artist or the novelist. The result is thoroughly bad for art. The free movement of genius is arrested. The novelist writes, not to please himself, not to fulfil his own ideals, but to please his public. He becomes stereotyped both in theme and method. Editors of journals, who naturally think more of the condition of the market than of the claims of art, discourage the novelist when he seeks to strike out a new path for himself. He who has written a detective story must go on writing detective stories to the end of his days, or run the risk of losing his public; for is it not only fair that the public who pay the piper should also call the tune? No real progress in English fiction can be anticipated while these conditions prevail. There is but one rule of life possible to the man of genius who seeks the full development of his powers: he must write to please himself; he must care more for the perfection of his art than for its rewards; he must live the self-respecting life of the artist, unseduced by the glitter of social ambitions; he must realise that he is the appointed teacher of the public, and he must not become its slave. The man who acts thus rarely fails to come to his own, if he have the patience to persevere. He who acts otherwise may gain the praise and reward of a day, but he travels to oblivion.

Should prose fiction be included in the highest category of the literary art? Any doubt on such a subject probably arises from the ease with which a certain skill in fiction may be attained by writers not remarkable for any high qualities of intellect. With nothing to teach, with no philosophy to unfold, with no extensive knowledge of life, and often with an education both narrow and defective, it is, nevertheless, possible for men and women to write novels which attract attention and secure popularity. But such examples are misleading. Between the productions of such writers and the works of a Meredith or a Hardy there is the kind of difference which exists between the smooth and even verse of the minor bard and the poetry of Shelley, the clever dialogue of the modern playwright and the drama of Shakespeare. A great artist can make a great thing of any form of art. Prose fiction, in the hands of its greatest masters, has proved itself a vehicle for the expression of the most serious thoughts, the noblest visions, the profoundest philosophic teachings which genius can communicate to the world. It has displaced the drama; it is not impossible that it may in time displace poetry too, as the most popular means of instructing man through the imagination. It has great advantages over poetry as a means of expression—a wider canvas, a more catholic choice of material, and freedom from the bondage of rhythm. Already we see that many persons gifted with some power of feeling and imagination, who in an earlier age would have been content to publish verse, now express their ideas in fiction. It seems not unlikely that poetry will decay in the ratio that fiction advances. It seems yet more likely that the time will come when every man who has anything to say on art or science, on religion or sociology, will seek to say it in fiction. These tendencies will inevitably produce a more general perception of fiction as a serious form of literature. We shall regard it less as a means of amusement than of instruction. Through the novel new ideas will be disseminated and new solutions of life expounded. Its influence will thus steadily increase; and the more seriously it is accepted as a high form of art, the greater will be the care taken to perfect its form and develop its scope.

Nevertheless, we should remember that the prime aim of all art is to please. This may serve as a consoling axiom for the multitude of novelists who have no creed to impart and no philosophic message to unfold. He has not written in vain who is content merely to lighten the tedium of life with a cheerful wit, to stimulate the fancy, to gild the passing hour, to provide a refuge for the weary mind, to summon to his mimic stage those who need some pleasurable and brief distraction from monotonous and anxious thoughts.

Melancholy seizes on the mind in the recollection of the mass of excellent and faithful work done by novelists whose names are now totally forgotten. If no fame is reached so easily as that of the novelist, none withers so quickly. Books that once were read by every one are now read by no one; and in that immense grave of buried reputations, where the novelists and novels of other generations lie, it is difficult to disinter the merest evidence of their existence. Let it be remembered that these graves of an army nevertheless cover many strong and noble hearts that wrought well according to their measure. They served their own generation; they spoke in living accents once; and, in communicating some element of pleasure to their own generation, they did the one task possible to them, and they helped forward the art they loved. Of fiction, as of poetry, it may be said, in Wordsworth's pregnant phrase, that its true mission is "to console the afflicted; to add sunshine to daylight by making the happy happier; to teach the young and gracious of every age to see, to think and feel, and therefore to become more actively and sincerely virtuous."

As the atmosphere of the world grows greyer and more sombre above the anxious stress of modern life, he who can relieve the stress, if only for a moment, by taking men out of themselves into some peopled realm of fancy, he who can attract the lonely and the brooding eye from self-contemplation to the spectacle of other lives even though they be imaginary, he who can add to the hard prosaic daylight of commonplace existence one brief shaft of sunlight by his own gift of gaiety or humour, has a work to perform of incomparable value to his race, in the right performance of which is exceeding great reward. The work of the imaginative writer, whether poet, dramatist, or novelist, is always necessary to the growth of the finer qualities of the human mind; and it is more than ever necessary in our age as a relief from grinding labour, as a sedative to nerves overstrung in material pursuits, as a means of quickening those finer sympathies which materialism represses; and it is because the novel thus answers an increasing need in modern life that we judge its destiny to be secure and immeasurable.

By NORMAN DUNCAN

Doctor Luke ^{of} *The* *Labrador*

12mo, Cloth, $1.50.

N. Y. Evening Post: "Mr. Duncan is deserving of much praise for this, his first novel. . . . In his descriptive passages Mr. Duncan is sincere to the smallest detail. His characters are painted in with bold, wide strokes. . . . Unlike most first novels, 'Dr. Luke' waxes stronger as it progresses."

Henry van Dyke: "It is a real book, founded on truth and lighted with imagination, well worth reading and remembering."

Review of Reviews: "Mr. Duncan has added a new province to the realm of literature. This strong, beautiful love story moves with a distinctive rhythm that is as fresh as it is new. One of the season's two or three best books."

Hamilton W. Mabie, in the Ladies' Home Journal: "Full of incidents, dramatically told, of the heroism and romance of humble life; strong, tender, pathetic; one of the most wholesome stories of the season."

Current Literature: "Beyond a peradventure, ranks as one of the most remarkable novels issued in 1904. Stands out so prominently in the year's fiction that there is little likelihood of its being overshadowed."

London Punch: "Since Thackeray wrote the last word of 'Colonel Newcome,' nothing finer has been written than the parting scene where Skipper Tommy Lovejoy, the rugged old fisherman, answers the last call."

Saturday Evening Post: "There is enough power in this little volume to magnetize a dozen of the popular novels of the winter."

Sir Robert Bond, Premier of Newfoundland: "I shall prize the book. It is charmingly written, and faithfully portrays the simple lives of the noble-hearted fisher folk."

Brooklyn Eagle: "Norman Duncan has fulfilled all that was expected of him in this story; it establishes him beyond question as one of the strong masters of present-day fiction."

FOURTH EDITION

THE HUBBARD EXPLORING EXPEDITION
By DILLON WALLACE

The Lure of the Labrador Wild

ILLUSTRATED 8VO CLOTH $1.50 NET.

New York Sun: "A remarkable story, and we are much mistaken if it does not become a classic among tales of exploration."

Chicago Evening Post: "Two continents became interested in the stories that came out of the wild about the hardships of the Hubbard expedition Wallace's story and record—they are inseparable—possesses in its naked truth more of human interest than scores of volumes of imaginative adventure and romance of the wild."

Review of Reviews: "The chronicle of high, noble purpose and achievement and it appeals to the finest, best, and most virile in man."

Chicago Record-Herald: "One of the most fascinating books of travel and adventure in the annals of recent American exploration. Every man or boy who has ever heard the 'red gods' of the wilderness calling will revel in these graphic pages, in which the wild odor of the pines, the roar of rapids, the thrill of the chase and of thickening dangers come vividly to the senses."

New York Evening Post: "The story is told simply and well. It may be added that for tragic adventure it has scarcely a parallel except in Arctic exploration."

New York Evening Mail: "A chronicle of the expedition from first to last, and a fine tribute to the memory of Hubbard, whose spirit struggled with such pitiable courage against the ravages of a purely physical breakdown The story itself is well told."

Chicago Inter-Ocean: "In the records of the explorations of recent years there is no more tragic story than that of Hubbard's attempt to cross the great unexplored and mysterious region of the northeastern portion of the North American continent Wallace himself narrowly escaped death in the Labrador wild, but, having been rescued, he has brought out of that unknown land a remarkable story."

Brooklyn Eagle: "One of the very best stories of a canoe trip into the wilds ever written."

FOURTH EDITION